THE I TATTI
RENAISSANCE LIBRARY

James Hankins, General Editor

BECCADELLI

THE HERMAPHRODITE

ITRL 42

ANTONIO BECCADELLI
◆ ◆ ◆
THE HERMAPHRODITE

EDITED AND TRANSLATED BY
HOLT PARKER

THE I TATTI RENAISSANCE LIBRARY
HARVARD UNIVERSITY PRESS
CAMBRIDGE, MASSACHUSETTS
LONDON, ENGLAND
2010

Series design by Dean Bornstein

Library of Congress Cataloging-in-Publication Data

Beccadelli, Antonio, 1394–1471.
[Hermaphroditus. English & Latin]
The Hermaphrodite / Antonio Beccadelli ; edited and
translated by Holt Parker.
p. cm. — (The I Tatti Renaissance library ; 42)
In Latin, with English translations on facing pages.
Includes bibliographical references and index.
ISBN 978-0-674-04757-0 (alk. paper)
1. Erotic poetry, Latin (Medieval and modern) — Translations
into English.   2. Intersexuality — Poetry.   I. Parker, Holt N.   II. Title.
PA8475.B4H413 2010
871′.4 — dc22   2010002227

Contents

ॐ१?ॐ

Introduction

ക്ക്ക്

Repulsive though the subject be, we must speak of his
"Hermaphroditus" or collection of epigrams, because the spirit of
the false Renaissance is here manifested in all its hideousness.
"The Book," says the Historian of Humanism, "opens a view
into an abyss of iniquity, but wreathes it with the most beautiful
flowers of poetry." The most horrible crimes of heathen antiquity,
crimes whose very name a Christian cannot utter without
reluctance, were here openly glorified. The poet, in his facile
verses, toyed with the worst forms of sensuality, as if they were
the most natural and familiar themes for wit and merriment.
"And moreover, he complacently confessed himself the author of
this obscene book, justified it by the examples of the old Roman
poets, and looked down upon the strict guardians of morality as
narrow-minded dullards, incapable of appreciating the voluptuous
graces of the ancients." Cosmo de' Medici accepted the dedication
of this loathsome book, which is proved by the countless copies
in the Italian libraries to have had but too wide a circulation . . .
No writing of the so-called Humanists, however, equals
Beccadelli's collection of epigrams in impurity. The false heathen
Renaissance culminates in this repulsive "Emancipation of the
Flesh," sagaciously characterized by a modern historian as the
forerunner of the great Revolution, which in the following
centuries shook Europe to its centre.

Ludwig Pastor, *History of the Popes* (3rd ed., 1906), I: 23–24.[1]

Such is the reputation of the book in your hands: one so loath-
some that it (eventually) set off the French Revolution or worse —
Protestantism.

Antonio Beccadelli (1394–1471)

Beccadelli belonged to what Rabil has called the "heroic age" of humanists, that third generation of Italian scholars, after Petrarch (1304–74) and Boccaccio (1313–75), and the second generation typified by Salutati (1331–1406). Beccadelli was a pioneer in rediscovering the power of the epigram and exploring Latin for its resources of abuse and louche eroticism.

He was born in Palermo, whose Latin name, Panormus, gave him his preferred cognomen, Panormita (the man from Palermo). Sicily was something of a cultural backwater at the time, but it had already produced one distinguished humanist in Beccadelli's older contemporary and life-long friend, Giovanni Aurispa (1376–1459), and would have to wait for Lucio Marineo (c. 1444–c. 1533) for its next.

His grandfather had fled Bologna, where Beccadelli would return, and his father became a prosperous merchant and senator in Palermo. We know little of his early life. His enemies later claimed that he had married there and wasted both his patrimony and his wife's dowry, but these charges are as baseless as their taunts that his father was a butcher and his mother a baker.[2]

In 1419/20, at the relatively advanced age of 27, he set out to pursue his studies with a recommendation from Aurispa to Pope Martin V (b. 1368/9, pope 1417–31), who was staying in Florence from February 1419 to September 1420.[3] He had been awarded a grant of six gold oncie (30 florins) a year from the university of Palermo to study abroad.[4] He continued on from Florence to Padua in 1420, where he studied with Gasparino Barzizza (c. 1360–1431).[5] Among Gasparino's previous students had been Leon Battista Alberti (1404–72) who had studied there from around 1416 to 1418 (see poem 1.21). Beccadelli continued on to Siena. He lived there from 1421 to 1424, and studied with the great scholar of canon law, Nicolò Tudisco (or Todeschi), a fellow Sicilian, and later archbishop of Palermo 1434–50. Plague hit Siena in 1424 and Beccadelli makes frequent mention of it and its victims (1.24, 1.25, 1.30, 1.32, 2.13, 2.31). Beccadelli left Siena for Bologna, another city famous for the study of law, and stayed from 1424 to 1427.[6]

The poems of *The Hermaphrodite*, his first work, reflect his time in Florence and Siena, and the initial version of the complete collection was dedicated to Cosimo de' Medici (1389–1464) and made public in Bologna over the winter of 1425/26.[7] Copies were made and quickly spread through humanist circles. Giovanni Lamola (c. 1405–49) gave a copy to his teacher Guarino da Verona (1374–1460) (see Prefatory Letter).[8] Guarino sent back a letter praising Beccadelli's style and defending his subject matter, the first shot in the war that would erupt over the book. Lamola also sent a copy to Poggio Bracciolini (1380–1459) in Rome, who passed it on to the senior humanist Antonio Loschi (c. 1368–1441), gathering praise but also a cautious warning to turn to higher topics (letter after Book I). Beccadelli would place these letters and his response in later editions of *The Hermaphrodite*. Poggio replied with a letter of mild reproof for the misuse of classical authority, which Beccadelli did *not* include (Appendix, II). Beccadelli's friend Santio Ballo (Xantius Ballus) sent a copy to Francesco Filelfo (1398–1481), who expressed his delight (see *Herm.* 1.27).[9]

Despite Beccadelli's appeal to the ancients, the circulation of such poetry was perhaps overdaring at the very moment when Bernardino da Siena (1380–1444) was fulminating against sodomy.[10] Aurispa expressed his admiration for the man and the work but cautioned Guarino against letting his favorable opinion be generally known.[11]

Hopes for *The Hermaphrodite* to be an entrée to a court appointment, however, proved delusive. Cosimo de' Medici was not forthcoming. In 1426, Aurispa recommended his friend to Gian Francesco Gonzaga (1395–1444) in Mantua, who however had already installed Vittorino da Feltre (1378–1446) as tutor to the ducal children.[12] Beccadelli continued to study law at Bologna.[13] In the following year, Guarino recommended him to the Este in Ferrara, which he visited, but the job as tutor went to Aurispa.[14] Beccadelli toured through Venice, Bologna, Genoa, and Florence. During this time he was hard at work on classical studies, and important copies of Propertius, Tibullus, Lucretius, and probably Cicero's *De oratore* came from his pen.[15]

He had set his eyes on the patronage of the Visconti of Milan, asking his friends, especially Lamola and Cambio Zambeccari of Bologna (jurist, poet, and manuscript collector), for help.[16] Perhaps his most influential friend was Bartolomeo della Capra, humanist, manuscript hunter, and from 1414 to 1435 archbishop of Milan. Capra had heard about *The Hermaphrodite* from Lamola in November 1426 and requested a copy. Beccadelli acceded to his request, with the apology that the book was a work of his youth (see Appendix, III).[17] The archbishop went to work on Beccadelli's behalf, recommending him to Francesco Barbavara and Luigi Crotti in the Visconti chancellery, not as a poet but as a historian, arguing that Leonardo Bruni's *History of the Florentine People* and his funeral oration for Nanni Strozzi, together with various Venetian versions of events, were working as propaganda against Milan and needed counterbalancing.[18] Capra proved prophetic: Beccadelli's greatest triumphs would come as a panegyrist. Beccadelli himself was in two minds about *The Hermaphrodite*, both promoting it and deprecating it. In a letter to Lamola (20 Sept. 1427) Beccadelli wrote from Florence asking for help with the Visconti:

> *The Hermaphrodite* seems to me to be too obscene a thing to send to such important people, and the author regrets and is ashamed that he ever published it. But the gods should grant

that the poet actually benefits from it, as long as they look with favor on our Caesar [the Duke].[19]

Capra then encouraged Beccadelli to visit the curia of Pope Martin V in 1428. He spent the rest of the year in Rome, where he met Poggio face to face, as well as Lorenzo Valla (1407–1457), sending a copy of Valla's famous (but now lost) *De comparatione Ciceronis Quintilianique* back to friends in Florence.[20] Valla in turn made "Panormita" the spokesman for Epicureanism in the first version of *De voluptate*, setting the third day of the dialogue in Beccadelli's house in Rome.[21] On all these travels, he was accompanied by a young man he had met in Bologna, Tommaso di Bazalerio Tebaldi (c. 1415–75), whom he called Ergoteles, and took with him to Venice, Florence, Rome, and ultimately Pavia.[22] We have one of Beccadelli's poems to him (see Appendix, X). Guarino described Ergoteles as remarkably civilized,[23] and he would grow up to become a leading diplomat for Milan.[24] A friend of Beccadelli's, a monk named Giacomo, left a vivid anecdote about him:

> As I was writing, I recalled . . . that boy of yours, Ergoteles, who was endowed with nobility of mind no less than bodily beauty. When he sang poetic verses at dinner during the meal so sweetly and charmingly, I often hung on his lips so completely that I nearly forgot to eat.[25]

Beccadelli wrote directly to Duke Filippo Maria Visconti promising immortality in poetry.[26] Eventually, the recommendations and networking of his friends paid off. On 10 December 1429, Beccadelli was appointed court poet (*poeta aulicus*) to the duke, with a rich stipend of 400 gold florins a year. He dutifully produced an oration comparing his patron to the sun.[27] He did not stay put, however, and traveled to Genoa and Pavia, where he delivered orations on the duke's behalf and completed his law studies in 1430–

31 on Capra's advice. The duke arranged for him to be appointed to a lectureship there, thus transferring to the university the task of paying the huge salary.[28] When plague hit Pavia, Beccadelli escaped into a miserable refuge at Stradella, and from there called on his old friend, the lawyer Catone Sacco to help arrange a post for Valla, and asked the author for a copy of his *De voluptate*.[29] Beccadelli also used his new friend Antonio Cremona, who had influence with both Duke Filippo Maria and the imperial court, to arrange an audience with the emperor. This period of his life culminated in May 1432 when he was crowned poet laureate by Emperor Sigismund (1368–1437) at Parma.[30] Guarino composed congratulatory verses.[31]

While at Pavia, he continued work on a vast and never-to-be-completed series of studies on Plautus (*Indagationes*), which he made with a copy of Plautus borrowed from Guarino and not returned.[32] He also produced a work which was to be important for the history of later literature, his *Poematum et prosarum liber*.[33] This was arguably the first anthology by a humanist of his own work, and contained two further epigrams to young men, suggestive but not explicitly erotic (Appendix, XI–XII). Its clear purpose was to be a portfolio showing his potential and vast range to future clients, especially King Alfonso of Aragon.[34] Around this time, the future Pius II included Beccadelli's name in a poem suggesting those who might be for hire to sing the praise of the newly crowned king of France, Charles VII.[35]

The calling card was needed. At the end of 1432, his Maecenas at court, Barbavara, fell from the duke's Secret Council and went into exile.[36] Beccadelli was demoted and returned to the university of Pavia in 1432–33 as professor of rhetoric, at the lowly salary of only 30 florins a year. It was around this low point in his life that Beccadelli married his first wife, Filippa, who gave birth to a daughter, Agata.[37]

His fame, however, remained high. Guarino wrote him (20 May 1433) with the remarkable story of how some bizarrely dressed "Calabrian or Sicilian" had strolled into Verona, and before an admiring crowd had launched into an extempore oration adorned with bits of Beccadelli's poetry and the works of the most learned contemporaries. When asked his name he replied, "My name is Antonio Panormita, and Sicily is my native soil." He was embraced and fêted by the Podestà and other leading citizens. Some, however, were not taken in and wrote a description of the squinty imposter to Guarino. The charlatan was whipped out of town.[38]

Pier Candido Decembrio (1399–1477), Milanese ambassador and secretary to Filippo Maria Visconti, may have played a role in Beccadelli's demotion. Guarino had praised Carmagnola. Decembrio attacked Guarino for praising a traitor. Beccadelli rose to Guarino's defense. Decembrio continued the quarrel by writing a dialogue in which he mocked Beccadelli's "Oration on the Image of the Sun," and reminded everyone how Beccadelli supposedly praised the enemy Venetians.[39] It was time to go.

The Controversy

The storm over *The Hermaphrodite* had been building for some time. In late 1427–early 1428, Antonio da Rho ('Raudensis', 1395–1447), a Franciscan from Milan, wrote an attack on certain of his enemies within the order. In the course of defending his reading of the poets, he mentioned "our contemporary, a certain Antonio Panormita, whose genius will not be condemned but his life someday will be unless he writes serious verses subsequent to his filthy ones (as Vergil did)." Rho had not yet read *The Hermaphrodite* but its fame was already widespread.[40] So famous was it that the great Franciscan preacher Bernardino da Siena staged public burnings of it in Milan, Bologna, and Ferrara.⁴¹ Beccadelli himself was burned twice in effigy, at Bologna and Milan.⁴² A feud broke out between Rho and Beccadelli, based perhaps on these remarks. By mid-1429 a poem, "The Prostitutes of Pavia," attacking the author of *The Hermaphrodite*, was circulating (see Appendix, VI). Beccadelli got to hear of it and assumed Rho was the author.⁴³ He responded in March–April 1430 with a set of lost "Priapeia," which he alternately denied and boasted about. An anonymous invective responded to these, which Rutherford convincingly attributes to Rho.⁴⁴ In this, the author claims (with what truth we cannot know) that Beccadelli had attempted to get a letter of recommendation from Gasparino Barzizza but in vain, and that Leonardo Bruni, Rho, and Cencio dei Rustici had all expressed their disapproval of his work.⁴⁵

Beccadelli answered with an open letter to Rho in 1431, in which he both defends *The Hermaphrodite* by the examples of Catullus, Vergil, Martial, and Juvenal, and dismisses it as a work of youth (see Appendix, VII).⁴⁶ Rho paid him back the next year with a vast and blistering *Philippic*, accusing Beccadelli, among other things, of a) wasting his patrimony among sodomites while a youth in Sicily, b) then burning through a wife's dowry, c) before abandoning her, d) having been driven out of Siena by the virtuous citizens, e) prostituting his boy Ergoteles while in Rome, f) having written "The Prostitutes of Pavia" himself, g) trying to get special "Fuckarian" laws passed to benefit whores, catamites, and *cinaedi*, and perhaps most insulting of all, h) plagiarizing Guarino da Verona for his commentary on Plautus. Rho further claimed that Cosimo de' Medici had read *The Hermaphrodite* only to toss it in the fire (the presentation copy, of course, remains in the Medici library to this day).⁴⁷

Rho's attack on Beccadelli was primarily personal and *The Hermaphrodite* merely provided ammunition.⁴⁸ However, *odium philologicum* was a major participatory sport for the humanists, and people rapidly chose sides. Beccadelli's enemies picked up on Rho's charges. Decembrio produced the invective (1431–32) *Novis monstris infamis scatet insula* ("The infamous island swarms with new monsters"), repeating the rumors about Beccadelli's wife and Ergoteles, and telling (somewhat obscurely) a tale, set in Bologna, where Beccadelli sees the handsome son of an innkeeper, lays in wait for him in a brothel, and is caught literally with his pants down. Hauled before the court, he defends himself by the example of Vergil.[49] Decembrio's poem "The Epitaph of Antonio Panormita" belongs to this period (Appendix, XV).[50] Valla, who would eventually quarrel with everyone (including Rho), broke with Beccadelli between February and June 1432, and wrote him out of the new version of *De voluptate*, now more cautiously named *De vero et falso bono* (*On the True and False Good*), handing his role over to Maffeo Vegio.[51] Valla increased the stakes by accusing Beccadelli of murdering a first wife and divorcing a second (preferring her son).[52] He called Beccadelli a "pimp for boys" (*puerorum mangone*) and added corroborative details: that his boyfriend had helped Beccadelli poison and rob their host, Miniato da Lucca, a papal secretary, before they fled Rome together.[53]

Beccadelli in turn tried to turn Guarino against Valla.[54] The legal scholar Catone Sacco (the Stoic spokesman in Valla's revised *On the True and False Good*), also defected to Rho and Decembrio.[55] Even his old friend and fellow poet, Antonio Cremona, had become an Observant Franciscan, and wrote him a long letter repeating the slanders of his enemies.[56] The wear on Beccadelli was great. He longed to escape to Barbavara's Villa Ridibovana since "the conspiracy of my enemies is growing day by day."[57] He blasted the trio of Rho, Valla, and Sacco in a bitter exchange of poetic invective (Appendix, VIII).[58]

The new pope, Eugenius IV (b. 1383, pope 1431–47), is said to have threatened any readers of *The Hermaphrodite* with excommunication.[59] Cardinal Cesarini (1398–1444) was more forgiving.

Vespasiano da Bisticci (1421–98) recounts the anecdote of how the cardinal found his secretary reading *The Hermaphrodite*. The priest tossed the book into a chest but not fast enough and was speechless when confronted. Cesarini made him take it out and destroy it, but kindly remarked, "If you had known how to respond, perhaps you wouldn't have had to tear it up. What you should have answered me was that you were searching for a precious stone in a dunghill."⁶⁰

Alberto da Sarteano gave his Lenten sermons of 1434 at Ferrara, demanding a retraction by Guarino of his letter praising *The Hermaphrodite*.⁶¹ Not until 1 January 1435 did Guarino comply—in rather cringe-making terms. In his letter, Guarino was reduced to pretending that Beccadelli cut out several passages without his knowledge or permission, and that when he praised the book as having been "written with such skill and polish" (*prudenter et polite conscriptus*), he was referring to the handwriting.⁶² Though his version of events has sometimes been given credence, it is clearly false.⁶³

In the end, around the same year, Beccadelli surrendered and wrote a recantation of his dedication to Cosimo (after Book II). It makes for sad reading. *The Hermaphrodite* continued to be enjoyed and copied, but its father had disowned his misbegotten child.⁶⁴ Yet his friends were still willing to call on the abandoned work as testimony to his genius.⁶⁵

In the King's Service

The remainder of Beccadelli's life will be more quickly related.⁶⁶ In late 1434, he left Milan for Genoa, and thence returned to Palermo, where with the help of the royal secretary, Giacomo Pellegrini, he entered the service of King Alfonso V of Aragon and Naples (1396–1458) as a counselor and confidant. The king was busy snapping up scholars and had already acquired Guiniforte Barzizza (c. 1406–63), the son of Beccadelli's old teacher, from Visconti in Milan.[67] The king gave the new arrival a sinecure, the post of *gaito* (overseer) of customs at Palermo. He followed the king to Messina, Ischia, and the siege of Gaeta. Beccadelli persuaded the commander of that fortress to surrender, but before the terms could be carried out, the commander was replaced, and at the Battle of Ponza (5 August 1435), the king was taken prisoner. After he was freed by the Milanese, Beccadelli brought him the news of the surrender of Gaeta. Alfonso then sent Beccadelli in the spring of 1436 as ambassador to Florence and Siena in company with his old enemy Valla, who had joined Alfonso's court and had also been present at the Battle of Ponza.[68] Beccadelli's task was to persuade the Republics not to form a league with Venice and Genoa against his old employer, Filippo Maria Visconti of Milan, Alfonso's ally in the reconquest of Naples. Though he played up Florentine distrust of the Genoese, the mission was unsuccessful. His work as ambassador and humanist, secretary and spokesman, companion and military adviser paid handsomely—a salary of 450 ducats a year (in 1437–39) and the gift of the Palazzo della Zisa in Palermo.[69] In 1440, he visited the anti-Pope Felix V in Savoy, in order to get him to recognize Alfonso's claim to the throne.[70] During his next mission in 1441, he convinced the city of Caiazzo to surrender peacefully. Beccadelli told the anecdote of how he and Alfonso were so caught up in a friendly debate about Viriatus, the Iberian guerilla leader who defeated the Romans, that the king turned away the prefect of the camp for interrupting.[71]

Besides his formal duties, Beccadelli served as tutor, reader, and confidant to Alfonso. He told how once when the king was sick at Capua, he brought his own medicine: Curtius Rufus's *Life of Alexander*. The king was so interested that he began to feel better and Beccadelli continued to read to him three times a day until he was completely well and the book was finished.[72]

On 26 February 1443, Alfonso entered Naples. Beccadelli and Valla walked behind the triumphal cart and helped organize the elaborate pageantry.[73] This initiated a long and rich period of his life, marred by an increasingly vicious quarrel with Valla. Valla undertook brilliant philological work in his years in the king's service, not least his *Declamation on the Donation of Constantine*, written to aid Alfonso's claim to the crown of Naples.[74] But even so grand a court was perhaps too small for the titanic egos it fed. Beccadelli and Valla scored off each other in public, competed like children for the king's attention, and exchanged poetic insults. Valla denounced Beccadelli to Decembrio, accusing him of buggery and beating his wife (Appendix, XIX–XX).[75] Beccadelli's old friend Bartolomeo Facio (c. 1405–57) arrived in 1444 as ambassador from the new Doge of Genoa, Raffaele Adorno, and decided to stay. He too felt the lash of Valla's disdain and hoped to take over the task of writing Alfonso's *res gestae*, a task which Valla had been pottering about with while writing the life of Alfonso's father, Ferdinand I of Aragon.

In that same year, Cosimo de' Medici sent a royal gift to Alfonso, which was to prove a further apple of discord. Petrarch's own compilation of Livy was the most complete text seen since antiquity but it was based on deeply corrupted sources. Petrarch had begun emending it, and the king entrusted the rest of the task to Facio and Giacomo Curlo. Valla mocked their attempt and produced a vastly superior text.[76] Facio and Beccadelli lay in wait for their revenge. While Valla and the king were away in the summer of 1445, they got the royal librarian to loan them Valla's draft copy of the first three books of his history of the king's father, the *Gesta Ferdinandi Regis Aragonum*. When Valla returned, they publicly charged him with poor Latin style and having made over two hundred errors in the first ten pages alone.[77] Facio made the quarrel even more public by circulating four books of *Invective in Laurentium Vallam* throughout Italy, accusing Valla (inter alia) of having plagiarized *De voluptate* from his uncle, the papal secretary Melchior Scrivani.[78] Valla finally was sent a copy and responded with his own *Antidotum in Facium* (1447), which included many sideswipes at Beccadelli.[79] The death of Eugenius IV and the election of Pope Nicholas V allowed Valla to return at last to Rome in 1448.

Beccadelli's wife, Filippa, had died in early 1444 and in April–May 1447 he married his second wife, the sixteen-year-old Laura Arcella, somewhat to the surprise of Aurispa. He wondered at someone risking shipwreck twice, and wrote to Alfonso, "I don't know why he isn't shunning marriage, since he's always held the entire female sex in the greatest contempt."[80] Laura bore him a daughter, Caterina Pantia (Pantheia), and a son, Antonio (Antonino).[81] Part of these years was spent back home in Palermo.[82]

Following Valla's departure, Beccadelli enjoyed an undisputed position and increased riches. He held his previous posts, was granted citizenship and immunity from taxes, and his annual salary was increased to 600 (1450), then to 900 ducats (1454). He was master of ceremonies for the king's elaborate annual religious pageants and other pomps.[83] He was sent as ambassador to Florence in 1451, where he delivered a memorable Latin address.[84] Beccadelli continued on to Ferrara and Venice in 1451–52, where he met Francesco Barbaro. He stopped in Padua, where he was given a relic to present to Alfonso: the arm bone of Livy.[85] The next year, he was in Rome to deliver an oration at the coronation of Emperor Frederick III. In October 1453, he urged the Genoese to join a crusade again the Turks, and from 1454–69 he served tirelessly as the royal secretary.

During these years, he presided over a court of scholars at Naples which eclipsed even its former grandeur. Alfonso wanted the best and paid for them: 20,000 ducats in the year of his death according to Vespasiano.[86] The most splendid light was one of the first: Giovanni Pontano (1429–1503), who joined Alfonso while the king was still at war in Tuscany in 1447, and entered Naples with him in 1448.[87] Decembrio visited Naples at various points between 1443 and 1458 to drop off translations and pick up money. Porcellio Pandoni (d. post 1485), who had met and broken with Beccadelli in their Rome days, now became secretary and poet in 1450 but left three years later after a renewed quarrel with his former friend. Three of his early attacks on Beccadelli and *The Hermaphrodite* are included in the Appendix (XVI–XVIII).[88] Flavio Biondo (1392–1463) came in 1451–52. Filelfo (1398–1481) visited in 1453, and was given the laurel crown. Giannozzo Manetti (1396–1459), after a lifetime of serving as ambassador from Florence, went into exile at Naples in 1455, where he produced translations of Aristotle's ethical works.[89] Greek scholars were richly rewarded. Gregorio Tifernate (i.e. from Città di Castello, 1419–69) worked in Naples in the period 1447–50, as did George of Trebizond (1395–1486) in 1452 to 1455, while Beccadelli continued his interest (and the king's) in military science by collaborating with Theodore Gaza (c. 1400–75) on a translation of Aelian's *Tactics*, which Gaza dedicated to him (1456; living in Naples 1455–58). There even was an attempt to lure Leonardo Bruni (1370–1444) from Florence in his final years. Those who could not come themselves sent books, especially translations from the Greek with an eye to a king's education: Bruni sent Aristotle's *Politics*; Poggio, Xenophon's *Cyropedia*: Lapo da Castiglionchio, Plutarch's *Fabius Maximus*.

Beccadelli was busy enriching the king's library and his own. The story of how he used Alfonso as a book agent, selling a farm to buy a copy of Livy for 120 florins, became a famous anecdote.[90] His major accomplishments as a humanist in these years were two.[91] The first is *De dictis et factis Alphonsi regis* (1455), for which the king gave him a thousand ducats. Though Beccadelli claimed Xenophon's *Memorabilia* as his inspiration, the truer model is Valerius Maximus, with various anecdotes about Alfonso arranged under rhetorical headings of *Fortiter, Iuste, Moderate*, etc. The implication is plain: one need not scour antiquity but look no farther than Alfonso for an exemplar of all the virtues. The immediate model for the king is Augustus, especially the human and humane ruler of Suetonius's anecdotes.[92] The book became immensely popular and helped set the image of the ideal Renaissance prince: the warrior who relaxed by reading Livy and Vergil, discussed philosophy with his circle of scholars, built with a copy of Vitruvius in hand, and was so eager for a book that he broke into his own royal library after hours.[93] Aeneas Silvius Piccolomini, later Pius II, wrote a *Commentary* on it — in essence, a set of further anecdotes — as soon as it appeared (1456).[94]

Beccadelli's other great accomplishment was founding the first of the Academies that would nurture intellectual life in the following centuries, the Academia Neapolitana. By 1447 Beccadelli was planning a formal recreation of the Academies of the ancient world. There had already been literary meetings in the royal library, to which Beccadelli made many contributions. The new venue, a setting which favored open and unstructured discussions, was the remains of the Roman arches in the Strada dell'Anticaglia near his home, which came to be called the Porticus Antoniana.[95] Towards the end of Beccadelli's life, the running of the academy passed to Pontano, and it came to be called the Accademia Pontaniana. This fell into desuetude in 1542, was revived in 1808, was repressed by the fascists in 1934, again revived by Croce in 1944, and continues today.

The passing of the throne from Alfonso (†1458) to his less generous (and more embattled) illegitimate son Ferrante (Ferdinand I, 1424–94) created a time of crisis for Beccadelli. Though he served Ferrante in diplomatic missions to Milan (1458) and to Pius II at the Congress of Mantua (1459–60), he briefly considered retiring to Sicily or seeking other posts in Rome or Spain. His talent as humanist and propagandist was solicited by Ferrante's rival claimant for the throne, Jean d'Anjou.[96] By 1462, however, his

situation improved, with a new house, a new garden, new reve-
nues, and a new appointment as tutor to the heir, Duke Alfonso
of Calabria (Alfonso II, 1448–95). He continued to edit and as-
semble his letters in two collections, the *Epistolae Gallicae* (which
carried the working title of *Liber familiarum*) and the *Epistolae
Campanae*, covering his years in Naples, together with his official
correspondence as secretary to the king, which would be published
posthumously.[97]

He wrote a final work, *Liber rerum gestarum Ferdinandi regis*
(1469), but his plans to continue the chronicle were cut short by
his death in 1471, following a urinary disease long and patiently
borne.[98]

After Beccadelli's death, Filelfo looked back on the glory days
of Alfonso's court as being when Beccadelli debated various views
of the philosophers on human happiness, in sessions of the Acad-
emy with the king in attendance.[99]

The Hermaphrodite: Contents, Language, Style

Beccadelli explained his choice of title (1.42):

> I have divided my book into two parts, Cosimo,
>   For the Hermaphrodite has the same number of parts.
> This was the first part, so what follows is the second.
>   This stands for the cock, the next will be cunt.

But the title does not really make sense this way, nor is the
promised division fulfilled. It is certainly not the case that "cock"
equals boys and "cunt" equals girls as objects of lust, or that only
boys are treated in Book I and only girls in Book II. Rather,
Beccadelli's inspiration seems to be Boccaccio's *Genealogies of the
Gods* (3.21):

> Albericus [that is, the Third Vatican Mythographer] takes
> Hermaphroditus, since he is born from Mercury and Venus,

to symbolize speech that is unnecessarily lascivious, which when it ought to be manly, seems effeminate because of the excessive softness of the words.[100]

Even that is an imperfect guide to this miscellany of verse. There are the usual dedicatory and introductory verses (1.1–4, 1.42–43, 2.1–2, 2.33, 2.35, 2.38) and programmatic poems in defense of writing dirty poems (1.10, 1.20, 1.23, 2.11).

We have poems to friends: Leon Battista Alberti (1.21), Santia Ballo (1.27), Francesco Pontano (1.38). Giovanni Aurispa (1.41 asking for a copy of Martial; 2.22 to Cosimo de' Medici in praise of Aurispa), an unnamed young poet-soldier (2.13), a certain Sanseverino (2.14); and attacks on enemies: the schoolmaster Mattia Lupi da San Gimignano (1.10, 1.11, 1.16–17, 1.26, 1.36, 2.15–16, 2.19, 2.24, 2.27) and the possibly fictional Oddo (1.20, 2.11, 2.20). We find the poet hunting for copies of Martial (1.41) and Catullus (2.23) but hocking his Plautus (2.29).

There are the traditional targets of classical and medieval satire: the cuckold (1.6), the drunkard (2.12), the miser (2.36), the blocking character of the girl's mother (2.4). But vignettes of how his poetic inspiration was broken by a peasant relieving himself (1.40) and obscure anecdotes about the ignominious burial of a cook (2.21) or an old horse dying of hunger (2.36) make odd companions for moving (if mechanical) epitaphs for young girls who died of the plague (1.24–25, 1.32. 2.32) and noble old warriors (1.37).

However, it is the poems about sex that have kept this collection infamous. The cast of characters is wide: a grotesque female love, Ursa, the embodiment of insatiable female desire (1.5, 1.8, 1.21, 2.7–10); an ideal love, Alda, whom Beccadelli nevertheless needs to degrade (1.18, 1.35, 2.3, 2.5); another named Lucia (1.29–31, 2.25), threatened by sickness and childbirth; and miscellaneous unnamed others (1.9, 2.13, 2.31; 2.26: gender unspecified). Beccadelli mocks the man obsessed with women he can't get (1.22) and the one who doesn't mind a crowd of onlookers (2.24). There is the "Epitaph for Nichina of Flanders, the Famous Whore" (2.30) and "To His Book, That It May Go to the Brothel in Florence" (2.37), destined to become anthology pieces.

Above all, it is the poems on sodomy that have shocked (or raised the need to pretend to be shocked). Mockery of active pederasts (1.7, 1.19, 1.26, 1.36, 2.6) and attacks on the adult passives (1.12, 1.13, 1.33, 2.20) combine with celebration of the act (1.9, 1.14–15, 1.28, 1.34) and poems of seduction ostensibly written on behalf of friends (2.17–18, 2.28, 2.34). It is these poems that Beccadelli was at special pains to disavow later (Beccadelli's Recantation 3–4: *quos natura fugit*, "those deeds which nature shuns").

Beccadelli tells the reader indirectly how he wishes all these poems to be read: they are after-dinner entertainments, a form of mental relaxation, verses that he claimed to have written under similar sympotic circumstances (1.1, 1.27, 1.38, 1.43, 2.1).

From Catullus, Martial and Pliny, Beccadelli reanimated the classic defense of the obscene poet: my life and my verse are separate.[101] He cited Catullus, Vergil, Martial (or Cicero), Ovid, Marsus, and Pedo (the last two merely names to Beccadelli) for precedent.[102] Though Beccadelli claimed Catullus as an authority and has been called a Catullan writer, his model for the individual epigrams was "almost exclusively Martial."[103] He has read Catullus but made no use of him.[104] Vergil, as the supposed author of the *Priapeia*, was a particularly potent name to invoke, since he provided a model of youthful sportiveness followed by an epic maturity (2.11, final line). Beccadelli's *Hermaphrodite* thus offers to any prospective patron a combination of current amusement and future glorification.[105]

The search for classical models, however, should not obscure Beccadelli's debt to more recent poetry. Italian had a rich tradition of comic realism in prose and poetry. *The Hermaphrodite* shares some of the tone and subject matter of the so-called "comic-realistic" poetry of the *poeti giocosi*, who were not "realistic" so much as anti-courtly: parodying and inverting the perfect world of *poesia aulica*.[106] Like the Latin Goliardic poets, they were not afraid to visit the rougher parts of town: the market, the tavern, the brothel.[107] Beccadelli shares this satiric (and satyric) strain and, despite his genuine devotion to the new learning, he seems more at home in this late medieval world of the *fabliaux* and *novelle* than in the equally robust but decidedly more classical world that Filelfo and Pontano would explore.

In some ways, Beccadelli seems to be trying to outdo the *poeti giocosi*. So, for example, while his Ursa may owe a literary debt to Becchina, Cecco Angiolieri's anti-Beatrice, she is presented as a real person with a will of her own, while Ursa is merely grotesque — a collection of misogynistic commonplaces.[108] For the other side of love, the comic-realistic poets are quick to accuse others (and each other) of sodomizing and being sodomized.[109] But a celebration of the pleasures (and sorrows) of loving handsome youths is rarer and tends to employ the tropes of the courtly tradition, rather than the more carnevalesque world that Beccadelli depicts.[110] In *The Hermaphrodite*, even the boys are ugly.

The resemblance, then, lies less in any specific feature than in the general idea that the grubby side of life might be celebrated in verse. At his best, Beccadelli can for short stretches resemble the poets of the so-called "poesia borghese."[111] So, for example, our most vivid evocations of the market in Florence are Beccadelli (2.37) and Antonio Pucci (c. 1310–88). But there is a sharp contrast: Pucci's topics are those of everyday life, and he lacks the obscenity and even the misogyny of Beccadelli and the *giocosa* tradition.[112]

Beccadelli also shares the meter (elegiac couplets), certain topics (notably sodomy), possibly the name of a heroine (Alda), and a little of the sportive spirit of the new Latin comedies, both the Ovidian plays of the middle ages and the new humanist dramas of the universities.[113] Some indeed have gone so far as to attribute the rash of new Latin comedies in Pavia, several with pederasty as a theme, to Beccadelli's professorship there.[114] The differences, however, are far greater. Beccadelli is working strictly in the mode of epigram, and even his longer pieces lack narrative, dialogue, or the beloved practical jokes that are the centerpieces of the comedies and stories. In the comedies, sex is there because it is part of basic human absurdity. In *The Hermaphrodite*, sex is there because it is sex. As with *poesia giocosa*, the resemblance is due to their common background in the world of Goliardic poetry and the *novelle*.

After all the hyperbole of praise and condemnation, the reader's initial reaction may be disappointment. The truth of the matter is, despite Valla's praise of him (when they were getting along) as the best poet of his age, he was not especially good.[115] He was usually competent in his meter and holds closely to the disyllabic law for the pentameter.[116] However, he never ventures beyond the conventional elegiac couplet, well-thumbed in the medieval tradition, to try the new meters he encountered in Martial and others.[117] His Latin is at best serviceable (this may have been at the heart of his quarrel with Valla).[118] He had almost no idea of pronouns, and frequently misuses the reflexives (a fault shared with his contemporaries). Tenses are virtually meaningless; subjunctives are used as meter demands or model provides. He uses the wrong word, usually for metrical reasons.[119] All of these things combine to make exactly what he was trying to say a little obscure in places. There is a certain amount of redundancy and padding.[120] He is also largely tone-deaf.

However, the main problem with Beccadelli is that he lacks wit. One need only compare his warning "To Married Women and Chaste Virgins," with its original in Martial. Beccadelli bluntly informs his readers (1.4.3–6):

I'm taking off my clothes. See, already from my open pants my
member springs out!
My muse is buried in so much pure wine.
Let Nichina stay, read, and praise my salacious verses
and Ursa who is accustomed to see naked men.

But Martial concludes after a similar warning to the respectable
woman (3.68.11–12):

If I know you well, you were already bored with my long
book and were just about to set it aside: now you'll read the
whole thing with close attention.

Similarly, it is hard to see the *point* of some of Beccadelli's epi-
grams.

Beccadelli suffers by comparison with later poets, but his flaws
are not entirely those of a trailblazer, and contemporaries were
writing less rebarbative verse.[121] Humanist praise, like humanist
vituperation, strove for hyperbole. Still, a number of his contem-
poraries felt that something new was here, that he had "roused
from sleep the Latin Muses, who have been so long dormant"
(Poggio in his prefatory letter to Beccadelli). Beccadelli's work
served both as a license and a warning. Pontano's *Pruritus* ("The
Itch," 1449) was directly inspired by *The Hermaphrodite*, but the
change in atmosphere can be sensed when the author suppressed
the earlier work in favor of his more lyrical *Parthenopeus
(Amores)*.[122] A later title is more telling still: *De amore coniugali*
(1480–84).[123] Beccadelli's directness proved a dead end. Erotic
themes could now be explored with the blessing of the ancients
but poets were more careful of their expression and content. The
subject matter moved from sex to love, the mode from satiric to
celebratory, the model from Martial to Catullus (and even more
to Propertius). One need only contrast Giovanni Marrasio's

Angelinetum (c. 1429),[124] Piccolomini's *Cinthia* (c. 1431),[125] Tito Vespasiano Strozzi's *Eroticon* ("Anthia," 1443),[126] Landino's *Xandra* (1443–44),[127] Pontano's less domestic but still relatively mild *Baiae* (1470s–1503),[128] Girolamo Angeriano's *Erotopaegnion* (1512),[129] and Johannes Secundus's *Elegies* and *Basia* (1531–36).[130]

After an initial flurry, *The Hermaphrodite* sank into a certain obscurity, overshadowed perhaps by better poems in more cautious times.[131] The full text was not printed until 1790 and then in 1791,[132] and from the many inaccurate summaries of its contents (some of which continue today), one suspects the work was more infamous than read. The book, however, may have a more important place in the history of reception and the study of sexuality than in Latin literature. Friedrich Karl Forberg (1770–1848), while librarian in Coburg, ran across a manuscript of *The Hermaphrodite* "unnoticed and covered in dust" and resolved to give it a full edition and commentary.[133] In his study, he gathered up so many passages from Greek and Roman authors that he had to issue them as an appendix, which he called *Apophoreta* ("Party Favors," the title Martial used for Book 14). In doing so he became the founder of the systematic study of sex in antiquity.[134]

Despite its flaws, *The Hermaphrodite* remains an important and influential work. It is an act of homage and of defiance; a provocation and an embarrassment; a forbidden thriller and an object of scholarship to this day.

Text, Language, and Translation

Forberg's edition was the basis of all subsequent editions and translations until Coppini's meticulous reexamination of the manuscripts (1990), on which this translation is based. We are fortunate in possessing two manuscripts personally supervised by the poet himself. Coppini's edition, therefore, is also important for showing the horrors that can happen even to a nearly autograph manuscript, executed by a professional scribe, in humanist script, in the course of transmission.

Among the many renderings, O'Connor's 1997 English translation, the only one based on Coppini's edition, stands out for scholarship and for capturing the flavor of the author's world. Thurn's 2002 German translation (also based on Coppini) is both elegant and metrical.

Beccadelli's sometimes rough syntax and uncertain command of vocabulary raises some interesting questions of translation. In my own versions, I have usually given him the benefit of the doubt and translated more what he meant to say than what he wrote. However, I have occasionally translated with stricter literalness when it seemed important to give the reader the smack of his style.

I am much indebted to Martin Davies, Associate Editor of the I Tatti Renaissance Library, for his careful editorial work on this volume.

NOTES

1. Citing Voigt 1880–81: 481 (1893: 477) and Gregorovius 1870: 7, 509, 543–44, respectively.

2. Sabbadini 1891: 16–17; Natale 1902: 10; see below on the marriages. Decembrio's attack is merely a pun on the name Beccadelli (cf. regional Italian *beccaro, beccaio,* "butcher"), though the name actually refers to "battlements" *(beccatello).*

3. The main evidence comes from Antonio da Rho's attack, but his purpose is to claim that Beccadelli failed to gain a position *despite* the support of eminent men. See Rutherford 2005: 141 for the text. See also Sabbadini 1891: 17; Natale 1902: 10–12; Corso 1953: 145 argues that Beccadelli went straight to Siena.

4. Document cited in Colangelo 1820: 18; Corso 1953: 138.

5. Resta (1965: 400) cautiously says "forse," but see Sabbadini 1891: 17; Natale 1902: 11.

6. He writes from Bologna to Roselli on 9/10 Dec. 1424 (cf. *Herm.* 1.9); see Coppini 1990: lxxviii–lxix.

7. See Coppini 1990: lxxiii–lxxiv for an assessment of Sabbadini's dating. The firmest dates are between Sept. 1424, when Aurispa goes to Florence (*Herm.* 1.41) and the letter from Guarino da Verona to Giovanni Lamola praising the book, dated 2 February [1426]. Coppini 1990: lxxviii–lxxix argues convincingly that Beccadelli was adding poems and putting the finishing touches on the book as late as Dec. 1424. Lorenzo Valla in *Antidotum in Facium* 4.14.2 claimed incorrectly (and too neatly) that the first book of *The Hermaphrodite* was written at Siena and the second at Bologna (Valla 1540: 630; Regoliosi 1981a: 394–95). Despite some speculation (Kidwell 1991: 40; O'Connor 1997: 1003), the collection was not added to after this point and only minor corrections (to meter and orthography) were made.

8. Also *Epistolae Gallicae* 4.6 (Beccadelli 1553: 75r–76r = 1746: 176–77); Sabbadini 1891: 21.

9. Sabbadini 1891: 20–21 (a letter of 1433).

10. Mormando 1999, esp. 109–163. See below for Bernardino's burnings of *The Hermaphrodite*. For a subtle analysis of Beccadelli's defense of his subject matter and its effects on Renaissance rhetoric, see O'Connor 1997.

11. Sabbadini 1915–19: 1, 512 (no. 350, Feb. 1426); cf. 1915–19: 1, 43.

12. Sabbadini 1910b: 102; 1916: 6; 1931: 39–40. See also O'Connor 2001: 6; Rutherford 2005: 27.

13. Sabbadini 1915–19: 1, 537 (no. 371).

14. Sabbadini 1891: 27–28; Resta 1965: 401; O'Connor 2001: 6.

15. Butrica 1984: 66–95; Heyworth 1986: 16–17, 69–73, 164–65; Heyworth 2007: xxix–xxx; Reeve 1990: 25–26. Hausmann 1986: 619.

16. For this period, see Ramorino 1883, esp. 257–60; Sabbadini 1916. For Cambio Zambeccari, see Frati 1909: 367–74.

17. Beccadelli had just missed seeing him in Rome. Beccadelli, *Epistolae Gallicae* 2.23 (1553: 38r–39r = 1746: 107–8); Sabbadini 1891: 25–26; Valla 1977: 21.

18. Baron 1955: 359, 618 n. 3; Sabbadini 1891: 40–41, 1916: 26–28, 1922: 83–84.

19. Sabbadini 1891: 36 (also 1916: 21): "Hermaphroditus res nimis obscena mihi visa est, quam viris gravissimis mitterem, sed auctorem pudet pigetque editionis. Sed di dabunt ut et poeta ipso perfrui possit, modo di Caesarem nostrum fortunent."

20. Sabbadini 1891: 38; Mancini 1891: 8, 18.

21. Valla 1977: 16–26. For the background, see Fubini 2003: 140–44.

22. Beccadelli, *Epistolae Gallicae* 3.36 to Valla (1553: 68r–69v = 1743: 164–67); Sabbadini 1931: 76 (mid-1431); Valla 1984: 131–32; see also Sabbadini 1916: 25 (*Epistolae Gallicae* 4.25). On Ergoteles, see Frati 1909: 359–67. The boy was nicknamed after the subject of Pindar *Olympian* 12. Since at that point only Guarino and Aurispa had access to Pindar, Sabbadini (1915–19: III, 317) suggests that the name was bestowed by Guarino in 1424–25, when all three were living in Bologna. It appears that Ergoteles stayed behind at the court of Filippo Maria Visconti in 1432: Regoliosi 1981: 267 n. 33 with full bibliography on the affair.

23. "singularis humanitatis homo, ut fama est": Sabbadini 1915–19: II, 204, no. 661 (Nov. 1434).

24. Frati 1909: 359–67; Garin 1955: 593–94; Kendall and Ilardi 1970: I, xlv–xlvii, li.

25. "Venit nunc scribenti mihi in memoriam . . . Ergotilis illius tui adolescentuli, qui non minori ingenii nobilitate quam forma corporis erat ornatus; quo versus poeticos ad mensam inter prandendum blande suaviterque cantante persaepe ipse totus pendens ab eius ore exstiti comedendi prope oblitus." Sabbadini 1891: 39–40 (from Bologna, Biblioteca Universitaria, MS 2948 (Miscellanea Tioli), vol. 29, p. 250).

26. Beccadelli, *Epistolae Gallicae* 1.2 (Beccadelli 1553: 1v–2v). See Ramorino 1883: 260–61; Voigt 1893: 1, 447 n. 1, 481–82, 510; Tenenti 1957: 23; Murphy 1997: 138–39, 279. For the duke's somewhat cagey reply, see Beccadelli 1553: 3r–3v.

27. Text at Rutherford 2005: 285–99.

28. Corbellini 1930: 35; Fubini 2003: 141, 276 n. 6 for the details of his appointment. Barzizza was paid only 60 gold florins.

29. *Epistolae Gallicae* 3.33 of summer 1431 (Beccadelli 1553: 66r–v = 1746: 161). *Epistolae Gallicae* 3.34 (1553: 66v–67r = 1746: 162–63). *Epistolae Gallicae* 4.2 (Sabbadini 1891: 58–60, who dates it to summer-autumn 1430). Natale 1902: 46–47; Valla 1977: 21–22; Regoliosi 1981a: xxii; Valla 1984: 117, 119, 131–32. Fubini 2003: 141–42. Beccadelli and Catone Sacco would part ways over *The Hermaphrodite*.

30. For these events, see Sabbadini 1891: 40–43; Resta 1965: 401; O'Connor 2001: 6–7.

31. Sabbadini 1915: II, 138 (May 1432).

32. Guarino was still trying to get it back as late as 1445: Sabbadini 1915–19: II, 200–2 (no. 658–59), 204 (no. 661), 316–20 (no. 711–13), 432 (no. 781, 452 (no. 793); Questa 1962: 216–17; Cappelletto 1988: 200–23. See Natale 1902: 51–53. Additions to Plautus's *Bacchides* (to make it playable) have been ascribed to Beccadelli (Ritschl 1845: 402, Perosa 1965: 33) but on no good evidence (Stäuble 1968: 152, 201 n. 1; Braun 1980: 114).

33. Genoa, Biblioteca Durazzo, B IX 5; London, British Library, Harl. 3933, fasc. 2, fols 30–120.

34. Resta 1965: 402; Ryder 1976b: 124. See Beccadelli's letters in Sabbadini 1916.

35. Arnaldi et al. 1964: 136–39, beginning, "Sis licet invictus multaque in proelia victor." Pius suggests Beccadelli, Giovanni Marrasio, and Maffeo Vegio.

36. Raponi 1964: 142; Sabbadini 1891: 44–45.

37. Beccadelli, *Epistolae Gallicae* 4.5, Naples, c. March 1443 (1553: 73r–75r = 1746: 173–76); see Sabbadini 1910b: 12, 158–59, who dates the marriage to late 1433-early 1434; Laurenza 1912: 7, 11; Regoliosi 1981a: 194. The

statements about Beccadelli's marriages and children in early (and some recent) works are often in error.

38. Sabbadini 1915–19: II, 155–7, no. 614. The poetry can only have been *The Hermaphrodite*.

39. Francesco Bussone, called Il Carmagnola (c. 1380–1432), had helped reconquer Milan for the duke. In 1426 he defected to Venice and played the foes against each other, until on 5 May 1432 the Venetians lost patience and executed him. See Sabbadini 1891: 16 n. 1; Rutherford 2005: 35, 279–84 (Decembrio's letter of 1432).

40. Rutherford 2005: 29, 217 (Rho, *Apology* §31). For Rho, see Fubini 1961.

41. Mormando 1999: 154 (and 305–06 n. 186). Beccadelli is not mentioned in the surviving works of Bernardino, but Valla attests the public burning (Valla 1540: I, 364, *Antidota in Pogium*, Bk. 4, an attack on Poggio): "cur non autorem librumque ad ignem vocatis? imitantes Berardinum et Robertum, qui opus Antonii Panhormitae in concione Mediolani, Bononiae, ac Ferrariae concremarunt. . . . Et Panhormitam fortasse poenitebat pigebatque operis sui." Bernardino's follower Alberto da Sarteano (1385–1450) joined the denunciations: Rutherford 2005: 27. The repeated claim that Roberto da Lecce (Roberto Caracciolo), probably born in the year of *The Hermaphrodite*'s publication (c. 1425–95) and who never heard Bernardino preach (Mormando 1999: 38), also condemned Beccadelli seems to rest only on this passage (most subsequent references can be chased back to Symonds 1877: 256). Since Valla's attacks on Poggio date to 1452–53, some twenty years after the likely date of the events, it seems probable that Valla's *Robertum* here may be an error for *Albertum*. Roberto da Lecce may have toasted Beccadelli, but he did so years later (Campbell 1997: 44).

42. Again according to Valla, who hoped for a third, more successful, attempt: 1540: I, 630: *Antidotum in Facium* 2.9.28, 4.14.2 (Regoliosi 1981a: 194–95, 394–95).

43. Sabbadini 1910b: 99–100 (letter of Aug. 1429); Rutherford 2005: 29, 265–68 for his edition of the text. Some manuscripts attribute it to Vegio on no good evidence.

44. Sabbadini 1910b: 81–82, 99–102, 137, 145–46; Rutherford 2005: 29–30, 258–63 for text of the "Anonymous Invective."

45. Rutherford 2005: 263.

46. Rutherford 2005: 248–55 for text and translation.

47. Rutherford 2005: 30–31, text and translation at 50–189. Specific charges at Rho, *Philippic* §§41, 120, 132, 137 = Rutherford 2005: 80–81, 130–31, 140–43, 146–47; Sabbadini 1891: 39. There is no evidence that Beccadelli was married in Sicily. The "Fuckarian" laws (*Futuariae*: a pun on the Roman Agrarian Laws) on the other hand are most probably based on a real joke by Beccadelli, since Rho mocks his pastiche of archaic Latin. See Rutherford 2005: 33. It may be that Beccadelli's composition survives unrecognised as the 'Lex de re futuaria', placed among the *inscriptiones falsae* of CIL VI.5 17*, and often earlier printed, e.g. in Valerius Probus 1499, dɪv–2r.

48. Rightly emphasized by Rutherford 2005: 36.

49. For partial texts and analysis, see Sabbadini 1891: 33–34, 39–40; Gabotto 1893: 292; Rutherford 2005: 35, 102 n. 180, 142 n. 338 (citing the manuscript). O'Connor dates this earlier, to 1427, but sees quite rightly that it is no more than Decembrio turning bits of *The Hermaphrodite* into biography.

50. Cinquini and Valentini 1907: 51.

51. Valla 1977: 23; Regoliosi 1981a: xxii; Valla 1984: 120–21, 240–41; Fubini 2003: 142.

52. Valla *Antidotum in Facium* 2.9.27 (Regoliosi 1981a: 193). This is the mythical first Sicilian wife, and then his wife Filippa. Valla also accuses him of buying his third, the young Laura Arcella, whom he married in 1447.

53. Valla 1540: I, 476, 630: *Antidotum in Facium* 3.8.34, 4.14.2 (Regoliosi 1981a: 266–67 with notes, 394–95): Venit mihi ex hoc loco in mentem Miniati cuiusdam qui fuisse dicebatur insignis aleator et eo questu in numerum papalium pervenisse scribarum, quem Antonius Panormita, cum ab eo in hospitium acceptus esset, veneno sustulit et bonam partem ex mortui (immo necdum mortui) censu compilavit, adiutus Hyla suo,

per quem ut alios ita miserum Miniatum illexerat atque inescaverat. Rem loquor minime obscuram. ("I am reminded at this point of a certain Miniato who was said to be a notable gambler and who had managed to become one of the papal secretaries with his winnings. Antonio Panormita, after he had been taken in as his guest, murdered him with poison and stole a good part of the dead—or rather not quite yet dead—man's money, with the aid of his boy Hylas, whom he used to seduce and entrap the poor Miniato like so many others. I'm talking about a well-known business.") Rutherford 2005: 34 points out that this "Hylas" is simply another name for "Ergoteles," and not Beccadelli's lover, Enrico, whom he had only in Naples, nor is he to be confused with the humanist Enrico da Prato (Hylas Pratensis), to whom Beccadelli also addressed poems.

54. Sabbadini 1915–19: II, 161–62, no. 618; Resta 1954: 199, no. 318.

55. See the poem Appendix, VIII.

56. Sabbadini 1891: 3, 42–43; 1910b: 32–34. See Hankins 1990: 129.

57. "usque adeo in dies crescit inimicorum coniuratio": Sabbadini 1891: 5 n. 4 (dated to 1431, but it is probably later: see O'Connor 1990: 12, 27 n. 28).

58. Dated to 1432 before the fall of Barbavara.

59. Vespasiano's anecdote (cited in the next note) is our only source for the papal threat: "sappiendo che l'era iscomunicatione papale a chi lo leggessi, fatta da papa Eugenio" ("knowing there was a papal excommunication against anyone who read it, made by Pope Eugenius"). Lopez (1972: 62) and Rozzo (2001: 194) date the pope's prohibition to 1431, citing Zaccaria (1777: 130–31). Zaccaria, however, merely dates the prohibition to *after* 1431 ("dopo il 1431"), the first year of Eugenius's papacy. Zaccaria, in turn cites Ménage (ed. La Monnoye 1729: 4, 329), who makes no mention of the pope, but merely repeats the familiar story that it was burned by Bernardino and Roberto da Lecce.

60. "se tu m'avessi saputo rispondere, per aventura tu nollo aresti [avresti] istraciato : la risposta che tu mi dovevi fare si era, che tu cercassi una pietra pretiosa in uno monte di litame." Waters 1926: 128–29: Greco 1970–76: 1, 147–48.

61. See Martène and Durand 1724–1733: III, 775–77 for a letter of uncertain date from Alberto condemning *The Hermaphrodite* as a corrupter of youth and asking for copies of Poggio and Beccadelli's correspondence.

62. Sabbadini 1915–19, vol. 2, 209–14, no. 666; 3, 321.

63. Cinquini and Valentini 1907, 55–56; see Rutherford 2005, 27. See the Notes to Guarino's Prefatory Letter.

64. His reputation, however, continued. Lorch (1970: xxxvii n. 71) quotes from a letter from Gerardo Landriani, bishop of Lodi, to Beccadelli (from Lodi, January 1431; no further citation) about his friendship with Francesco Piccinino, warning him against "voluptuosa amicitia, sed qualem virtus parere consuevit." A certain Manfredo Balsamo, hearing that Beccadelli had influence in Alfonso's court, planned to send him his cousin Giovanni. In a letter of 1435 he writes (Sabbadini 1910b: 144 n. 1): "Unum tamen humanitati tue recordor, ut non ut Ergotiles seu Hilas tractetur, sed ut Hypolitus ille aris deorum consecratus: aliter mihi et tibi esset in futurum maximum scandalum." "However, I rely on your kindness, that he will be treated not as Ergoteles or Hylas but as a Hippolytus consecrated to the altars of the gods. Otherwise it will be a great scandal for me and for you."

65. So Pontano as late as 1452 is still writing praise for *The Hermaphrodite* (Appendix, XXI).

66. The best modern sources are Sabbadini 1891, Starrabba 1902 (important documents), Natale 1902 (largely derivative; the manuscript transcriptions are occasionally inaccurate), Laurenza 1912, Resta 1954 and 1965, Ryder 1976b, Santoro 1984. Bentley 1987: 84–100 is outstandingly useful. I have drawn on his account and readers are referred there for full documentation.

67. Ryder 1976a: 221.

68. Valla 1984: 142.

69. Beccadelli served as lieutenant (*locumtenens*) for the royal protonotary, lieutenant for the royal logothete, and as a president of the *Sommaria* (i.e., a legal adviser to the office of the auditor). See Ryder 1976a: 219, 23–34; 1976b: 126–28. As a comparison, papal secretaries drew 250–300 duc-

ats in 1415 (D'Amico 1983: 28). In 1431, Carlo Marsuppini's salary as professor of rhetoric in the university of Florence was 140 florins (raised to 350 florins in 1451: Chambers 1976: 73).

70. Ryder 1976b: 129.

71. Beccadelli 1538: 13–14 (1.42). Viriatus's long hit-and-run campaign culminated in the defeat of the army of general Q. Fabius Maximus Servilianus, which Viriatus spared. The source is Appian, *Iberica* 60–72; Beccadelli's enemy Pier Candido Decembrio was at work on a Latin translation during these years.

72. Beccadelli 1538: 14–15 (1.43).

73. For the account see Beccadelli's "Alphonsi Regis Triumphus," an appendix to the *De dictis et factis Alphonsi Regis* (1538: 129–39 misnumbered as 229–39). For a fascinating analysis of the elaborate allegorical floats, see Stacey 2007: 183–86. See also Helas 1999: 61–71 for Beccadelli's role in this and later pageants.

74. Bentley 1987: 108–22.

75. For Valla's side of the story, see Sabbadini 1891: 101–3; Regoliosi 1981a: 303–22; Valla 1984: 226–7, 238–41.

76. Billanovich 1951; Regoliosi 1981b. Valla included all his emendations of their emendations in his *Antidotum in Facium*: Regoliosi 1981a: 303–70.

77. The book was composed in only two months, apparently soon after April 1445: Valla 1540: 464–65; Gabotto 1892: 144–48, 275; Besomi 1966: 77–78; Resta 1968: 19–20; Besomi 1973: x–xv; Regoliosi 1981a: xl (for the date of the king's departure), 14–18; Ryder 1990: 324–25.

78. Valla 1977: 16–17; Rao 1978 and reviews by Regoliosi 1980, Ribuoli 1981; Fubini 2003: 163.

79. Valla 1984: 264, 272–73. The source and background of these attacks on Beccadelli have to be taken into consideration. Ryder 1990: 320–25 for a brief account of the atmosphere at court.

80. Sabbadini 1931: 110: "At nescio quo pacto is ab re uxoria non abhorreat qui omne feminarum genus iampridem summo odio habuit."

81. Beccadelli *Epistolae Campanae* 27 (1553: 108r–v = 1746: 351–52); Sabbadini 1910b: 158–59; 1915–19: 107–16; Laurenza 1912: 11–14; Resta 1954: 34, 57 n. 10; Regoliosi 1981a: 194; Valla 1984: 227.

82. Ryder (1976b: 130) placed him away from court for the entirety of September 1444 to early 1449, but then (Ryder 1990: 324–25) correctly notes that Beccadelli was near or present in Naples throughout the quarrel with Valla (as Valla himself makes clear: Valla 1540: 464–65), then placing his departure for Sicily in the aftermath. Resta (1965: 403) more correctly, I think, places the return to court in 1445 (the text misprints 1455). In a letter dated after 27 June 1445 he is planning to join the king on campaign, and we find him in the field in Tuscany by early 1448 at the latest: Laurenza 1912: 13–14; Resta 1954: 231 (no. 515).

83. Beccadelli 1538: 11 (1.35); 108–9 (4.4) on the visit of Holy Roman Emperor Frederick III to Naples in 1452. See also Ryder 1990: 349 and Tuohy 1996: 10–12.

84. Alas, the anecdote wherein he was so persuasive that the people called Alfonso "not King Alfonso, nor King of Aragon, but King of Quiet and Peace" is not borne out. The people in their relief were shouting the words even as the embassy came into town. See Duprè Theseider 1956: 106; Ryder 1990: 283–4.

85. Sabbadini 1910b: 157–58.

86. Greco 1970–76: I, 91, 100–01; Waters 1926: 63, 72.

87. Beccadelli and Pontano had a long exchange of poetic teasing at some point, a corrupt text filled with neologisms and obscure private references, but apparently touching on a boy named "Monophilas." See Cinquini and Valentini 1907: 47–49, Sommer 1997: 222–32.

88. For the quarrel, see Sabbadini 1917.

89. Ryder 1990: 327–28.

90. Beccadelli wrote to Aurispa to get copies of Caesar, Diogenes Laertius, Donatus on Terence, and Cicero for the royal library. He sold it his own copy of Ptolemy's map of the world (Ryder 1990: 321). Beccadelli, *Epistolae Campanae* 45 (1553: 118r–v = 1746: 370): "Significasti mihi nuper ex Florentia extare T. Livii opera venalia, literis pulcherrimis, libri pre-

tium esse CXX aureos. Quare Maiestatem tuam oro, ut Livium, quem Regem librorum appellare consuevimus, emi meo nomine, ac deferri ad nos facias; interim ego pecuniam procurabo, quam pro libri pretio tradam. Sed et illud a prudentia tua scire desidero uter ego an Poggius melius fecerit : is ut villam Florentiae emerit, Livium vendidit, quem sua manu pulcherrime scripserat ; ego ut Livium emam, fundum proscripsi." ("You have recently written me from Florence that there are works of Livy for sale, in good handwriting, and that the price of the book is 120 florins. Therefore I beseech your Majesty to buy this Livy, whom we are accustomed to call the King of books, in my name and have it sent to me; meanwhile I'll find the money for the purchase price. But I want to know who, in your opinion, did better, I or Poggio? He sold a Livy, beautifully written in his own hand, to buy a villa at Florence; I, to buy a Livy, have sold a farm.") For the copy of Livy, see Ullman 1933: 286–87 (who points out that the Livy Poggio sold and the Livy Beccadelli bought are not necessarily the same).

91. There was a lost *Vocabulario* of 1451; Ryder 1976b: 133.

92. Bentley 1987: 224–27 for a judicious summary; Ryder 1990: 306–07.

93. E.g. Beccadelli 1538: 6 (1.16), 10 (1.31–32), 12 (1.39), 13–15 (1.42–44), 19 (1.47), 40 (2.13–15), 50–51 (2.37) 110 (4.15), 112 (4.18), 115 (4.31).

94. Beccadelli 1538; Pius II 1571: 472–499.

95. Pontano's dialogue *Antonius* is a pleasant tribute to the early days: Pontano 1943, esp. 49–50. See Bentley 1987: 94–95; Furstenberg-Levi 2006: 37–41 (who clearly differentiates what we know of the meetings in Beccadelli's day from the later forms of the Accademia under Pontano); Santoro 1975: 159–61. The arches are in the short section of the Strada dell'Anticaglia (the ancient Decumanus superior) between vico Giganti and via San Paolo. They ran between the baths and the ancient theater. Beccadelli had a palazzo being rebuilt nearby at via Nilo, 26 (the older vicolo degli Bici). See Colangelo 1826: 111; Santoro 1975: 160.

96. Bentley 1987: 97–98.

97. Resta 1954: 404–05; Beccadelli 1475, 1553, 1746.

98. Resta 1954: 404; 1968: 33–34.

99. Filelfo 1502: 238v–239v.

100. "Hermofroditum ex Mercurio et Venere genitum vult Albericus lascivientem preter oportunitatem esse sermonem, qui, cum virilis esse debeat, nimia verborum mollicie videtur effeminatus." See O'Connor 2001: 17, Rutherford 2005: 91 n. 136.

101. Martial praef. 1, 1.4; Catullus 16; See Gaisser (1993, 20–23, 228–29) and O'Connor (1997) for Beccadelli's place in this literary topos.

102. 1.20, 2.11. Tibullus, Propertius, and Juvenal are also invoked in his letter to Poggio (after Book II).

103. Coppini 1998: 7. Ludwig (1989: 163, 165, 168–70; 1990: 188) disposes of any imitation of Catullus.

104. See Ludwig 1989, 1990 for a careful study of the influence of Catullus.

105. The idea of the personal epic was very much in the air and there was a sudden outpouring about twenty-five years later. The most famous (if still unpublished) of these is probably Francesco Filelfo's *Sforziad* (on Francesco Sforza, 1451–63 and after), but there was another *Sforziad* by Antonio Cornazzano (after 1454). In addition, there were a *Hesperis* (on Sigismondo Pandolfo Malatesta) by Basinio Basini da Parma (c. 1450–57), a *Borsiad* (on Borso d'Este) by Tito Vespasiano Strozzi (begun c. 1460), a *Feltriad* (on Federico da Montefeltro) by Giovanni Antonio Pandoni ("Porcellio"), a *Gonzagiad* (on Lodovico Gonzaga) by Gian Pietro Arrivabene, and a *Borgiad* (on Giovanni Borgia) by Giovanni Battista Cantalicio. In the next generation, Francesco Filelfo's son, Giovanni Mario Filelfo, managed a *Cosmiad* (on Cosimo de' Medici), a *Lorenziad* (on Lorenzo de' Medici), a *Martiad* (Federico da Montefeltro) and even an *Amyris* (on Mahomet II). There were papal epics by Marco Girolamo Vida, who, besides the *Christiad*, wrote two lost works, the *Felsinead* and the *Juliad* (on Julius II), and by Camillo Querno, who wrote an *Alexiad* (on Leo X).

106. Petrocchi 1965; Lanza 1985; Kleinhenz 1986: 157–200; Botterill 1996: 115 (for a concise overview). Orvieto and Brestolini 2000.

107. E.g. Rustico di Filippo 21, 26–29 (Marti 1956: 53, 58–61); or the sonnets attributed to Cecco Angiolieri with the overheard conversation of traders, an invective on women and make-up, or a repulsive and antaphrodisiac old woman.

108. Though, of course, these themes have a distinguished classical ancestry (Marti 1956: 248–49). For the theme of "the ugly woman," see Bettella 2005.

109. E.g. Rustico di Filippo mocking an addiction to sodomy or accusing an enemy of being an effeminate *(comare)* 1–2, 30 (Marti 1956: 33–34, 148), and being teased in turn by his pupil Jacopo da Lèona, 1 (Marti 1956: 97); Meo de' Tolomei, 4 (Marti 1956: 268–69), possibly the earliest attestation of *finocchio* in the sense of "homosexual;" Jacomo (Granfione) de' Tolomei, 1 (Marti 1956: 289, 299); Lapo Farinata degli Uberti responding to Guido Cavalcanti, saying that when he wrote he met a pretty shepherdess *(pasturella)*, he should have written "a handsome shepherd," if he wanted to tell the truth (De Robertis 1986: 178).

110. So the sonnets dubiously attributed to Cecco Angiolieri on various pretty boys (118–21, Marti 1956: 240–43); Meo de' Tolomei (12–13; Marti 1956: 268–69); Niccola Muscia (2–3; Marti 1956: 292–93). The Meo poem is especially interesting, as it depicts sodomy as a rich man's pastime, associated with aristocratic decadence *(luxuria): Sie certo ch'i' sapre' mangiar pernici / e giucar e voler lo mascolino, / sì come tu:* ("It's clear I know how to eat partridge, and gamble, and desire the male as well as you"). On the theme in general, see Marti (1953: 179–83), who views it primarily as a product of the 1300s, though accusations of sodomy continue to fly about in various *tenzoni* (poetic exchanges) of the following centuries.

111. Martin 1991: 18–20; Classen 1991: 145–72.

112. Ferri 1909: esp. 194 for a poem actually in praise of wives.

113. A number of the medieval comic tales (mostly in elegiacs) with their plots of sexual intrigue made their way from the Loire valley to Italy (see Bertini 1976–2000 for the details). One important manuscript containing the racy plays *Alda* and *Lidia* (plus *Geta*, a reworking of *Amphitruo*) was copied by Boccaccio, who used *Lidia* for the story of *Decameron* 7.9

(Bertini 1998a: 37–38, Gualandri and Orlandi 1998: 197–200). See Orlandi 1990 on the classical roots, and Elliott 1984 for a good introduction to the genre and English translations. Italy produced its own additions to the corpus, such as Richard of Venosa's *De Paulino et Polla* (the misadventures of a lawyer trying to set up a marriage between two old people, c. 1228–31), and the sexier *De Cerdone* (a wily priest gets the wife and the better of her husband) by one Jacobus, probably Jacobus de Benevento OP (13th cent.). See Haskins 1928: 147–48; Pandolfi and Artese 1965: 1–29; Pittaluga 1986; Doglio 1990, Bertini 1998b. Of the humanist comedies, *De Cavichiolo* (anon.) features a husband given to boys, while *Janus Sacerdos* (anon.) and *De falso hypocrita* (by Mercurino Ranzo) star pederastic priests. The first ends happily for all concerned. The last two do not. For studies of these (and other) works, see Pandolfi and Artese 1965 (Latin texts and Italian translations); Perosa 1965 (Italian translations); Stäuble 1968. See Grund 2005 (Latin texts and English translation) for a selection of humanist comedies.

114. So Pandolfi and Artese 1965: xii (where Pandolfi seems to want to attribute to him the rebirth of Italian theater generally) and Stäuble 1968: 206. Lorch 1968 attributes the anonymous *Janus Sacerdos* to him on the basis of a doubtful name in one manuscript. See Viti 1982: 1–9 and Limbeck 2000: 70 for a balanced account. Viti 1999: 65–68 argues for *The Hermaphrodite* as at least a source for the *Janus*, but the supposed parallels are too general to convince. The verbal echoes are better explained as borrowings from shared sources.

Alberti had completed his first major work, the morally improving allegorical play *Philodoxeos*, while in Bologna in 1424, where he knew Beccadelli (*Herm.* 1.21). In a later version, Alberti claims that a friend borrowed the manuscript, botched the copying and added some obscene bits before circulating it without the author's permission. Some have been tempted to see Beccadelli in this role (Grayson 1954: 291; Stäuble 1968: 29) but the charge is easily refuted (Cesarini Martinelli 1977: III n. 3).

115. In the original version of *De voluptate* (Lorch 1970: 143): "nullum scio hac tempestate meliorem vel historicum vel poetam" ("I know no better historian [Bruni] or poet [Panormita] in this age.").

116. Though he had to fix various mistakes in his first edition: 1.40.21, 2.26.21, etc.

117. Contrast Filelfo who works his way systematically through all the meters of Horace.

118. Ryder's assessment (1976b: 130), though harsh, is fair: "Money and possessions clearly meant a lot to him, and the steady accumulation of offices gave him much more than he could have hoped for from a simple pension or sinecure. Also he was a person of strictly limited creative ability: he possessed sparkling talent for the vivid sketch of character and incident in verse or prose, but lacked the breadth of vision and power of composition to carry through a major work. His achievement was one of style and form; he had no original ideas to put forward. Such a man could make no creative use of prolonged leisure, and might indeed have become demoralised by it. The very presence of Valla may have driven Beccadelli into a flurry of bureaucratic activity in order that he might be spared humiliating comparison with his rival."

Mancini (1891: 195) claimed that in their disputes before the king, Valla would speak in Latin and Beccadelli would reply in Italian, "implicitly confessing himself inferior to his rival." This is incorrect, since Paolo Cortesi, a brilliant Ciceronian, praised Beccadelli's Latin conversation to the detriment of Valla's (*Quid ergo est causae, si tam diligenter Valla de ratione verborum Latinorum scripserit, ipse non bene satis loqui Latine videatur?* "So why was it that though Valla wrote so carefully on Latin usage, he didn't actually seem to speak it very well?"); see Appendix, XXIII. Were it so, Valla, who was not slow to claim that he often made Beccadelli look ridiculous to the king, would have made the most of it (e.g. Valla 1984: 239; Regoliosi 1981a: xxii–xxiv, 304–5). In fact, Valla does not go that far, merely saying "loquebar autem ego litterate, Antonius illitterate" when Beccadelli offered his silly interpretations of Latin verses (Valla 1540: I, 595; Regoliosi 1981a: 308). The king told them both to shut up (Regoliosi 1981a: 309).

119. See the notes for examples.

120. E.g., 2.36.5–6: *vide . . . videas*; 2.36.37–38: 2.36.37: *mage malim . . . quam . . . velim*; 2.36.43: *fauces inhiant ut asellus hiascens*. For padding: 2.36.27: *ocius affectem* for *malim*, etc.

121. Cortesi in giving him modest praise adds the telling phrase "illis temporibus non contemptus" ("Not bad for those times"). See Appendix, XXIII.

122. Later subtitled *Amores*. Ludwig 1990: 189–92 for a glimpse of the original form. A selection in Arnaldi et al. 1964: 394–447.

123. Thurn 2002. A selection in Arnaldi et al. 1964: 448–527.

124. Resta 1976. A selection in Arnaldi et al. 1964: 104–13. Marrasio, a fellow Sicilian, however, does have one poem (not included in the *Angelinetum*; Resta 1976, *Carmina varia* 21) that has the title: "Ad Panhormitam divum poetam, ut solvat duo problemata quae ei Venus ante oculos adiecit: unde est <ut> unus gallus centum gallinarum sufficiens fututor sit, centum homines non unius feminae; alterum ut pulcherrima puella uni paediconi superabundans sit, milia vero epheborum vix sufficiunt." ("To Panormita, the divine poet, so that he might solve two problems that Venus has set in front of him. One: How come one rooster is enough to fuck one hundred hens, but one hundred men are not enough for one woman? The other is: How come one beautiful girl is more than enough for someone who likes butt-fucking, but a thousand boys are scarcely enough?").

125. Charlet 1997. A selection in Arnaldi et al. 1964: 126–31.

126. Mesdjian 1997. A selection in Arnaldi et al. 1964: 252–95.

127. Chatfield 2008. A selection in Arnaldi et al. 1964: 166–209.

128. Dennis 2006, of which one can rightly say with Porcellio (Appendix, XVII.3): *mentula, cunnus abest* ("Prick and cunt, there are none"). A selection in Arnaldi et al. 1964: 600–63.

129. Wilson 1995.

130. See Ludwig 1989, 1990; Fantazzi 1996; O'Connor 1997: 1006–9. For Secundus, see Godman 1988 and 1990; Murgatroyd 2000. See O'Connor 1997 for an excellent survey of later defenses of dirty poetry. Pacifico Massimi (Pacificus Maximus, c. 1410–c. 1505) was unaffected and contin-

ued to write more openly obscene verse. There is a new edition of his second *Hecatelegium* by Daude 2008.

131. For details of the manuscripts, see Coppini 1990. The vast majority (69) of the manuscripts are fifteenth century. Dated: L_3 (1434), W_1 (1450), V_4 (1452), Ma (1454), P (1455), V_1 (1461), Be_2 (1466), Pa_2 (1466), V_8 (1466), H (1469), Be_4 (1473), Pan (1475).

XV_{ex}: Par.
XV–XVI: E, Fe, Ox, Pa3, Vo, We, Wi. Dated: Bu (1522)
XVII: Ma_1, Q_2.
XVIII: Br, Or, Raw. Dated: Q (1718), Pa_1 (1722), Q_1 (1738), Ac (1790).

132. Jacodetius 1790, followed by the more widely disseminated Mercier 1791.

133. Forberg 1908: xiv n. 4.

134. English translation: Forberg 1884. See Halperin, Winkler, and Zeitlin 1990: 8–10 for Forberg's place in classical and sexual scholarship.

THE HERMAPHRODITE

Guarini in Hermaphroditon iudicium

Guarinus Veronensis suavissimo Iohanni Lamolae
plurimam salutem dicit.

1 Posteaquam alteras ad te descripseram, tuae et graves et ornatae
redditae mihi sunt, quae eo accumulatiores venerunt, quo etiam
comitem habuerunt libellum vere Ἑρμαφρόδιτον. Adeo pruden-
ter et polite conscriptus est, ut sane Mercurio iuncta Venustas
videatur, quod et ipsum Graece sapit vocabulum. Mirari profecto
licet suavissimam carminis harmoniam, dicendi facilitatem, inela-
borata verba et inoffensum compositionis cursum; nec idcirco mi-
nus carmen ipsum probarim et ingenium quia iocos, lasciviam et
petulcum aliquid sapiat: an ideo minus laudabis Apellem, Fabium
ceterosve pictores quia nudas et apertas pinxerunt in corpore parti-
culas natura latere volentes? Quid si vermes, angues, mures, scor-
piones, ranas, muscas fastidiosasque bestiolas expresserint? Num
ipsam admiraberis et extolles artem artificisque solertiam? Ego
mediusfidius hominem probo, ingenium miror et ludente delector,
flente <fleo, ridente>[1] rideo, lupanari medio scortantem laudo ver-
sum.

2 Plus valet apud me conterranei mei vatis non illepidi auctoritas
quam imperitorum clamor, quos nil nisi lacrimae, ieiunia, psalmi
delectare potest, immemores quod aliud in vita, aliud in oratione
spectari convenit. Ut autem ad meum conterraneum revertar, ille
hunc in modum ait:

PREFATORY LETTER

Guarino's Opinion about the Hermaphrodite

Guarino da Verona sends greetings to his dearest
Giovanni Lamola.[1]

After I had written a second letter to you, I received your serious 1
and elegant letter, which arrived all the more richly laden in that it
had as its companion a book, truly a Hermaphrodite! It is written
with such skill and polish that it certainly seems to be Mercury
united with Elegance, as the Greek word itself suggests.[2] One may
admire its sweet harmony of song, its ease of diction, its elaborate
word choice, and the unimpeded flow of its composition. And so I
would not approve less of the poem itself and the author's talent
just because it smacks of jokes, playfulness, and something a little
wanton. Would you therefore praise Apelles, Fabius, and other
painters the less because they painted naked and open to view
those parts of the body which by nature prefer to be hidden?[3]
What if they painted worms, snakes, mice, scorpions, frogs, flies,
and disgusting vermin?[4] Wouldn't you admire and praise their art
and the skill of the artist? I in truth praise the man, admire his
talent, delight when his verse plays around, when he cries <I cry,
when he laughs> I laugh,[5] praise it when it goes whoring in the
middle of a brothel.

The authority of my fellow countryman, a not inelegant poet,[6] 2
carries more weight with me than the shouting of the ignorant,
who can delight in nothing but tears, fasting, and psalms,[7] and
who forget that things ought to be looked at differently in life than
in speech. And to return to my countryman, he spoke to this
effect:

3

Nam castum esse decet pium poetam
ipsum, versiculos nihil necesse est,
qui tum denique habent salem ac leporem
si sint molliculi ac parum pudici
et quod pruriat incitare possint.

3   A qua quidem sententia et noster Hieronymus non abhorret, homo castimonia et integritate praeditus in primis, qui, cum in meretricis sermonem incidisset, quantam lascivienti ac vere scortanti calamo permisit usurpare licentiam!: "Quo cum, recedentibus cunctis, meretrix speciosa venisset, coepit delicatis stringere colla complexibus, et, quod dictu quoque scelus est, manibus attrectare virilia, ut, corpore in libidinem concitato, se victrix impudica superiaceret." Quis leno impudens flagitio magis linguam involveret? Habeo mille et quidem locupletissimos testes, graves, continentes et Christianos homines, qui spurcissimo uti sermone nihil expaverunt, cum res postulabat: sed in re certa supervacuum est testes citare minime necessarios.

4   Laudo igitur non modo ἐποποιίαν sed et poetam nostrum, ita enim appellare velim.

Musarum decus, Antoni, per saecula salve!
Theocriton, antiquum Siculae telluris alumnum,
effingis, prisca revocans dulcedine vatem.
Sicilidas Latio per te dabit Aetna Camenas.

5   Vale, mi Iohannes, et litterarum mearum λακωνισμῷ da veniam. Haud enim me sinunt occupationes μακρολογεῖν. Quid nostri sentiant de hominis ingenio faxo sentias cum eos in voluptatis partem vocaro. Vale iterum.

Veronae IIII nonas februarias.

For it's right that a proper poet be pure,
himself, but there's no need for his verses to be,
which can only have wit and charm
if they are a little on the lax side and not too modest
and can stir up what makes you itch.[8]

This was an opinion that even our own St. Jerome did not dis- 3
agree with, a man of the most exceptional chastity and rectitude,
who, when he chances to be speaking about a courtesan, what li-
cense does he allow his playful, even whorish pen to use: "After ev-
eryone had left him, a beautiful courtesan came to him, and began
to stroke his neck with sensuous embraces, and (though it is a sin
even to mention it) to fondle his manhood with her hands, so
that, once his body was roused to lust, the lewd woman might be
the victor and mount him."[9] What shameless pimp would get his
tongue around a more disgraceful act? I have a thousand very
trustworthy authorities, serious, self-controlled and Christian
men, who were not afraid to use the vilest language when the oc-
casion demanded it. But in a case that's already been decided, it's
pointless to call unnecessary witnesses.

So I praise not only the poetry, but our poet, as I should like to 4
call him:

Hail, glory of the Muses, Antonio, for ever.
You imitate Theocritus, the ancient son of the land of Sicily,[10]
recalling the poet with the sweetness of old.
Etna will give Sicilian Muses to Latium through you.

Farewell, Giovanni, and pardon the Laconic quality of my let- 5
ter. My business doesn't allow me to talk at length. What people
here think about the fellow's talent, I'll be sure to let you know
when I get them to join Pleasure's party.[11] Farewell again.

Verona, 2 February [1426].

LIBER I

: I :

Quod spreto vulgo libellum aequo animo legat,
quamvis lascivum, et secum una
priscos viros imitetur

Si vacat a patrii cura studioque senatus,
    quicquid id est, placido lumine, Cosme, legas.
Elicit hoc cuivis tristi rigidove cachinnos
    cuique, vel Hippolyto, concitat inguen opus.
5   Hac quoque parte sequor doctos veteresque poetas,
    quos etiam lusus composuisse liquet,
quos et perspicuum est vitam vixisse pudicam,
    si fuit obsceni plena tabella ioci.
Id latet ignavum volgus, cui nulla priores
10   visere, sed ventri dedita cura fuit;
cuius et hos lusus nostros inscitia carpet:
    o, ita sit! Doctis irreprehensus ero.
Tu lege tuque rudem nihili fac, Cosme, popellum;
    tu mecum aeternos ipse sequare viros.

BOOK I

: I :

That He May Ignore the Crowd and Read This Book
Sympathetically, Even Though It Is Naughty, and
So Join the Author in Imitating the Ancients[1]

If you have a break[2] from your care and concern for the senate
    of our country,
    please read this for what it's worth,[3] Cosimo, with an
      indulgent eye.[4]
This work rouses laughter from anyone, no matter how stiff
    and serious,
    and stirs anyone's loins, even Hippolytus's.[5]
And in this I follow the example of the learned poets of old,   5
    who, it is clear, composed trifles
and, it is evident, lived modest lives,
    even if their pages were full of obscene jokes.[6]
The lazy crowd fails to notice this, who have no care to look
    to the ancients
    but whose only care has been given to their belly.   10
Their ignorance will pick at my trifles too:
    So be it — the learned will not reproach me.
You read them, Cosimo, and don't give a toss for the rude
    rabble.
    Follow with me the men who live forever.

: II :

Ad semet ipsum loquitur et respondet

Cosmus habet dios et lectitat usque poetas:
    quid studium turbas, rauce poeta, suum?
Cosmus habet lautas epulas: quid oluscula coenat?
    Una quidem ratio est et studii et stomachi.

: III :

Ad Cosmum, virum clarissimum, de libri titulo

Si titulum nostri legisti, Cosme, libelli
    marginibus primis, "Hermaphroditus" erat.
Cunnus et est nostro, simul est et mentula, libro:
    conveniens igitur quam bene nomen habet!
5 At si podicem vocites, quod podice cantet,
    non inconveniens nomen habebit adhuc.
Quod si non placeat nomen nec et hoc nec et illud,
    dummodo non castum, pone quod ipse velis.

: IV :

Ad matronas et virgines castas

Quaeque ades, exhortor, procul hinc, matrona, recede;
    quaeque ades hinc pariter, virgo pudica, fuge:
exuor, en bracis iam prosilit inguen apertis

: II :

He Talks to Himself and Answers

Cosimo possesses the divine poets and reads them through
    and through.
    So why do you disturb his study, noisy poet?[7]
Cosimo has elegant banquets, so why does he dine on
    vegetables?
    He has the same plan for study and stomach.

: III :

To the Noble Cosimo, on the Title of His Book

When you read the title of our book, Cosimo,
    at the top of the page, it was "Hermaphroditus."
Our book has at the same time a cunt and a cock,
    so how very fitting a name it has!
But if you call it "Ass" because it sings with its ass,   5
    it will still have a not unfitting name.
But if neither this name nor that pleases you,[8]
    give it any title you want—as long as it's not a chaste one.

: IV :

To Married Women and Chaste Virgins[9]

If there are any married women present, I beg you, go far
    away from here.
    Likewise any modest virgin who is present, run away.

et mea permulto Musa sepulta mero est.
5   Stet, legat et laudet versus Nichina procaces,
assueta et nudos Ursa videre viros.

: V :

De Ursa superincubante

Quum mea volt futui, superincubat Ursa Priapo:
ipse suas partis sustineo, illa meas.
Si iuvat, Ursa, vehi, moveas clunemque femurque
parcius, aut inguen non tolerabit onus;
5   deinde cave reduci repetas ne podice penem:
quamvis, Ursa, velis, non mea virga volet.

: VI :

De Corvino, vinum accurate custodiente,
non uxorem

Corvinus vegetem custodit clave seraque;
non cohibet cunnum coniugis ille sera.
Zelotypus vegetis, cunni sed prodigus ille est:
haustu nam cunnus non perit, illa perit.

I'm taking off my clothes. See, already from my open pants my
    member springs out!
  My muse is buried in so much pure wine.
Let Nichina[10] stay, read, and praise my salacious verses,   5
  and Ursa who is accustomed to see naked men.[11]

: V :

On Ursa, Who Likes Being on Top

When my Ursa wants to be fucked, she climbs on top of
    Priapus.
  I play her role; she plays mine.
If you want to be carried, Ursa, move your buttocks and
    pussy[12]
  more cautiously, or my member won't bear the load.
Finally, please don't try to put my cock back up your ass.   5
  However much you want it, Ursa, my yardstick does not.[13]

: VI :

On Corvinus, Who Carefully Guards His Wine,
but Not His Wife

Corvinus guards his barrel[14] with lock and key,
  but he doesn't confine his wife's cunt with a lock.
He's stingy with the barrel but lavish with the cunt:
  the cunt can't be exhausted by dipping; the other can.[15]

: VII :

Epitaphium Pegasi claudi paediconis

Si vis scire meum nomen votumque, viator,
    Pegasus hac ego sum claudus humatus humo.
Vota deinde scias, nomen quum sciveris; audi,
    sic desyderio tu potiare tuo:
5   quum paticum quemquam paedicaturus ephebum es,
    illud in hac tumba, quaeso, viator, agas
atque ita mis animas coitu, non thure, piato:
    scilicet hanc requiem Manibus, oro, dato.
Hoc apud infernas genus est leniminis umbras
10   praecipuum, prisci sic statuere patres:
quippe ita Chironis cineres placabat Achilles,
    sensit et hoc podex, flave Patrocle, tuus;
gnovit Hylas, patrio percisus ab Hercule busto.
    Tu mihi maiores quod docuere lita.

: VIII :

De Ursae tentigine et naso

Si multus multae est nasus tentiginis index,
    Ursae tentigo tenditur usque pedes.
Quin si multa ampli nasi tentigo sit index,
    nasus ad usque tuum tenditur, Ursa, genu.

: VII :

Epitaph for Pegasus, the Lame Pederast

If you wish to know my name and my prayer, traveler,
    I am Pegasus, the lame, buried beneath this earth.
Now that you know my name, listen and learn my prayer:
    So may you enjoy your own desire.
When you're about to butt fuck your submissive youth,   5
    please do it on this tomb, traveler,
and so honor my[16] soul with fucking, not with incense.
    Grant this rest to my spirits, I pray.
This type of solace counts the most among the shades,
    as established by the fathers of old.   10
Thus Achilles satisfied the ashes of Chiron,[17]
    and your ass felt it too, blond Patroclus,[18]
Hylas knew it, spitted by Hercules on his father's burial
    mound.[19]
    Perform for me the rites our ancestors taught us.

: VIII :

On Ursa's Clit and Her Nose[20]

If a big nose is a sign of a big clit,
    then Ursa's clit hangs down to her feet.
But if a big clit is a sign of a big nose,
    then, Ursa, your nose hangs down to your knees.

: IX :

Ad Cornutum respondet quare relicta Etruria tristior sit

Quaeris ab unanimi, dulcis Cornute, sodali,
    cur videor licta tristior Etruria,
cur lusus abiere iocive et pallor in ore est,
    muta quid hic subito facta Thalia mea est.
5   Pene potens agit hic Gallus, qui cruscula solus
    quaeque velit, solus basia quaeque velit;
is sibi habet quodcunque natis vel podicis urbe est,
    quicquid et e Tuscis aut aliunde venit;
munera dat, Chroeso nummato qualia sat sint,
10   muneribus blandas adiicit illecebras;
inde edicta suis scribit quasi praetor ephebis:
    "Ne sine te tangi, ne sine te subigi";
non potes ergo loqui puero, ni indulgeat ille,
    ni velit is, puero non potes ipse frui.
15   Tu contra ingenuas mulieres, tu quoque servas,
    tuve bonas vexas inguine tuve malas;
vix tibi quae natum sacro de fonte levavit,
    vix sacra vixque soror, vix tua tuta parens;
tu futuis viduas, futuis nuptasve maritasve
20   et tibi vis cunni quicquid in urbe manet.
Tu tibi vis igitur tota quid mingit in urbe,
    ille sibi tota quicquid in urbe cacat.

: IX :

He Tells Cornutus Why He Is Sad to Have Left Tuscany[21]

You ask of your devoted comrade, sweet Cornutus,
    why I seem so sad to have left Tuscany,
why my trifles and jokes have vanished and there's pallor in my
        face,
    why my comic Muse has suddenly become mute.[22]
The Frenchman, mighty in cock, rules here.[23] He's the only   5
    one who has
    whatever thighs[24] he want, who has whatever kisses he
    wants.
He keeps for himself whatever bum and asshole is in the city,
    and whatever comes from Tuscany or elsewhere.
He gives gifts that would be enough for rich Croesus,
    and adds sweet nothings to his gifts.   10
Then like a praetor he writes orders to his youths:
    "Don't allow yourself to be touched, don't allow yourself to
    be done."
So you can't talk with a boy unless he allows it.
    If he doesn't want it, you can't enjoy a boy.
On the other hand, freeborn women and serving girls,   15
    the good and the bad, *you* can assault with your member.[25]
The woman who has lifted her baby from the baptismal font
    is barely safe from you, barely safe is your sister and your
    own mother.
You fuck widows, you fuck fiancées or brides,
    you want for your own all the cunt that remains in the   20
    city.[26]
In short, you want for your own everything in the whole city
    that pisses.
    He wants everything in the whole city that shits.[27]

Et mihi quin etiam iam constat mentula, qualem
    qui superat certe non homo, mulus erit;
25   et mihi nimirum constant viresque vicesque,
    quales qui vincit non homo, passer erit:
cur mihi non igitur futuendi copia fiat,
    nec sit quae coleos hauriat ulla meos?
Quare, agedum, nobis de partis cede puellam
30   aut unam aut unam tu mihi quaere novam.
Tunc me conspicias laetum lautumque licebit,
    candida tunc pulchrum nostra Thalia canet.

: X :

In Mathiam Lupium claudum maledicum

Nescio quis nostram fertur carpsisse Camenam:
    si non decipior, Lupius ille fuit.
Illa sibi solita est nimium lasciva videri;
    confiteor: vitae congruit ergo suae.
5   Est vir is obscenus, nostrae est lascivia Musae,
    illa levis versu, moribus ille levis.
Adde quod id monstri pedibus non ambulat aequis,
    imparibus constat nostra Camena modis.
Si culpat versus, et se culpare necesse est:
10   si sapis, ergo, tace, prodigiose senex.

For me, my cock stands so firm,
  that anyone who surpasses it is definitely a mule, not a
    man.
And truly my strength and condition[28] is so firm   25
  that he who conquers them is not a man, but a sparrow.[29]
So why shouldn't I have a supply of fucking?
  Why is there no one to drain my balls?
So come on, loan me a girl from your possessions
  or find me a new one.   30
Then you'll be able to see me happy and healthy,
  then my shining Thalia will sing beautifully.

: X :

Against Mattia Lupi, the Cursed Cripple[30]

Some nobody is said to have attacked my muse.
  If I'm not mistaken, it's Lupi.
She tends to appear too wanton to him;
  I admit it — that's because she suits his way of life.
The man himself is dirty; my wantonness is in my muse.   5
  She is easy in verse, he in morals.
Add the fact that this monster[31] does not walk on equal feet.
  Our muse is made of unequal measures.[32]
If he finds fault with our verse, he must also find fault with
    himself.
  So you'll shut up if you have any sense, you freakish old   10
    man.

: XI :

In eundem loripedem

Dic mihi, cur longo, Lupi, vestiris amictu?
    An vitium surae vis operire toga?
Nil agis, o demens: humeri latera atque moventur
    ut tumida nullo remige lembus aqua.

: XII :

In Mamurianum, postremae turpitudinis virum

Si tot habes scapula penes quot sorpseris ano
    et perfers, vincis, Mamuriane, boves.

: XIII :

In Lentulum mollem, elatum et postremae
turpitudinis virum

Solus habes nummos et solus, Lentule, libros,
    solus habes pueros, pallia solus habes,

: XI :

Against the Same, the Gimp

Tell me, Lupi, why do you dress in a long cloak?
    Do you think you can cover up the deformity of your leg
        with a toga?
It's not working, you idiot. Your shoulders and sides move
        around
    like a boat without an oar in a swollen sea.

: XII :

Against Mamurianus, a Man of the Lowest Vice[33]

If you took on your shoulders all the cocks you've sucked into
        your ass
    without collapsing, Mamurianus, then you're stronger than
        bulls.

: XIII :

Against Lentulus, the Effeminate, the High and Mighty, and a Man of the Lowest Vice[34]

You keep your money to yourself, Lentulus, and your books to
        yourself,
    you keep your boys to yourself, you keep your coats to
        yourself,

solus et ingenium, cor solus, solus amicos:
    unum si demas, omnia solus habes.
5   Hoc unum est podex, quem non tibi, Lentule, solus,
    sed quem cum populo, Lentule mollis, habes.

: XIV :

Lepidinus ab auctore quaeret cur qui semel paedicare
coeperit haudquaquam desistit

Cur qui paedicat semel, aut semel irrimat, auctor
    nugarum, nunquam dedidicisse potest?
Imo Brito et bardus, cum vix gustaverit, ultro
    certat in hoc ipsas vincere amore Senas.
5   Parthenope Gallis cedit, Florentia Cimbris,
    si semel iis puerum sors tetigisse dedit!

: XV :

Ad Lepidinum responsio et quare
ursus cauda caret

Accipe ridiculam, dulcis Lepidine, fabellam,
    et quae quod poscis dissoluisse queat.
Fertur ab orticola divam quaesisse Priapo
    (seu Venus in dubio est, seu dea Flora fuit)
5   cur, quum velentur quasi quaeque animalia cauda,

your talent to yourself, your heart to yourself, your friends to
    yourself.
  You keep everything to yourself, except for one thing.
That one thing is your asshole, Lentulus, which you do not   5
    keep to yourself,
    but share with everyone, effeminate Lentulus.

: XIV :

Lepidinus Asks the Author Why Once Someone Begins to Butt Fuck He Never Stops[35]

O author of trifles, why is a man never able to give it up
  once he's fucked someone in the ass or the mouth?
In fact, even a blockhead Breton,[36] when he's had barely a
    taste,
  willingly competes with Siena itself in this sort of love.
Naples yields to the French, Florence to the Germans,   5
  once they get the chance to touch a boy.

: XV :

The Author's Response to Lepidinus and the Story of Why the Bear Is Missing His Tail[37]

Listen, sweet Lepidinus, to this silly story,
  which can solve the riddle that you pose.
They say a goddess asked the garden god Priapus
  (it's uncertain whether it was Venus or the goddess Flora)
why, when nearly every animal veils with a tail   5

21

ursus non cauda membra pudenda tegat.
Ille refert: "Escam cupide dum quaereret ursus,
    in tempestivos incidit ille favos;
nec comedit primum, licet ipse famelicus esset,
10   quandoquidem merdas credidit esse favos.
At, stimulante fame, mox haeret, libat et instat:
    mel sapit, et tandem non edit, imo vorat.
Rusticus advortit, properat, strepit; ursus obaudit
    (rusticus is custos mellis et Argus erat).
15   Denique robusti cauda subnititur ursi
    et trahit; ille novo non trahit ora cibo.
Pauperiem timet hic, timet hic de melle moveri,
    ille suo perstat proposito, ille suo.
Verum adeo trahit hic, adeo hic contrarius obstat,
20   manserit ut stupida cauda revulsa manu."
Hic deus hortorum, dum subdere plura pararet,
    arrigit, et pepulit mentula tenta deam.
Sic qui forte mares semel inclinaverit, idem
    haud facinus coeptum destituisse potest.

: XVI :

In Mathiam Lupium

Annua publicitus tibi larga pecunia, Lupi,
    solvitur: et pueris quot legis ipse? Tribus!

its unmentionable members, the bear does not cover them.
He replies, "When a bear was looking eagerly for food,
    he chanced upon some ripe honeycombs.
Yet he didn't eat them at first, even though he was starving,
    since he believed the honeycombs were turds.   10
But driven by hunger, he soon stopped, nibbled, and set to.
    He tasted the honey, and didn't just eat, he devoured.
The farmer noticed, ran up, yelled. The bear paid no heed.[38]
    (This farmer was an Argus when it came to watching the
      honey.)
So then he grabbed hold[39] of the tail of the mighty bear,   15
    and pulled; but he could not pull its mouth away from the
      new food.
This one feared poverty; this one feared to be moved from the
      honey
    That one persisted in his purpose; that one in his.
Finally, this one dragged so hard, that one stood its ground so
      obstinately
    that the tail tore away and remained in his amazed hand."   20
And here the god of gardens, while he was preparing to add
    further details,
    became erect, and his swollen cock drove the goddess away.
So once someone bends males over,[40]
    he can't give up the misdeed once he's begun.

: XVI :

Against Mattia Lupi[41]

A large stipend is paid you every year, Lupi,
    from public funds. And how many boys do you lecture to?
    Three!

: XVII :

In eundem litterarum ignarum

Inde tui libri sint, inde scientia, Lupi:
    qui non desipiat, mallet habere libros!

: XVIII :

Laus Aldae

Aldae oculis legere domum Charitesque Venusque,
    ridet et in labiis ipse Cupido suis.
Non mingit, verum si meiit, balsama mingit;
    non cacat, aut violas, si cacat, Alda cacat.

: XIX :

*Ad Coridonem ardentem Quintium, turpem
et deformem puerum*

Quintius is, Coridon, quem vesanissime flagras,
    siccior est cornu pallidiorque croco;
aridus in venis extat pro sanguine pulvis
    deque suo gracili corpore sudor abest;
5   Aethiopi perhibet gens concubuisse parentem
    atque ideo gnatos edidit illa nigros;
si risum elicias, rictum inspicies sibi qualem
    prodit in aestivo tempore cunnus equae;

: XVII :

Against the Same Ignoramus[42]

You got your learning from the same place you got your books,
  Lupi.
  Anyone with sense would prefer to have the books.

: XVIII :

Praise of Alda[43]

Venus and the Graces have chosen their home in Alda's eyes.
  And in her[44] lips Cupid himself smiles.
She doesn't piss, but if she did piss, she pisses balsam.
  She doesn't shit, but if Alda did shit, she shits violets.

: XIX :

To Coridon, Lusting for Quintius, a Foul and Ugly Boy[45]

That Quintius, for whom you are madly on fire, Coridon,[46]
  is drier than horn[47] and paler than crocus.
There is dry dust in his veins instead of blood,[48]
  there's no sweat in his thin body.
People say that his mother slept with an Ethiopian   5
  and so she bore black children.
Provoke a laugh and you'll see a gape
  like a mare's cunt produces in summertime.[49]

si buccam olfacias, culum olfecisse putabis,
10 verum etiam culus mundior ore suo est;
mentula perpetuo tibi quam contracta iacebit,
  tu sibi dumtaxat basia fige semel!
I procul hinc, Quinti, foedum putensque lupanar,
  atque alio quovis ista venena feras!
15 Quis numeret quot hians absorpserit inguina podex?
  Quot naves Siculo littore Scylla voret!
Ipse palam patitur (pudet heu!) muliebria cuivis,
  ipse palam tota prostat in urbe puer.
Qui puerum hunc igitur quit paedicare, profecto
20 is poterit rigidas supposuisse feras!

∶ XX ∶

In Hodum mordacem

Hodus ait nostram uitam non esse pudicam:
  e scriptis mentem concipit ille meis.
Non debet teneros Hodus legisse Catullos,
  non vidit penem, verpe Priape, tuum.
5 Quod decuit Marcos, quod Marsos quodve Pedones,
  denique quod cunctos, num mihi turpe putem?
Me sine cum tantis simul una errare poetis,
  et tu cum vulgo crede quid, Hode, velis!

If you smell his mouth, you'll think you've smelled his ass,
　　but even his ass is cleaner than his mouth.[50]　　　　　10
Your cock will just lie there shriveled forever,
　　the minute you plant kisses on him.[51]
Go far away from here, Quintius, you dirty, stinking brothel,
　　And take your venom elsewhere—anywhere else.
Who can count the number of members your gaping asshole　15
　　has swallowed?
　　As many as the ships that Scylla devoured by the Sicilian
　　shore.
He openly takes the woman's passive role for any man (the
　　shame of it!)
　　The boy openly whores himself throughout the city.
The man who can butt fuck this boy, in fact,
　　would be capable of mounting bristling beasts!　　　　20

: XX :

Against Oddo, the Backbiter[52]

Oddo says my life is not pure.
　　He imagines my mind from my writings.
Oddo must not have read the tender[53] Catulluses;
　　he has not seen your cock, well-endowed[54] Priapus.
What was fitting for the Marcuses, the Marsuses, the　　　5
　　Pedones,[55]
　　in short everyone, do you think is shameful for me?
Let me make *my* mistakes in the company of these great poets
　　and *you* believe what you like with the crowd, Oddo.

: XXI :

Ad Baptistam Albertinum de Ursae luxuria

Comis es et totus pulcher totusque facetus,
    litterulis totus deditus ingenuis
atque Albertorum claro de sanguine cretus,
    nec morum quisquam est nobilitate prior;
5   cum placeas cunctis raris pro dotibus, idem
    tu mihi pro vera simplicitate places.
Veridicus cum sis et apertae frontis amicus,
    in parili nostro casmate dic quid agas:
si mihi sint epulae totidem, quot in alite plumae,
10   uno luxurians has edet Ursa die;
si mihi sint totidem vegetes, quot in aequore pisces,
    uno subsitiens ebibet Ursa die;
si mihi sint totidem loculi, quot littore arenae,
    hos omnis uno depleat Ursa die;
15   si mihi sint totidem libri, quot in aere pennae,
    hos omnis uno foeneret Ursa die;
si mihi sint totidem penes, quot in arbore rami,
    hos omnis uno sorbeat Ursa die.
Denique si nasis essem, Baptista, refertus,
20   hos faetore omnis imbuet Ursa suo!

: XXI :

To Leon Battista Alberti, on Ursa's Extravagance[56]

You are kind and completely handsome and completely clever,
　　completely dedicated to the liberal arts,[57]
and sprung from the famous blood of the Alberti,[58]
　　nor is there anyone superior to you in nobility of morals.
Though everyone likes you for these rare gifts, I myself like　　5
　　you
　　for your true candor.[59]
You are truthful and an open-hearted friend,
　　tell me what you would do in a disaster[60] like mine.
If I had as many banquets as a bird has feathers,
　　Ursa in her extravagance would eat them all in a day.　　10
If I had as many barrels as there are fish in the sea,
　　thirsty[61] Ursa would drink them in a day.
If I had as many money chests as there are grains of sand on
　　the shore,
　　Ursa would empty them all in a day.
If I had as many books as there are wings beating in the sky,　　15
　　Ursa would hock them all in a day.
If I had as many cocks as there are branches on a tree,
　　Ursa would suck them all dry in a day.[62]
And finally if I were stuffed full of noses, Battista,
　　Ursa would fill them all with her stench!　　20

: XXII :

Ad Quintium quomodo possit arrigere

Ad non dilectas, Quinti, tibi mentula tenta est,
  si tibi iocunda est, non potes arrigere.
Qui volt posse, suum digitos intrudat in anum:
  sic perhibent Helenae concubuisse Parim.

: XXIII :

Ad Minum quod libellum castrare nolit

Mine, mones nostro demam de carmine penem:
  carmina sic cunctis posse placere putas.
Mine, meum certe nolim castrare libellum:
  Phoebus habet penem Calliopeque femur.

: XXIV :

Epitaphium Horiectae Senensis puellae
bellissimae ac moratissimae

Postquam marmoreo iacet hoc Horiecta sepulchro,
  ipsa deum credam numina posse mori.
Non fuit absimilis forma aut virtutibus ipsis
  caelitibus, Senae gloria magna suae.
5   Heu heu, non probitas species aut unica quenquam
  abs inclementi demere morte potest!
Quod si clara deos faciat mortalia virtus

: XXII :

To Quintius: How He Can Get It Up[63]

For women you don't like, Quintius, your cock is stiff.
    If one really attracts you, you can't get it up.
If you want to be able to do it, jam your fingers up your ass.
    That's how, they say, Paris slept with Helen.

: XXIII :

To Mino, That He Should Not Castrate This Book[64]

Mino, you advise me to take the cock out of my book.
    That way you think my songs will please everyone.
Mino, please don't castrate my book.
    Phoebus has a cock. Calliope has a pussy.[65]

: XXIV :

Epitaph for Orietta of Siena, a Most Beautiful and Moral Girl[66]

Now that Orietta lies here in this marble tomb,
    I can believe that the very powers of the gods can die.
In her beauty and virtues she was like to the very
    inhabitants of heaven, a great glory to her city Siena.
Alas, alas, even goodness and unique beauty   5
    cannot keep anyone from pitiless death.
But if bright virtue can make mortal bodies

corpora, si caelum simplicibus pateat,
non dubitem, per vim modo non sibi iura negentur:
10   deiiciet supera sede puella Iovem.

: XXV :

Epitaphium Baptistae virgunculae sororis Horiectae

Hic tumulus, longe tumulo felicior omni,
    Baptistae auricomae virginis ossa tegit.
Dulciter haec agili pulsabat cymbala dextra
    movit et artifices saltibus apta pedes,
5   omnibus et cantu plus quam Philomena placebat;
    matre quidem pulchra pulchrior illa fuit;
indolis egregiae, minimo pro errore rubebat,
    sparsa rubore placens, fusa rubore decens.
Quum satis haec fecit naturae luce suprema,
10   transierat vitae vix duo lustra suae.

: XXVI :

In Mathiam Lupium paediconem

Ergo tua, Lupi, si pascitur Hisbo culina,
    cur non obsequitur iussibus ille tuis?
Etsi grammatica instituas hunc arte magister,
    cur tibi dat tenera verbera crebra manu?
5   Nescio Thiresiae sortes, nec aruspicis artes,
    sed coniectura hoc et ratione scio:

into gods, if heaven is open to the pure in heart,
I am sure, provided her rights are not denied her by violence,
   that this girl will throw down Jove from his high throne.   10

: XXV :

Epitaph for the Young Girl, Battista, Sister of Orietta[67]

This tomb, far more blessed than all tombs,
   covers the bones of Battista the golden-haired girl.
Sweetly she struck the cymbal with her agile hand
   and adept at the dance she moved her skillful feet.
She pleased everyone with her song more than Philomena.[68]   5
   She was even more beautiful than her beautiful mother.[69]
Of exceptional talent, she blushed at the least little mistake,
   pleasing when sprinkled with blushing, lovely when suffused
     with blushing.
When she paid her debt to nature on her last day,
   barely ten years of her life had passed.   10

: XXVI :

Against Mattia Lupi, the Pederast[70]

So, if Hisbo[71] gets fed in your kitchen, Lupi,
   why doesn't he obey your orders?
And though you're the teacher and instruct him in the art of
    grammar,
   why does he give you frequent blows with his soft hand?[72]
I don't know Tiresias's lots or the arts of the soothsayer,[73]   5
   but this I know by conjecture and reason:

qui nocte est facilis, durus sit luce necesse est;
    quem non paedicas est tibi morigerus.

: XXVII :

Ad Sanctium Ballum, versuum suorum cultorem

Sancti, nugarum lector studiose mearum,
    cui plus quam satis est nostra Camena placet,
desine mirari versus quos inter edendum
    edimus, aut hora carmina lusa brevi.
5   Testis es ut, quum iam versu defixior essem,
    e digitis calamos subtrahat Ursa meis;
carmina iam nosti strepitu persaepe foroque
    condita sint medio qualiacunque legis:
cum platea dubius peterem verbumque locumque
10   factus sum monitu certior ipse tuo;
verum adeo longe me diligis, ut tibi vatis
    Thraicii videar concinuisse lyra.
Si qua tamen nostrae dederit sors otia pennae
    et me tranquilla scribere mente sinat,
15   est animo versus quos nulla oblitteret aetas
    conficere, ingenii ni mihi vana fides.
Interea felix et amans, mi Balle, valeto,
    fiant et parcae ferrea fila tuae,
et tua crudelis deponat Masia fastus,
20   atque iterum felix, compatriota, vale.

he who is easy by night, must of necessity be hard by day.
The one you're *not* butt-fucking is nice to you.

: XXVII :

To Santia Ballo, an Admirer of the Author's Verses[74]

Santia, devoted reader[75] of my trifles,
   you who like my Muse even more than you should,
stop wondering at the verses I've produced while eating,
   the playful songs of a brief hour.
You are witness, when I was focused on composing a verse,   5
   how Ursa would take the pen from my fingers.
You know how the songs you read, such as they are,
   were often composed amid noise and in the middle of the
      forum.[76]
When in the street I would hesitate over a word or a passage
   I was given the right answer by your advice.[77]   10
Truly you love me so much that to you I seem
   to have played on the lyre of Thracian Orpheus.
Yet if fate will give my pen some leisure
   and allows me to write with a tranquil mind,
I have in mind to make verses that no age will erase,[78]   15
   unless the faith I have in my talent is vain.
In the meanwhile, my happy and loving Ballo, farewell.
   May the threads of your Fate be made of iron,[79]
and may your cruel Masia drop her pride[80]
   and happy once more, my compatriot, fare you well.   20

: XXVIII :

Lauridius ad auctorem de flagrantissimo amore suo

Me vexat Perusinus amor vincitque Senensem.
    Heu capit, heu vexat me Perusinus amor!
Collibeat summo proles Perusina tonanti,
    grata foret superis stirps Perusina deis!
5   Karolus, insignis forma natoque decore,
    me tenet et tenero sub pede colla premit.

: XXIX :

Ad Lauridium responsio de amore suo

Ut lubeat Perusinus amor te verset et angat:
    me mea Senensis Lutia nympha capit.
Gens tibi gensque Iovi placeat Perusina superno,
    me mea dumtaxat nympha Senensis amet.
5   Nil mortale tenet, divas et moribus aequat
    et specie, et Iovis haec digna rapina foret.

: XXVIII :

Lauridio to the Author, about His Most Burning Love

A love from Perugia attacks me and conquers the love from
    Siena.
    Alas he captures me, he attacks me, the love from Perugia.
The son of Perugia would delight the Thunderer above,
    the offspring of Perugia would please the gods on high.
Carlo, famed for beauty and natural grace,   5
    captures me and presses my neck beneath his tender foot.[81]

: XXIX :

The Author's Response to Lauridio, about His Own Love

Let the love from Perugia attack and torment you as he
    wishes:
    my Lucia, the maiden of Siena, holds me.
Let the race of Perugia please you, please Jove above,
    as long as my maiden of Siena loves me.
She has nothing mortal about her, and in her ways and looks   5
    she equals the goddesses. She would be plunder fit even for
    Jove.

: XXX :

Sena civitas Etruriae loquitur et Iovem orat
ut saltem sibi Lutiam nympham servet
mortalitatis expertem

Iupiter, omnipotens et clementissime divum,
    exaudi fundit quas tua Sena preces.
Iusta precor: iustas audi, iustissime, voces
    urbis, et, o, miserae commiseresce, deus!
5   Postquam me affligi tantorum morte virorum
    et nuruum placuit, vivat alumna precor;
vivat alumna precor, quam scis prolixius unam
    mater amem: stabile est matris alumna decus.
Nympha diu superet, patriae faustissima proles:
10   est honor et dos, spes, gloria, fama mei est.
Ut peritent cuncti et maneat modo nympha superstes:
    damna potest patriae restituisse suae.
Si vivit, mecum est virtus, victoria, mos, pax,
    nobilitas et cum nobilitate salus.
15   Sin migrat, sane cuncta haec et plura peribunt:
    mors sua mors nobis omnibus acris erit.
Non amor aut cultus, nec erit iocus ullus in urbe,
    plausus nec risus, laeta nec ulla dies;
gymnasium pariter solvetur, gloria Senae,
20   quod mea iocundo lumine nympha tenet.
Credite vos, superi, celebris curate puella
    vivat: longaevo est digna puella die.

: XXX :

The City of Siena in Tuscany Speaks, and Prays to
Jove That He Would Keep the Maiden Lucia
Untouched by Mortality for Her

Jove, omnipotent and most merciful of gods,
    listen to the prayers your Siena pours out.
I ask for justice. Listen, most just, to my just cries,[82]
    and, O God, pity a wretched city.
Since it has pleased you to afflict me with the deaths of so   5
    many men
    and women, let one foster daughter live, I pray.
Let the foster daughter live, I pray, whom you know I love
    with all my heart
    as a mother loves her only child. The foster daughter is her
    mother's enduring glory.
Let the girl live longer, the most blessed offspring of her
    fatherland.
    She is my honor, dowry, hope, glory, and fame.   10
Let all the others perish and let the girl alone survive.
    She can restore the losses to her fatherland.
If she lives, I have virtue, victory, morals, peace,
    nobility and with nobility, security.
If she passes on, all these things and more will perish.   15
    Her death will be bitter death for us all.
No love or culture, no fun will be in the city,
    applause nor laughter, no day will be happy.
The university[83] will be dissolved, the glory of Siena,
    which my girl looked on with kind eyes.   20
Believe me, gods on high, make sure that this famous girl
    may live: the girl is worthy of a long life.

Diique deaeque, iterum moneo, servate puellam,
　　et sinite Etruria stet decus urbe suum.
25　Credite, si nigrae truncent sua pensa sorores,
　　ingens caelicolis pugna deabus erit,
suscipiet siquidem caelestis regia nymphen
　　atque opus est proprio cedat ut una polo:
aut sibi promeritae decimum statuetis Olimpum
30　(nympha quidem caelo est Lutia digna novo),
aut pellat quamvis propria de sede necesse est
　　(digna quidem caelo est Lutia nympha suo).
Dicite vos, caelum si pro virtute secutae
　　sitis: an ulla poli munere digna mage est?
35　Nulla fuit vestrum, veniam date, purior illa,
　　moribus, ingenio vel pietate prior.
Denique centenos operam date victitet annos,
　　neu cedat vestris mors sua forte malis.
Ergo simul, divae, mecum exorate tonantem
40　ut praestet nymphae tempora longa meae.

: XXXI :

Ad Cosmum Florentinum virum clarissimum

Quam modo sensisti si non tibi grata fuit vox,
　　Cosme, nihil miror: Sena locuta fuit.

Gods and goddesses, again I warn you, save the girl,
    and allow its glory to remain in the Tuscan city.
Believe me, if the black sisters cut short her thread,[84]   25
    there will be a great battle among the goddesses in heaven.[85]
If the heavenly hall receives the nymph
    and one of them has to yield her proper sphere,
then either you will set up a tenth Olympus for her — she has
        earned it —
    the nymph Lucia is worthy of a new heaven,   30
or it is necessary to push some goddess from her place;
    the nymph Lucia is worthy of her own heaven.
Tell me, if you goddess have reached heaven because of your
        virtue,
    is any girl more worthy of the prize of a heavenly sphere?
None of you (begging your pardon) was purer than she   35
    in morals, or better in talent or piety.
So see to it that she lives[86] for a hundred years
    and that her death does not turn out to your misfortune.
So goddesses join me in praying to the Thunderer
    that he grant my nymph a long life.   40

: XXXI :

To Cosimo, the Florentine Nobleman

If the voice you just heard was not pleasing to you,
    Cosimo, I am not surprised: Siena spoke.[87]

: XXXII :

Epitaphium Catherinae puellae ornatissimae

Hoc iacet ingenuae formae Catherina sepulchro:
  grata fuit multis scita puella procis.
Morte sua lugent cantus lugentque choreae,
  flet Venus et moesto corpore moeret Amor.

: XXXIII :

In Mamurianum Tuscum penisuggium

Tuscus es, et populo iocunda est mentula Tusco;
  Tusculus et meus est, Mamuriane, liber.
Attamen e nostro praecidam codice penem,
  praecidam simulac, Mamuriane, iubes:
5   nec prius abscindam, nisi tu prius ipse virilem
  promittas demptam suggere nolle notam.

: XXXIV :

Ad Amilum paediconem

Hunc paedicato qui portat, Amile, tabellam,
  et referas quae sit pulchra tabella magis.

: XXXII :

Epitaph for Catherine, a Most Talented Girl[88]

In this tomb lies Catherine possessed of great beauty.
   Learned, she was loved by many suitors.
At her death, songs grieve, and dances grieve,
   Venus weeps and Love mourns her mourned body.

: XXXIII :

Against Mamurianus, the Tuscan Cocksucker[89]

You're a Tuscan, and cock delights the Tuscan people.
   My book is also a little Tuscan, Mamurianus.
And yet, I'll cut the cock out of my volume,
   I'll cut it out, Mamurianus, as soon as you give the order:
But I won't cut it off unless you promise first   5
   that you won't try to suck the mark of manhood[90] after it's
   been removed.

: XXXIV :

To Amilus the Pederast[91]

Butt fuck the one who brings you this letter, Amilus,
   and tell me if you've had a more handsome letter.

: XXXV :

De villico stulto Aldam basiante

Porticus insignem facie dum sustinet Aldam,
    villicus incautae basia rapta dedit.
Hunc vulgus stolidum credit, sed stultius illo est
    volgus. Me miserum, quam bene, stulte, sapis!
5   Cum liceat stultis impune suavia nymphae
    figere, dii facerent stultus ut ipse forem!

: XXXVI :

In Mathiam Lupium paediconem

Lupius, indoctum dum paedicaret ephebum,
    dixit: "Io, clunes, dulcis ephebe, move!".
Hic ait: "Id faciam, uerbo si dixeris uno."
    Ille refert: "Ceve! Diximus, ergo move!".

: XXXVII :

*Epitaphium Sanzi Ligoris,
belli ac domi praecipui viri*

Temporibus luteis in me romana refulsit
    virtus prisca, domi militiaeque simul.
Nomen erat Sanzus, clara de stirpe Ligori:
    sarcophago hoc tegitur corpus, at umbra polo est.

: XXXV :

On the Stupid Bailiff Kissing Alda[92]

While Alda, famed for her beauty, lingered in the portico,[93]
   a bailiff snatched kisses from the unsuspecting girl.[94]
The crowd thought he was stupid, but the crowd is stupider
   than he.
   Woe is me, how smart you are, idiot.
Since it's allowed for idiots to plant kisses on a girl   5
   and get away with it, may the gods make me an idiot too!

: XXXVI :

Against Mattia Lupi, the Pederast

When Lupi was butt fucking an ignorant boy,
   he said, "O sweet boy, move your bottom!"
The boy said, "I'll do it, if you put it in one word."[95]
   He replied, "Wiggle![96] I've said it, so move it!"

: XXXVII :

Epitaph for Sanzio Liguori, an Outstanding Man in War and Peace[97]

In filthy times, the old Roman virtue
   blazed forth in me, at home and on military service.[98]
My name was Sanzio, from the famous family of Liguori.
   This body is covered by a tomb, but my shade is in heaven.

: XXXVIII :

Ad Pontanum Pollam semideam ardentem,
pro quo vehementer orat

Si vacat, Aoniis o vir pergrate Camenis,
    accipe quid pro te lingua animoque precer:
ut tibi dent annos superi (dignissimus aevo es,
    dignior est digno candida Polla uiro),
5   et tibi sit facilis tenera cum matre Cupido
    (dignior est tenerae Polla favore deae),
et visens nullo possis, Pontane, videri,
    dummodo semidea tu videare tua,
atque anus enervis quae semper murmurat in te
10   in fontes, urnae pondere tracta, cadat;
at via declivis fieri planissima possit,
    sentiat et gressus semper amica tuos;
etsi dulce canas, possit vox ipsa videri
    dulcior, et credat suavius esse nihil,
15   inque dies crescat calor hic, et possit amare
    strictius hic illam, strictius illa virum,
et tibi iam possit nymphe praeclara videri
    Tindaris, ac illi tu videare Paris;
hispidus actutum queat expirare maritus,
20   ni deus hortorum vir sit, ut esse putas;
sive sit ipse deus, seu non, tamen ipsa maritum
    te fingat, tecum seque cubare putet;
et tibi contingat demum inclusisse labellis

: XXXVIII :

To Pontano, on Fire for the Demigoddess Polla;
the Author Prays Earnestly for Him[99]

If you have a moment, O man most pleasing to the Aonian
    Muses,[100]
  hear what I pray for you with tongue and heart,
that the gods above give you years[101] (you deserve an eon,
    shining Polla is even more deserving of a deserving man)[102]
and may Cupid be kind to you, along with his tender mother;   5
  Polla is even more deserving of the favor of a tender
    goddess.
And as you look, Pontano, may no one look on you,
  while you are looked on by your demigoddess,
and the decrepit old woman[103] who's always muttering at you,
  may she fall into the well, dragged down by the weight of   10
    her bucket.[104]
May the road leading down become as smooth as possible,[105]
  and may your girlfriend always hear your footsteps;
and even if you sing sweetly, may your very voice seem
  even sweeter, and may she believe there's nothing sweeter,
and may this heat increase day by day, and he love her   15
  more intensely, she more intensely her man,[106]
and may the wonderful nymph seem to you
  a Helen, and you to her a Paris.[107]
May her hairy husband breathe his last immediately,
  if he's not the god of gardens you think he is.[108]   20
But whether he's a god or not, let her pretend
  that you're her husband, and dream that she's sleeping with
    you.
And may it befall you at last to enclose her tongue

et linguam et dominae sustinuisse femur.
25 Si forte unanimis pro me, Pontane, precari
    atque vicem votis reddere forte velis,
id, precor, assidue noctuque diuque precare,
    ut sit deformis nulla superstes anus.
Sit tibi nil mirum si inculta et dissona mitto
30   in risu et medio carmina facta ioco!

: XXXIX :

In maledicum

Est qui me coram meque et mea carmina laudet
    et me clam laniet, meque meosque sales.
Obticeat, ni se laniavero clamve palamve
    inque suas maculas ipse trilinguis ero.

: XL :

Ad Crispum, quod suas laudes intermiserit
rustico cacante

Arbor inest medio viridis gratissima campi,
    limpidus hinc constat rivulus, inde nemus.
Hanc avis adventat pulchraque sub arbore cantat,
    lenitur sonitu lucus et unda suo.

between your lips[109] and feel the weight of your mistress's
    pussy.[110]
If perchance you are willing to pray likemindedly for me   25
    and pay me back for my own prayers,
pray for this, I pray you, constantly day and night:
    that no ugly old woman may survive.
And don't wonder if I send you these uncouth and dissonant
    songs
    composed in the midst of laughter and jokes.   30

: XXXIX :

Against a Backbiter

There's a man who publicly praises me and my songs,
    and savages me privately, both me and my wit.[111]
Let him be silent, otherwise I'll savage him both publicly and
    privately,
    and I'll be triple-tongued against his blots.[112]

: XL :

To Crispus: How the Author Broke off Writing His Praises When a Peasant Took a Shit[113]

There is a tree most pleasing in the middle of a green field,
    On one side stands a clear stream, on the other a wood.
A bird came to it, and sang beneath the lovely tree
    Both grove and wave were soothed by the sound.

5   Hic de more aderam, versus dictare parabam,
       astiterat calamo Clio vocata meo.
    Crispe, tuos coepi sanctos describere mores,
       quive vales prosa, carmine quive vales,
    utque tua summus sis civis in urbe futurus,
10   ut meritum virtus sitque habitura suum.
    Rusticus interea satur egesturus in herba
       se fert; contigua pallia ponit humo,
    mox aperit bracas, coleos atque inguina prodit,
       leniter et nudas verberat aura nates;
15   inflectit genua ac totum se cogit in orbem,
       imposuit cubitos crure manusque genis;
    postera iam talos contingere crura videntur,
       se premit et venter solvitur, inde cacat;
    tunc ex vocali ventosa tonitrua culo
20   dissiliunt, strepitu tunditur omnis ager.
    Excutior, calamus cecidit, dea cessit in auras,
       ad crepitum trullae territa fugit avis.
    Deprecor ut primas plantes, male rustice, vites,
       postmodo, sat sitiens, non sua vina bibas;
25   rustice, sulcatae summittas semina terrae,
       nec panem, esuriens, nec, miser, esse queas.
    Ergo vale et tum, quum concinna reverterit ales,
       iam pergam laudes scribere, Crispe, tuas.

Here came I as is my custom, I was getting ready to compose   5
    verses.
    Clio had been summoned and stood ready by my pen.[114]
I began to write about your blameless morals, Crispus,
    how you excel in prose, how in verse you excel,
and how you are going to become the leading citizen in your
    town,
    and how your virtue will have its reward.   10
Meanwhile, a bloated peasant comes up to relieve himself[115]
    on the grass. He places his cloak on the ground nearby,
then opens his pants and pulls out his cock and balls:
    and the breeze gently lashes his naked buttocks.
He bent his knees and curled up into a circle,   15
    placing his elbows on his thighs and his hands on his
    cheeks.
Seeming to rest his heels on the back of his thighs,
    he squeezes, loosens his bowels, and then shits.[116]
At that from his talkative asshole windy thunders[117]
    break forth; the whole field is stricken by the crack.   20
I was shaken, my pen fell, the goddess betook herself to the
    breezes,[118]
    the bird fled terrified by the rumble of the fart.[119]
I pray,[120] evil peasant, that you first plant your vines,
    after, when you're very thirsty, that you not drink their[121]
    wine.
Peasant, may you plant seeds in the furrowed earth,   25
    and have no bread to eat, wretch, when you're hungry.
Farewell, and when the tuneful bird returns,
    then I'll go on to write your praises, Crispus.

: XLI :

De precibus pulchra Homeri fictio

Preces, ut tradit Homerus, divae sunt et puellae magni Iovis. Hae
et claudae et lippae sunt, hisque Ἄτης praevenit, idest Nocumen-
tum, quae sanis et validis pedibus constat ac longe anteit, nocens
hominibus per omnem terram; Preces vero post sequuntur. Qui
autem veneratur puellas Iovis prope venientes, maxime illum qui-
dem iuvere et rogantem exaudiunt. Qui vero eas aspernatur ac
dure repellit, orant abeuntes Iovem uti hunc insequatur Nocu-
mentum et damnatus det poenas.

Preces igitur oratum mittit Aurispam Siculum ut sibi
Marcum Valerium Martialem commodet

Ite Preces, gnatae magni Iovis, en praeit Ἄτης,
    Ἄτης quae vobis praevia monstrat iter.
Si multum validis Nocumentum passibus anteit,
    ite citae, lippae loripedesque Preces.
5   Ivit Ate, cuivis omnem nocitura per orbem,
    ite citae vestris gressibus, ivit Ate.
Est Florentina celeber tellure poeta,
    quem numerat genitis Sicilis ora suis.
Illius ex lepido cantant Heliconides ore,
10   illius ex digitis pulsat Apollo chelim.
Non peperit Latium, non Graecia, mille per annos,
    eloquio similem vel probitate virum.
Illi ego non parvo iampridem iungor amore,
    iampridem nobis mutuus extat amor.

: XLI :

On Prayers. A Beautiful Story by Homer[122]

Prayers, as Homer relates, are goddesses and the daughters of great Jove. They are lame and half-blind. And *Atê*, that is, Harm,[123] who stands on healthy and strong feet, precedes them and goes far ahead, harming people all over the earth. But the Prayers follow after. However, he who reveres the daughters of Jove when they come near, him above all have they helped and they hearken to him when he prays. But the man who spurns them and pushes them roughly away, when they leave they pray to Jove that Harm will pursue him and he will be condemned to pay the penalty.

So the Author Sends Prayers to Aurispa of Sicily That
He Would Lend Him Marcus Valerius Martial[124]

Go Prayers, daughters of great Jove, lo, *Atê* precedes,
    Atê leading the way who will show you the road.
If Harm goes far ahead with strong strides,
    go swiftly, half-blind and limping Prayers.
Atê has gone to harm everyone over the face of the earth.   5
    Go swiftly with your steps — *Atê* has gone.
There is in the Florentine land a famous poet,
    whom the Sicilian shore counts among her children.
The Muses of Helicon sing through his charming mouth,
    through his fingers Apollo strikes his lyre.   10
Latium has not borne, nor Greece, for a thousand years,
    a man like this for eloquence or honesty.
Long have I been bound to him by no small love,
    long has there been love in return for me.

15   Hunc petite, hunc vigili vos offendetis in aede,
        cantantem altisonis regia gesta modis.
    Hunc igitur magni Iovis exorate puellae —
        per si qua est scriptis fama futura suis —
    ut mihi concedat perrara epigrammata Marci:
20   illa libens relegam restituamque libens.
    Si facilis, divae, coram venientibus extet
        et meritus vobis exhibeatur honos,
    aeque adiutrices hunc exaudite rogantem,
        sitis et huic placidae parque referte pari.
25   Quod si vos nihili faciat dureque repellat,
        poscite confestim, turba repulsa, Iovem,
    hunc ut terribili Nocumentum voce sequatur
        et damnas poenas detque luatque graves.

: XLII :

Ad Cosmum virum clarissimum de libri divisione

In binas partes diduxi, Cosme, libellum:
    nam totidem partis Hermaphroditus habet.
Haec pars prima fuit, sequitur quae deinde secunda est:
    haec pro pene fuit, proxima cunnus erit.

Seek him out, you will find him in his wakeful house   15
   singing the deeds of kings in resounding measures.
So daughters of great Jove beg him,
   by whatever fame his writings will have in future,[125]
to lend me Martial's very scarce epigrams.
   Willingly shall I read them again and willingly return them.   20
If he is obliging to you goddesses when you come into his
     presence,
   and the honor you are owed is shown to you,
in return be his helpers and listen to him when he prays,
   be kind to him and give measure for measure.
But if he pays you no regard and rejects you roughly,   25
   when your company is rejected, ask Jove at once
that Harm harry him with her terrible voice
   and that condemned[126] he pay heavy penalties.

: XLII :

To the Noble Cosimo on the Division of his Book

I have divided my book into two parts, Cosimo,
   For the Hermaphrodite has the same number of parts.
This was the first part, so what follows is the second.
   This stands for the cock, the next will be cunt.

: XLIII :

Ad Cosmum virum clarissimum quando et cui legere libellum debeat

Hactenus, o patriae decus indelebile, panxi
convivae quod post prandia, Cosme, legas.
Quod reliqui est, sumpta madidis sit lectio coena,
sicque leges uno carmina nostra die.

HERMAPHRODITI LIBELLUS PRIMUS
EXPLICIT FELICITER

Poggius plurimam salutem dicit Antonio Panhormitae Siculo.

1   Lamola, adolescens, ut percepi, cum doctus tum studiosus tui, at-
tulit ad nos libellum epigrammatum tuorum quem inscribis Her-
maphroditum, opus et iocosum et plenum voluptate. Hunc cum
legisset primo vir clarissimus Antonius Luscus multisque verbis
collaudasset et ingenium et facilitatem dicendi tuam (nam liber est
suavissimus) misit deinde illum ad me legendum.

2   Delectatus sum, mehercle, varietate rerum et elegantia versuum
simulque admiratus sum res adeo impudicas, adeo ineptas, tam
venuste, tam composite a te dici atque ita exprimi multa turpius-
cula ut non enarrari, sed agi videantur, neque ficta iocandi causa,
ut existimo, sed acta existimari possint.

: XLIII :

To the Noble Cosimo: When and to Whom
He Should Read the Book

Thus far, unfading glory of your country,[127] I have composed
   something for you to read to a guest after lunch, Cosimo.
What's left is reading material for those in their cups when
   dinner is done.
That way you can read my poems in a single day.

HERE ENDS AUSPICIOUSLY THE FIRST
BOOK OF THE HERMAPHRODITE

Letter from Poggio to Beccadelli[128]

Poggio gives greetings to Antonio Panormita of Sicily.

Giovanni Lamola,[129] a young man as learned, I see, as he is zeal-   1
ous on your behalf, has brought us your book of epigrams, which
you entitled *The Hermaphrodite*, a playful work and full of pleasure.
The distinguished Antonio Loschi read it first and praised your
talent and ease of expression with many words (for the book is
very pleasant), and then sent it to me to read.[130]

   I was quite delighted by the variety of the subject matter and   2
the elegance of the verse and at the same time I admired the fact
that you had written about topics so immodest and so ridiculous
in a manner so charming and well put together, and that many
rather sordid matters are so well expressed that they seem to be
not just recounted but actually taking place and not just made up
for the sake of a joke but, in my opinion, one can imagine that
they actually happened.[131]

3   Laudo igitur doctrinam tuam, iocunditatem carminis, iocos ac
sales tibique gratias ago, pro portiuncula mea, qui Latinas musas,
quae iam diu nimium dormierunt, a somno excitas.

4   Pro caritate tamen qua omnes debitores sumus omnibus, unum
est quod te monere et debeo et volo, ut scilicet deinceps gra-
viora uaedam mediteris; haec enim quae adhuc edidisti vel aetati
concedi possunt vel licentiae iocandi: ita et Virgilius adolescens lu-
sit in Priapeia et multi praeterea qui post lascivos versus severiori-
bus vacarunt; ut enim Terentius noster refert, "haec aetas aliam vi-
tam, alios mores postulat." Itaque tuum est iam missam facere
lasciviam et res serias describere, ne arguatur vita impura libelli
obscenitate: scis enim non licere idem nobis, qui Christiani sumus,
quod olim poetis qui deum ignorabant. Sed fortasse "sus Miner-
vam": tu ipse hoc idem sentis, quod laudo proboque, et te ad
maiora hortor.

Haec bono animo accipias rogo: ego enim tuus sum; tu Pog-
gium ascribe in tuis.

Plura scripsissem si per otium licuisset; verum alias erimus lon-
giores, si haec non displicuerint tibi. Vale et me, quando id mu-
tuum fieri intelliges, ama.

Romae III nonas Apriles, manu festina.

So I praise your learning, the pleasantness of the poetry, the 3
jokes and the wit, and I give you whatever small thanks I can that
you have roused from sleep the Latin Muses that have been so
long dormant.

Nevertheless, in view of the kindly concern we all owe to each 4
other, there is one thing on which I must and want to advise you,
and that is that you next turn your mind to more serious matters.
The things you have produced so far can be granted to youth or to
the license allowed to humor, just as Vergil as a young man
amused himself with the Priapus poems,[132] and many other men
likewise who after producing licentious verses gave themselves over
to serious matters. As our friend Terence says, "This time of life
demands a different manner of living and different habits."[133] So
your job now is to put away playfulness and write about important
matters, so that an impure life is not inferred from the obscenity
of your book. You know that what was once allowed to the poets
who were ignorant of God is not allowed to us who are Chris-
tians. But perhaps I'm a pig trying to teach Minerva. You feel the
same way about what I am approving and praising, and I urge you
on to greater things.

I beg you to accept this in good part, as I am your friend — you
can put Poggio down among your intimates.

I would have written more had time permitted; I'll write at
greater length on another occasion if this letter doesn't displease
you. Farewell, and love me in return, once you realize it is mutual.

Rome, 3 April [1426], written in haste.

LIBER II

: I :

Quod civili iuri operam dare, et merito, pergit,
cum hac tempestate non sit
quisquam remunerator poetarum

Cosme, vir Etrurias inter celeberrime terras,
    si sileas, videor velle videre tuum:
malles, posthabitis iam iam lusuve iocove,
    clausissem forti strenua bella pede.
5   Ut tu magnanimus, sic et permagna cupiscis:
    hei mihi, sed nostro tempore Caesar abest!
Hic "Tibi sit largo pro Caesare gloria!", dices:
    sed tales epulas non meus alvus edit!
Laurea sit cuivis, dum sit domus aurea nobis:
10   auratam facient aurea iura domum.
Dant lites requiem, donant chyrographa nummos:
    hoc lex dat; voces gloria sola dabit.
Haec alit, haec fatuas dumtaxat inebriat aures:
    scilicet et venter carior aure mihi est!

BOOK II

: I :

That the Poet Continues to Pay Attention to
Civil Law, Rightly So, at a Time When
There Is No One Who Rewards Poets[1]

Cosimo, most famous man in the Tuscan lands,
    even though you are silent, I seem to see your wish:
now that games or jokes have been put aside, you would prefer
    that I had set strenuous wars in mighty meter.[2]
Just as you are great-hearted, so you desire great things.   5
    But alas for me, there is no Caesar in our time.
To which you will reply, "Instead of a generous Caesar, gain
    glory."
    But my stomach can't eat meals of that sort!
Let whoever wants them have laurels, as long as I have a house
    of gold.
    Golden laws will make a gilded house.   10
Lawsuits give ease, contracts[3] grant money.
    That is what the law gives; glory by itself will give mere
    words.
The one feeds; the other merely intoxicates empty ears.[4]
    And of course my belly is dearer to me than my ear.

15   Famaque quantalibet veniat post funera nobis:
          excipiam nullos mortuus aure sonos.
      Ergo sequor prudens leges ac iura Quiritum,
          prostituo prudens verba diserta foro.
      Quum vacat officio legali, ludicra condo
20   dum bibo, quae nobis immeditata fluunt.
      In mensa nequeunt heroum gesta reponi,
          non sunt implicitae proelia mentis opus.
      Sit mihi Maecenas: claros heroas et arma
          cantabo, et nugis prae fera bella feram.

: II :

Ad puellas castas

Vos iterum moneo: castae nolite puellae
    discere lascivos ore canente modos.
Nil mihi vobiscum est: vates celebrate severos.
    Me Thais medio fornice blanda legat.

: III :

Laus Aldae

Si tibi sint pharetrae atque arcus, eris, Alda, Diana;
    si tibi sit manibus fax, eris, Alda, Venus.
Sume lyram et plectrum: fies quasi verus Apollo;

And however much fame may come to me after my funeral,   15
    when I'm dead my ear will catch no sounds.[5]
So wisely I follow laws and statutes of the Romans,[6]
    wisely I prostitute my learned words in the forum.[7]
When I have time from legal business, I compose
        amusements[8]
    while I'm drinking,[9] things which flow from me   20
        spontaneously.
The deeds of heroes can't be put on the table;
    battles are not the job of a busy mind.
If I had a Maecenas, famous heroes and arms
    I'd sing, and prefer savage wars to trifles.[10]

: II :

To Chaste Girls[11]

Once again I warn you, chaste girls,
    don't learn lascivious verse from my singing mouth.
I have nothing to do with you. Celebrate serious poets.
    Let sweet Thais[12] read me in the middle of the brothel.

: III :

Praise of Alda

If you had a bow and quiver, Alda, you would be Diana.
    If you had a torch in your hand, Alda, you would be
        Venus.
Take up the lyre and the plectrum: you will become, as it were,
    a very Apollo.

si tibi sit cornu et thyrsus, Iacchus eris.
5   Si desint haec et mea sit tibi mentula cunno,
     pulchrior, Alda, deis atque deabus eris!

: IV :

In Aldae matrem

Ut mihi tu claudis, mater stomachosa, fenestram,
     sic tibi claudatur cunnus, iniqua parens!
Id tibi erit gravius, caelebs videare licebit,
     quam tibi si caeli ianua clausa foret.

: V :

Laus Aldae

Alda, puellarum fortunatissima, gaude:
     vincitur omnipotens igne Cupido tuo.
Alda deas omnis specieque et moribus aequat:
     sit minime mirum si capit Alda deos.

If you had the horn and thyrsus,[13] you would be Bacchus.[14]
If you didn't have these things and did have my cock in your   5
    cunt,
  you would be more beautiful, Alda, than the gods or
  goddesses.

: IV :

Against Alda's Mother

Just as you close the window against me, ill-tempered mother,
  so may your cunt be closed up,[15] cruel parent.
Though you seem to be single, that will be worse for you
  than if the gates of heaven were closed against you.

: V :

Praise of Alda

Alda, most fortunate of girls, rejoice.
  Almighty Cupid is conquered by your fire.
Alda is the equal of any goddess in beauty and morals,
  so it's little wonder if she takes the gods captive.

: VI :

Ad Philopappam deperientem Sterconum
virum turpem

Ni te detineat Sterconus, scire volebam
    an stomachus peni sit, Philopappa, tuo,
et stomachus certe talis qui digerat Aethnam,
    albicat hiberna quum magis Aethna nive.

5   Quid loquor in nebulis, qui non intelligor ulli?
    Simpliciter dicam quid, Philopappa, velim.
Est puer, hunc ardes, quin deperis: et puer ille
    sit tibi, terdecies qui nova musta bibit?
Iam pridem aegrotat: cur aridus instar aristae est,

10   et dubites vultus larva sit an facies?
Quamvis ipse gula sit longus, quum tamen offa
    proluit os, vellet guttur habere gruis.
Est sibi pro bello rubicundula tybia naso:
    ex patula cerebrum nare videre potes.

15   Cruribus atque ano densorum silva pilorum est,
    qua possit tuto delituisse lepus.
Mentis multivolae est, venalis, potor edoque,
    diligit et tantum munera, more lupae.
Ille (ita me dei ament!) sic est aut turpior: et tu—

20   proh pudor!—hunc plusquam viscera, caecus, amas.
Nescio quem volgus dicat flagrasse lucernam:
    derisi quondam, sed modo vera putem.

: VI :

To Philopappa, Desperately in Love
with Sterconus, a Filthy Man[16]

If you're not detained by Sterconus, Philopappa,
   I wanted to know if your cock has a stomach,
and a stomach in fact which could handle Etna,
   when Etna is completely white with winter snow.
Why do I talk amid the mists when I won't be understood by   5
     anyone?[17]
   I'll tell you plainly what I want, Philopappa.
There is a boy. You burn for him; no, you're crazy for him.
   Yet could he be a boy, when he's drunk thirty new
     vintages?[18]
He's been sick for a while already. Why is he as dry as an ear
   of wheat,
   and you can't tell whether his looks are a ghost or a face?   10
Though his throat is long, when he washes out his mouth
   with a bit of food,[19] he'd like to have the gullet of a crane.[20]
Instead of a nose he has a ruddy[21] flute.
   You can see his brain through his flared nostrils.[22]
On his shins and ass is a forest of thick hairs,   15
   where a hare could hide in safety.
He's got a slutty mind, he's for sale, a drinker, a glutton,[23]
   he loves only gifts, just like a whore.
That's what he's like — I swear to God — or worse. And you —
   for shame — love him more than your guts, you blind man!   20
People say that someone fell in love with a lamp.[24]
   I mocked it once, but now I think it's true.

Non erat in populo formosior alter Etrusco?
    Non erat Italico gratior orbe puer?
25   Caecus amor plerum mortalia pectora caecat,
    nec nos a falsis cernere vera sinit.
Cur edat ille fimum vulpes quaesivit asellum:
    "Nam memini — dixit — quod fuit herba fimus".
Sic, puto, tu referes cuivis fortasse roganti,
30   diligis hunc ideo, quod tener ante fuit!
Caecus es, et credis me cassum lumine, coram
    Sterconum eximiis laudibus usque ferens.
Crura licet pueri bombicia lautaque dicas,
    crura tamen siccae pumicis instar habet.
35   Iam modo crediderim te verpum posse Priapum
    scilicet et Lybicas accubuisse feras:
immanem ergo fovet stomachum tua mentula, verum
    nil videt, ut quae oculos ederit illa suos!

: VII :

Ad Aurispam de Ursae vulva

Ecquis erit, vir gnare, modus ne vulva voracis
    Ursae testiculos sorbeat ampla meos?
Ecquis erit, totum femur haec ne suggat hyrudo,
    ne prorsus ventrem suggat ad usque meum?
5   Aut illam stringas quavis, Aurispa, medela,
    aut equidem cunno naufragor ipse suo.

Was there no one better looking among the people of
    Tuscany?
  Was there no boy prettier in the Italian world?
Blind loves make most mortal hearts blind,   25
    And doesn't allow us to tell true from false.
The fox asked the ass why he ate dung.
  "Because I remember," he said, "when the dung was grass."
That's what I think you would say to anyone who might ask:
    You love him so much because he was of a tender age—   30
      once.
You are blind and you think that I've lost my eyesight,
    while you openly praise Sterconus to the skies.[25]
Though you say that his shins are silky and clean,
    yet his shins are like dry pumice.
Now I could believe you capable of sleeping with well-   35
    endowed Priapus,[26]
    or even the wild animals of Libya.[27]
Therefore your cock nurtures a huge stomach,[28] but
    it sees nothing, since it's eaten its own eyes.

: VII :

To Aurispa on Ursa's Cunt[29]

Is there any way,[30] learned man, to keep voracious Ursa's
    ample cunt from swallowing my balls?
Is there any way to keep that leech from sucking my entire
    crotch,[31]
    from sucking right up to my belly?
Either find some remedy to tighten it up, Aurispa,   5
    or I'll be shipwrecked in her cunt for sure.

: VIII :

Aurispae responsio

Si semper tantus spiraret in aequore faetor
    neminis ut nasus littora ferre queat,
quis vel in Adriaco, Scithico quis navita posset
    aut in Tyrreno naufragus esse mari?
5   Et tu ne timeas: nam, quum magis arrigis Ursae
    quumve magis cupias, vulva repellet olens.
Haec flat ita horrendum, quod pingue et putre cadaver
    Ursae cum cunno lylia pulchra foret;
haec flat ita ut, merdis si quisquam conferat inguen,
10   sit violae et suaves multa cloaca rosae.
Sin tuus hunc talem non horret nasus odorem,
    ut sit tunc vulvae strictior Ursa dabo.

: IX :

Ad Ursam flentem

Quid fles? En, nitidos turbat tibi fletus ocellos!
    Quid fles, o lacrimis Ursa decora tuis?
Forte quod adversus te acciverit ira Camenas,
    aut mihi quod tu sis non adamata putes?
5   Crede mihi, mea lux, tantum te diligo, quantum
    non magis ex animo quisquis amare queat!

: VIII :

Aurispa's Reply[32]

If such a stench always breathed on the ocean,
  so that no one's nose could bear the shore,
who could stand to be a sailor on the Adriatic or the Caspian,
  or shipwrecked on the Tyrrhenian sea?
But don't be afraid, for when you've really got a hard-on for   5
  Ursa,[33]
  or you really want her, her smelly cunt will put you off.
It smells so horrible that a bloated and putrid cadaver
  would be a beautiful lily compared to Ursa's cunt.
It smells so that if someone compared her groin to shit
  a great sewer would be violets and sweet roses.   10
If your nose doesn't shudder at such a smell,
  I will give you something so that Ursa will have a tighter
  cunt.

: IX :

To Ursa Crying[34]

Why are you crying? Look, weeping has clouded your shining
  eyes.[35]
  Why are you crying, Ursa, beautiful in your tears?
Perhaps because you think that my anger has summoned the
  Muses against you,[36]
  or that you are not loved by me?
Believe me, my light,[37] I cherish you so much   5
  that no one can love more from the heart.[38]

Tu quoque me redamas; dubium est quis vincat amore:
    alter utram vincit, vincitur alter utra.
Cur igitur credis vitio qui ductus iniquo
10   inter nos rixam dissidiumque cupit?
Iuro per has lacrimas et crura simillima lacti,
    perque nates mollis et femur, Ursa, tuum,
quod nunquam nisi quae te laudent carmina feci:
    sic sit versiculis gratia multa meis!
15 Ah, pereat, quaeso, tibi qui mendacia dixit!
    Ah, pereat falsum qui tibi cunque refert!
Terge tuos fletus, sine te dissabier, Ursa;
    parce mihi: luctu torqueor ipse tuo.
Tandem siste tuas[1] lacrimas curaque salutem:
20   namque ego, te domina sospite, sospes ero.

: X :

De poena infernali quam dat
Ursa auctori superstiti

Si calor et faetor, stridor quoque sontibus umbris
    sint apud infernos ultima poena locos,
ipse ego Tartareas dum vivo perfero poenas:
    id mihi supplicium suggerit Ursa triplex.
5 Nam sibi merdivomum stridit resonatque foramen,
    fervet et Ursa femur, putet et Ursa pedes.

And you love me back. It's uncertain which of us surpasses the
　　other in love:[39]
　each surpasses the other; each is surpassed by the other.
Why then do you believe someone who is led by resentful vice
　　and wishes to sow quarrels and disagreements[40] between　　　10
　　us?
I swear by these tears[41] and your milk-white thighs
　by your soft bottom and your pussy,[42] Ursa,
that I have never made poems except ones that praise you,
　— let that be the great grace of my verse.
Ah, may he perish,[43] I pray, who told these lies to you.　　　　15
　Ah, may he perish, whoever brings you false report.
Wipe away your tears and let yourself be smothered in
　　kisses,[44] Ursa.
　Spare me: I am tortured by your grief.[45]
Stop your tears[46] and take care for your health.
　For if you, my mistress, are well, then shall I be well.[47]　　　20

: X :

The Punishment of Hell That Ursa Gives
the Author While He Is Still Alive

If heat and stench and noise are the ultimate penalties
　for guilty ghosts in the infernal regions,
I while I'm living endure Tartarean penalties.
　Ursa supplies me with that triple punishment:
For her shit-barfing[48] hole shrieks and re-echoes,　　　　　　5
　Ursa's cunt is boiling, and Ursa's feet stink.[49]

: XI :

In Hodum mordacem

Quod genium versusque meos relegisve probasve,
    gratum est; quod mores arguis, Hode, queror.
Crede, velim, nostra vitam distare papyro:
    si mea charta procax, mens sine labe mea est.
5   Delitias pedibus celebres clausere poetae,
    ac ego Nasones Virgiliosque sequor.

: XII :

Epitaphium Haerasmi Biberii ebrii

Qui legis, Haerasmi sunt contumulata Biberi
    ossa sub hoc sicco non requieta loco.
Erue, vel saltem vino consperge cadaver;
    eripe: sic, quaeso, sint rata quaeque voles!
5   Ossa sub oenophoro posthac erepta madenti
    conde, natent temeto fac: requietus ero.

: XI :

Against Oddo, the Backbiter[50]

That you have approved my talent and reread my verses,
  is pleasing. That you attack my morals, Oddo, to that I
    object.
Please believe me, my life is different from my page.
  If my page is salacious, my mind is spotless.
Famous poets have set naughtiness in verse,   5
  and I follow those Ovids and Vergils.[51]

: XII :

The Epitaph of Erasmus Biberius, the Drunkard[52]

You who read this, the bones of Erasmus Biberius
  are entombed beneath this dry spot, but not at rest.
Dig them up, or at least sprinkle my body with wine.
  Rescue them, and thus, I pray, whatever you wish may be
    granted.[53]
Afterwards, bury my rescued bones in a dripping wine vat;   5
  make sure they swim in booze. Then I'll be at rest.

: XIII :

Ad amicum carum quod sui causa
Pistorium se conferat

Salve, vir populo spes certa ac maxima Tusco!
  Salve, praeclaros inter habende viros!
Salve, qui, longos si sis provectus in annos,
  tempora Phoebea virgine cincta feres!
5   Accipe si sileam tibi rem fortassis emendam
  quaeque animo nil non sit placitura tuo.
Nuper apud mollis Senas fit pestifer aer,
  quo fit ut ipse petam Pistoriense solum.
Sunt aliae Etruriis potiores montibus urbes,
10   sed tu non alios incolis ipse locos:
sis modo Pistorii, Romam vidisse fatebor
  quum magis illa armis floruit aucta suis.
Interea pathicam mihi, dulcis amice, puellam
  delige, quae vernas expuat ore rosas;
15   neve sit exiguus toto sub corpore nevus,
  sit quoque cui tenerum spiret amoma femur;
digna sit affectu, suavem quae norit amorem,
  quae velit et flammis reddere grata vices;
mersilis in vitium, vivens in amore iocisve
20   praeque proco cupiat postposuisse colos;
divitibus vates, praeponat carmina gazis,
  sit prae versiculo vilis arena Thagi;
denique sit pro qua sic possim dicere vere
  (pace dei dicam), "Pulchrior illa deo est!"

: XIII :

To a Dear Friend, for whose Sake
the Author Is Going to Pistoia[54]

Hail hero, the certain and greatest hope of the Tuscan people.
    Hail, you who are to be enrolled among the famous heroes.
Hail, you who, as you advance into further years,
    will have your temples circled by Apollo's maiden.[55]
Take as a gift, what you would perhaps have to buy, if I were   5
        silent,
    and which will not be displeasing to your mind.
Lately in soft Siena the air became pestilent,[56]
    so that I myself sought the soil of Pistoia.
There are other, more desirable cities in the Tuscan
        mountains,
    but you don't live in those other places.   10
Provided that you're at Pistoia, I shall say I've seen Rome
    when she was at her height, made great by her arms.
In the meantime, sweet friend, choose for me
    an easy girl, who spits spring roses from her mouth,[57]
nor should there be the slightest mole on her whole body,   15
    and let her tender pussy breathe forth perfumes too.
Let her be worthy of affection, one who knows sweet love,
    and one who wants to please by returning flame for flame.[58]
Sunk in sin, living in love and laughter,[59]
    who would put aside her spinning for a suitor.   20
Let her prefer poets to rich men, songs to treasure.
    In comparison to a line of verse let her hold the sands of
        Tagus cheap.[60]
Finally let her be one about whom I can truly say
    (and I say it with due respect to the god), "She is more
        beautiful than a god."[61]

25   Illam ego continuo nostris celebrabo Camenis,
        carmina si placeant, carmina mille dabo;
    quae si pro numeris ferat oscula, carmina condam
        qualia Virgilium composuisse putes;
    nec mihi Castalios latices petiisse necesse est:
30   sit mihi Castalius salsa saliva liquor.
    Haec ego praestiterim: tu tantum quaerito nymphen
        quae thyaso et cantu docta sit ante alias.
    Tandem perpetua, salve, mens digna salute,
        cum tua nimirum sit mea paene salus!

: XIV :

Ad Sanseverinum ut versus facere pergat

    Sanseverine, tuam legi bis terque Camenam,
        et placet et nullo claudicat illa pede;
    dii simulac facili praestant tibi pectora vena:
        hortor, Pierios condere perge modos.
5   Res sane egregia est, mortalia fingit et ornat
        pectora, post obitum miscet et illa deis.
    Tu, duce me, actutum vises Parnasea Tempe,
        deque sacro pleno pectore fonte bibes;
    nec te destituam, modo tu consortia vites
10   cum rudis atque hebetis, tum . . . rudis atque hebetis!
    Crassa quidem ruditas parvo te polluet usu
        inficietque tuos transitione sinus.

Her I shall celebrate ceaselessly with my Muse,   25
    if songs please her, I shall give her a thousand songs.
If she gives kisses for verses, I shall make such songs
    that you would think Vergil composed them.
There is no need for me to seek the Castalian waters.[62]
    Her salty saliva will be my Castalian liquid.   30
These things I would promise.[63] You just find the nymph
    who is learned above all the others in Bacchic song and
        dance.[64]
Finally, hail to a mind worthy of good health,
    since your well-being, of course, is almost my own.

: XIV :

To Sanseverino, That He May Continue to Make Verses[65]

Sanseverino, I have read your Muse twice and three times.
    She's pleasing and never puts a foot wrong.
At the same time, the gods grant you an easy vein of talent.[66]
    I urge you to continue to set down Pierian measures.[67]
It's a wonderful thing, it shapes and adorns the hearts of men,   5
    and after death mixes them with the gods.
With me as leader you will see at once Parnassian Tempe,
    and drink from the sacred fountain with full heart.
Nor will I desert you, provided you avoid mixing
    with both the ignorant and stupid, as well as . . . the   10
        ignorant and stupid.[68]
Crass ignorance will pollute you on the slightest contact
    and infect your bosom with its contagion.[69]

: XV :

In Mathiam Lupium claudum

Lupius, abs poscis me rara epigrammata Marci.
    Concedam: rectis passibus ipse veni!

: XVI :

In eundem grammaticum

Tris habet archana Mathias Lupius aula
    discipulos: unus de tribus est famulus.

: XVII :

Pro Marco Succino
ad Lucium Mauram

Pulchrior argento es, sed eris formosior auro,
    si bona reddideris verba, benigne puer.
Est pia vestra domus, fratres, germana, parentes:
    sis pariter mitis, si pia tota domus.
5   Est tua forma decens: mens sit quoque pulchra licebit;
    conveniant formae reddita verba tuae.

: XV :

Against Mattia Lupi, the Cripple[70]

Lupi, you ask me for the rare epigrams of Martial.
  I'll lend you them—just get your feet straight and come on
    over.

: XVI :

Against the Same, the Schoolteacher[71]

Mattia Lupi has three students in his private school[72]
  —and one of the three is his houseboy.

: XVII :

*A Poem to Lucio Maura, Written
on Behalf of Marco Sozzini*[73]

You are more beautiful than silver, but you will be handsomer
    than gold,[74]
  if you return kind words, generous boy.
Your family is good: brothers, sister, parents;
  you should be just as gentle, since your whole family is
    good.
Your appearance is handsome; let your mind be beautiful,   5
    too.[75]
  Let your words correspond to your appearance.

conservare viros perituros regia res est,
    haec nos caelitibus res facit esse pares:
ast ego Castalio deducam fonte sorores,
10   quae formam et mores et tua facta canant.
Quid melius Musa tribuam? Quid carmine maius?
    Si potius quid sit carmine, posce: dabo.
Quem sacri vates voluere, est fama perennis:
    tu quoque, ni fallor, carmine clarus eris;
15   namque ego doctiloquo vivaces carmine reddam
    semper amicitias (sit modo vita) pias;
quippe boni de te sument exempla minores,
    gaudebunt actus saepe referre tuos.
Lux mea, Maura, vale; tibi meque meamque Thaliam
20   dedo: velis uti. Lux mea, Maura, vale.

: XVIII :

Pro Marco Succino orat et ut speret
de Lucio Maura exhortatur

Dii faciles incoepta, precor, Succine, secundent,
    cum puero fautrix sit Cytharea suo,
ut responsa hilari sint convenientia formae
    et reddat pulcher verbula pulchra puer.
5   Est pia tota domus, fratres, germana, parentes:
    nescio quin speres, si pia tota domus.

It is a royal deed to save men who are about to die;[76]
    a deed such as this makes us equal to the gods.
As for me, I shall lead the Sisters down from the Castalian
    fountain,
    to sing of your appearance, your character, and your deeds.   10
What can I give that is better than the Muse? What is greater
    than song?[77]
    If there is anything preferable to song, ask and I shall give.
For him for whom the sacred poets have wanted it, there is
    eternal fame.[78]
    You too, if I'm not mistaken, will become famous in song.
I shall make your good friendships live forever   15
    in learned song, if life allows.
Therefore good young men will take their example from you;
    they will rejoice in always relating your deeds.
Maura, my light, farewell. I give you myself and my Muse.
    Please use them. My light, Maura, farewell.   20

： XVIII ：

The Poet Prays on Behalf of Marco Sozzini and Urges Him to Be Hopeful about Lucio Maura

May the kindly gods, Sozzini, I pray, look favorably on your
    undertakings.
    May Cytherea be your aid, along with her son,
so that his response matches his cheerful appearance.
    and the beautiful boy may give back beautiful little words.
His whole family is good: brothers, sister, parents;   5
    I do not doubt that you should hope, since his whole family
    is good.

Ipse pios longe superat pietate propinquos:
    nescio cur patri Maura sit absimilis.

: XIX :

In Mathiam Lupium

Lupius in pueros, si quis screat, intonat: idem
    dum comedit pedit, quum satur est vomitat.

: XX :

In Lentulum mollem

Si neque tu futuis viduas neque, Lentule, nuptas,
    si tibi nec meretrix, nec tibi virgo placet,
si dicas quod sis calidus magnusque fututor,
    scire velim, mollis Lentule, quid futuas.

: XXI :

Epitaphium Martini Poliphemi
coci egregii

Siste, precor, lacrimisque meum consperge sepulchrum,
    hac quicunque studens forte tenebis iter.
Sum Poliphemus ego vasto pro corpore dictus,
    Martinus proprio nomine gnotus eram;

He outdoes his good relatives in goodness.
　　I don't know why Maura should be any different from his
　　father.

: XIX :

Against Mattia Lupi

Lupi thunders at the boys if they clear their throats. But he
　　farts while he eats and vomits when he's full.

: XX :

Against Lentulus, the Effeminate[79]

If you don't fuck widows, Lentulus, and you don't fuck brides,
　　if no courtesan pleases you nor virgin,
if you claim that you're a hot and mighty fucker,
　　I'd like to know, effeminate Lentulus, what you *do* fuck.

: XXI :

Epitaph for the Exceptional Cook Martino,
Nicknamed "Polyphemus"[80]

Stop, please, and sprinkle my tomb with your tears,
　　if you're a student who by chance makes his way here.
I was called Polyphemus because of my huge body[81]
　　but I was known as Martino, my proper name.

5   qui iuvenes studiis devotos semper amavi,
        quem liquet et famulos et superasse coquos.
    Nunc ego funebri tandem spoliatus honore,
        thure carens, summa sum tumulatus humo.
    Me Mathesilanus tempesta in nocte recondi
10   iussit et exequias luce carere meas;
    nec cruce nec cantu celebravit nostra sacerdos
        funera, nec requies ultima dicta mihi,
    clamque fui sacco latitans raptimque sepultus,
        nec capiunt coleos arcta sepulchra meos.
15   Dum feror obstupui timuique subire latrinas
        nec loca crediderim religiosa dari.
    Oro pedem adiecta claudas tellure parumper,
        qui patet: heu, vereor ne lanient catuli!
    Continuo domini complebo ululatibus aedem
20   infaustis: poenas has dabit ipse suas.

: XXII :

Laus Aurispae ad Cosmum virum clarissimum

    Si quis erit priscis aequandus, Cosme, poetis,
        et si cui Phoebus Pyeridesque favent,
    si quis, quum loquitur vel splendida facta reponit,
        Mercurium iures eius ab ore loqui,
5   quive alios laudet cum sit laudabilis ipse,
        quive hedera merito tempora nexa ferat,

I always loved young men devoted to their studies,   5
    It was clear that I outdid all other servants and cooks.
But now at last I am robbed of my funeral service,
    lacking incense, I have been buried in shallow dirt.
Mathesilanus ordered that I be buried in the middle of the
        night,
    that my obsequies lack light.   10
No priest celebrated my funeral with cross or chanting,
    nor was the final requiem said for me.
Secretly and hastily I was buried, hidden in a sack.
    My narrow tomb didn't even cover my balls.
As I was carried out, I was amazed and feared I was going   15
        down into the latrines,
    nor did I think I was being put in holy ground.
I pray, at least quickly throw on some earth and cover my foot:
    it's sticking out. Oh, I'm afraid the dogs will tear at it.
Immediately I will fill the house of my master with ill-omened
    shrieks. He will pay his own penalty.   20

: XXII :

Praise of Aurispa, for the Noble Cosimo[82]

If there is anyone to equal the ancient poets, Cosimo,
    whom Phoebus and the Pierides cherish,
who, when he speaks or sets down splendid deeds,
    you would swear Mercury was speaking with his mouth,
who praises others, though he is praiseworthy himself,   5
    who deserves to wear the ivy wreath on his temples,

si quis erit linguae doctus Graiae atque Latinae:
    si non Aurispa est hic, periisse velim.
Quisquis in hoc mecum non senserit, arbiter aequus
10   non fuit, aut certe Zoilus ille fuit.

: XXIII :

Ad Galeaz, quem orat ut sibi
Catullum inveniat

Ardeo, mi Galeaz, mollem reperire Catullum,
    ut possim dominae moriger esse meae.
Lectitat illa libens teneros, lasciva, poetas,
    et praefert numeros, docte Catulle, tuos,
5   nuper et hos abs me multa prece, blanda, poposcit,
    forte suum vatem me penes esse putans.
"Non teneo hunc, — dixi — mea lux, mea nympha, libellum;
    id tamen efficiam: forsan habebis opus".
Instat et omnino librum me poscit amicum
10   et mecum gravibus nunc agit illa minis.
Quare ego, per superos omnis, o care sodalis
    (sic precibus lenis sit Cytharea tuis!),
te precor atque iterum precor: id mihi quaere libelli,
    quo fiam nostrae gratior ipse deae.

if there is anyone learned in the Greek and Latin languages,
    if it's not Aurispa here, may I die.
Anyone who disagreed with me was no sound judge,
    or was surely a Zoilus himself.[83]   10

: XXIII :

To Galeazzo, Whom the Author Begs to Find Him a Copy of Catullus[84]

I'm on fire, my dear Galeazzo, to find wanton[85] Catullus,
    so I can gratify[86] my mistress.
The lusty lass loves to read the tender poets,[87]
    and she prefers your verses, learned Catullus,[88]
and just now she sweetly asked me for them with many a   5
    prayer,[89]
    thinking that her favorite poet was perhaps in my house.
"I don't have the book," I said, "my light, my nymph.
    But I'll make sure I do. Perhaps you'll get the work."
She insists and asks me for the friendly book constantly,
    and treats me to dire threats.   10
Wherefore, by all the gods, dear friend
    (may Cytherea be just as kind to your prayers)
I beg you again and again: find this book for me
    so that I can make myself more pleasing to my goddess.

: XXIV :

Mathiae Lupii sententia. Ad Balbum

Balbe, scias calidi quae sit sententia Lupi,
    quam modo versiculis prosequar ipse meis:
"Si saepe efflictim cupiat mea mentula cunnum,
    interdum affectet cruscula cauda salax,
5   non tamen unquam adeo delira aut plena libido est
    ut popisma palam cumve cohorte rogem:
nolim cum populo compaedicare Iacincthum,
    cum multis ipsam non Helenen futuam".
Sic ait. Id digito dictum tibi, Balbe, ligato
10   et clam paedico clamve fututor agas.

: XXV :

Ad Memmum de partu Lutiae nymphae

Cum modo per dominae vicum mihi transitus esset,
    haec ego pro nympha parturiente precor:
"Nunc age, nunc, Lucina, meae succurre puellae,
    quae parit atque aliquem iam paritura deum est.
5   'Ah, dolor!', en clamat, supplex tua numina poscens,
    vocibus et lacrimas addit amara suis.
In me, dii, luctum dominae transferre velitis,
    etsi me miserum non minor angor habet!
Quid cessas? En, diva, tibi laus maxima, si tres

: XXIV :

The Opinion of Mattia Lupi: To Balbo[90]

Balbo, learn the opinion of clever Lupi,
    which I am now decking out with my verse:
"Even if my cock often desperately[91] wants cunt,
    or sometimes my dirty dick goes after boys' thighs,[92]
nevertheless my lust is not so crazy or swollen,[93]   5
    that I would ask for a bang[94] openly or in company.
I wouldn't want to bugger Hyacinthus in public,
    I wouldn't fuck Helen herself with a lot of people around."
That's what he says. This advice is for you, Balbo, so tie a
    string around your finger,[95]
and be a bugger or a fucker in private.[96]   10

: XXV :

To Memmo, on the Girl Lucia's Childbirth[97]

When I lately passed through my mistress's neighborhood,
    I uttered this prayer for the girl in labor.
"Come now, Lucina,[98] now, and help my girl,
    who is giving birth and even now is about to give birth to
    some god.[99]
'Oh, the pain,' she cries, a suppliant calling on your power,   5
    bitterly adding tears to her cries.
O gods, please transfer my mistress's pain to me,
    though no lesser worry holds me and makes me miserable.
Why do you hesitate? Goddess, look, the greatest praise will
    be yours,

10   incolumi nympha restituisse potes!
      Hei mihi, ne superi, si in te mala forte rogarim,
         audierint, votis et cruciere meis!
      Parcite moratam, superi, laesisse puellam
         et facite ut veniant in caput illa meum.
15   Quin vereor neu te dudum Venus effera vexet,
         sicque tua poenas impietate luas.
      Cernis ut ultricem durum est offendere divam:
         ergo tuo mitis sis facilisque proco!
      Quid tardas, Lucina? Veni faustissima nymphae,
20   lenis, io, nymphae prospera diva, veni!
      Postmodo solemnes certe tibi construet aras
         imponetque tuis menstrua thura focis".
      Haec ego. Sed, quoniam dea sit tibi promptior, oro
         ipse tuas praestes, splendide Memme, preces.
25   Nil dubito quin, flore dato votisque peractis,
         exsolvet partus molliter illa suos.

: XXVI :

De suo occulto amore

Uror, et occultae rodunt praecordia flammae:
   o ego, si sileam, terque quaterque miser!

if you can restore the three of us with my girl unharmed.   10
Woe is me, if perhaps the gods were listening when I called
    down curses on you, Lucia,
  and you are being tortured because of my curses!
Gods above, cease to hurt the girl who is having a hard
    delivery,[100]
  and make those things fall on my head!
Yet I am afraid that savage Venus has long been angry with   15
    you,
  and so you are paying the penalty for your impiety.[101]
You see how hard a thing it is to offend a vengeful goddess,
  so you be nice and kind to your suitor.
Why do you tarry, Lucina? Come and be as favorable as
    possible to the girl,
  propitious goddess, Oh, come and be gentle to the girl.   20
Afterwards, she will without fail erect solemn altars to you
  and every month place incense on your hearth."
So I spoke. But so that the goddess might be even quicker, I
    beg you,
  splendid Memmo, to offer your own prayers.
I have no doubt that, once the flowers have been offered and   25
    the vows fulfilled,
  she will have an easy delivery.[102]

: XXVI :

On His Hidden Love[103]

I burn, and the hidden flames gnaw at my vitals;
  Oh, if I'm silent I'm three and four times wretched.

: XXVII :

In Mathiam Lupium virum ignavum

Aonia rediens Mathias Lupius ora
    Castalidum steriles nuntiat esse lacus
et siccas laurus, nullam et superesse puellam:
    singula contatus, comperit esse nihil.
5   Impuri nequeunt oculi spectare sorores:
    scilicet ignavis Pegasis unda latet!

: XXVIII :

Pro Centio ad Contem
ut ex rure redeat

Centius hanc vidua tibi mittit ab urbe salutem,
    lux mea, mi Contes, dimidiumque animae.
Quid mihi laetitiae superest? Ubi rura petisti,
    spiritus est membris visus abire meis.
5   Id mihi laetitiae tantum est: puer urbe remansit
    inque suos vultus conspicor ipse tuos.
Ne fuge, care puer; sine te, germane, videri,
    dumque agit in sylva ne fuge, care puer!
Plura velim, sed plura loqui dolor impedit: ergo,
10   vivere si cupias me, cito rure redi!

: XXVII :

Against Mattia Lupi, the Lazy Man

Mattia Lupi, returning from the Aonian shore,
    declares that the pools of the Castalian[104] Muses are barren,
the laurels are dried up, and no Maiden[105] survives.
    Having investigated[106] them one by one, he discovers there
      is nothing.
Impure eyes cannot see the Sisters: 5
    of course the waters of Pegasus[107] are hidden from the lazy.

: XXVIII :

On Behalf of Cencio, to Conte, That He Should
Come Back from the Countryside[108]

Cencio sends this greeting to you from the city which you
    have left bereft,
    my light, my Conte, and half my soul.[109]
What happiness remains for me? When you set out for the
    country,
    my spirit seems to have left my body.
My only happiness is this: a boy has stayed in the city   5
    and I see your face in his.
Don't run away, dear boy;[110] let yourself be seen, brother,[111]
    and while *he* is off in the woods, don't run away, dear boy.
I want to say more, but my grief prevents me. So,
    if you wish me to live, come back from the country fast!   10

: XXIX :

Ad Leutium foeneratorem ut Plautum commissum habeat

Hunc tibi quam possim Plautum commendo, Leuti,
    Plautum, quem vocitat lingua Latina patrem.
Haud de te modicum, vates, oboleverat aetas:
    te modo pernities altera, foenus, edit.

: XXX :

Epitaphium Nichinae Flandrensis, scorti egregii

Si steteris paulum, versus et legeris istos,
    hac gnosces meretrix quae tumulatur humo:
"Rapta fui e patria teneris, pulchella, sub annis,
    mota proci lacrimis, mota proci precibus.
5 Flandria me genuit, totum peragravimus orbem,
    tandem me placidae continuere Senae.
Nomen erat, nomen gnotum, Nichina; lupanar
    incolui: fulgor fornicis unus eram.
Pulchra decensque fui, redolens et mundior auro,
10 membra fuere mihi candidiora nive,
quae melius nec erat Senensi in fornice Thais
    gnorit vibratas ulla movere nates.
Rapta viris tremula figebam basia lingua,
    post etiam coitus oscula multa dabam;

: XXIX :

To Leuzzi, the Pawnbroker, to Take Plautus as Security[112]

I commend this Plautus to you, Leuzzi, as much as possible,
  Plautus, whom the Latin language calls father.
O poet, age has obliterated no small part of you,
  and now another pest, moneylending, is eating up the rest.

: XXX :

Epitaph for Nichina of Flanders, the Famous Whore

If you will pause for a little while and read these verses,
  you will know the courtesan who is buried in this earth.
"I was carried off from my native land while still of tender
      years, a pretty little thing,
  moved by the tears of a suitor, moved by the prayers of a
      suitor.
Flanders bore me;[113] I wandered the whole earth;   5
  finally kind Siena detained me.
My name, my well-known name was Nichina; I lived in the
      brothel.
  I was the unique glory of the whorehouse.
Beautiful and graceful I was, sweet-smelling and cleaner than
      gold,
  my limbs were brighter than snow,[114]   10
no Thais in the whorehouses of Siena knew better than I
  how to shake her buttocks.[115]
I planted snatched kisses on men with flickering tongue;[116]
  even after sex I gave many kisses.

15 lectus erat multo et niveo centone refertus,
    tergebat nervos officiosa manus;
pelvis erat cellae in medio, qua saepe lavabar;
    lambebat madidum blanda catella femur.
Nox erat et, iuvenum me solicitante caterva,
20 sustinui centum non satiata vices.
Dulcis, amoena fui; multis mea facta placebant:
    sed praeter pretium nil mihi dulce fuit."

: XXXI :

Conqueritur quod propter pestem a
domina amotus sit

Quando erit ut Senas repetam dominamque revisam?
    Me miserum molli pestis ab urbe fugat!

: XXXII :

Optat pro Nichina defuncta

Oro tuum violas spiret, Nichina, sepulchrum,
    sitque tuo cineri non onerosa silex.
Pyeriae cantent circum tua busta puellae
    et Phoebus lyricis mulceat ossa sonis.

My bed was laden with many white quilts.   15
    My attentive hand rubbed cocks.
There was a basin in the middle of my room, where I washed
    myself.
    A sweet little lap-dog licked my wet pussy.
It was night, and if a crowd of youths asked for me,[117]
    I could turn a hundred tricks and not be satisfied.[118]   20
I was sweet and pleasant. My deeds pleased many,
    but except for my fee, nothing was sweet to me."[119]

: XXXI :

The Poet Complains that He Has Been Separated from His Mistress because of the Plague[120]

When will it be[121] that I can return to Siena and see my
    mistress again?
    Wretched me. The plague drives me from the city of
    pleasure!

: XXXII :

The Poet Prays for the Dead Nichina[122]

I pray that your tomb may smell of violets, Nichina,
    and that the stone may not lie heavy on your ashes.[123]
May the Pierian maidens sing around your tomb
    and Phoebus caress your bones with the sounds of the
    lyre.[124]

: XXXIII :

Laus Cosmi viri clarissimi

Cosme, quis est Latiis vir felicissimus oris
    coniugio, gazis, prole, parente, domo?
Quis patriae spes est? Quis sanguine clarus avito?
    Vates quis priscos servat amatque novos?
5   Pace quis Augustus, Caesar quis Iulius armis?
    Quis fiet mira pro probitate deus?
Cosme, quis hic est? Aut certe tu, Cosme, vir hic es,
    aut certe quis sit nescio: Cosmus, es hic.

: XXXIV :

Auctoris discipuli versus ad Lucium Mauram
quod non servet promissa

Cur non, Maura, venis? Cur non promissa fidemque
    solvis? Cur nullo pondere verba refers?
Nam, memini, dixti nobis venientibus ex te:
    "Ite alacres, cras hinc vos petiturus eam."
5   Cras venit, nec te aërea deducis ab arce,
    cras it, nec tu nunc, perfide Maura, venis.
Quod si nos flocci facias et ludere iam fas
    esse putes, noli spernere, Maura, deos.

: XXXIII :

Praise of the Nobleman Cosimo

Cosimo, who is the man most fortunate in Latin lands,[125]
  in marriage, treasure, offspring, parent, home?
Who is the hope of the fatherland? Who nobly born from his
    grandfather's blood?[126]
  Who protects the ancient poets and loves the new?
Who is an Augustus in peace, a Julius Caesar in arms?   5
  Who will become a god for his wondrous virtue?
Cosimo, who is that man? Surely you, Cosimo, are that man,
  or surely I don't know who is. Cosimo, you are that man.[127]

: XXXIV :

Verses of One of the Author's Pupils, to Lucio Maura,
Because He Has Not Kept His Promises[128]

Why don't you come, Maura? Why don't you keep your
    promises and your faith?
  Why do you utter words that carry no weight?[129]
For I remember, you said as we were leaving you,
  "Go quickly. Tomorrow I'll go from here to find you."
Tomorrow came, and you do not come from your airy   5
    citadel.[130]
  Tomorrow went, and you still do not come, faithless
    Maura.
Even if you don't give a damn for us and think it's okay
  to toy with us, don't spurn the gods, Maura.

Maura deos temnit: iuravit numina divum
10   quod nos Paganico viseret ipse solo;
Maura deos temnit memores fandi atque nefandi:
        spernit et ille viros, spernit et ille deos.
O levior foliis, avium ventosior alis!
        Femineum et turpe est fallere sic alios.
15 Si te, Maura, iuvat me fallere, falle; sed illum
        carmine qui claret ludere, Maura, cave.
Tu vatem et nomen, verum non dogmata nosti:
        nosce, capesse: cito carmine clarus eris.
Non mercede docet quemquam, non indigus auro est:
20   virtutis solum motus amore docet.
Me docuit doctor doctissimus edere versus:
        perdidici, et nunc iam carmina nostra legis.

ː XXXV ː

Ad libellum ne discedat

Quid vis invito domino discedere, quid vis?
        Quis te de nostra deiicit aede, liber?
Quo fugis, infelix? Degunt ubi mille Catones,
        mille quibus tantum seria lecta placent?
5   Cum censore, miser, rigido, laedere, rubesces,
        quumve minus poteris, laese, redire voles.
Vana tui, quaeso, domini praesagia sunto
        sitque timor vanus: thusque piperque teges.
I, verum auctoris rogitet si nomina lector,
10   immemorem nostri nominis esse refer.

Maura scorns the gods. He swore by the power of the gods
    that he would see us in person in Paganico.[131]   10
Maura scorns the gods, who remember right and wrong.[132]
    He spurns men, and he spurns the gods.
O lighter than leaves, windier than the wings of birds:[133]
    It is womanly and base so to deceive others.
If you like deceiving me, deceive away, Maura. But the one   15
    who is famous for song, Maura, beware of toying with
        him.[134]
You know the poet and his name, but not his teaching.
    Learn it, apprehend it; soon you will be famous in song.
He does not teach anyone for a fee, he needs no gold;[135]
    he teaches, moved only by the love of virtue.   20
The best-taught teacher taught me to produce verses.
    I learned it thoroughly and now you are reading my songs.

: XXXV :

To His Book, Not to Leave Him[136]

Why do you want to leave your unwilling master? Why?
    Has anyone thrown you out of my house, book?
Where are you running away to, unhappy one? Where a
        thousand Catos live,[137]
    a thousand who only like serious reading?
When you are hurt by a strict censor, then you'll blush,   5
    and once hurt, you'll want to return when you're least able.
May the forebodings of your master prove vain,
    and vain his fear—that you will be used to wrap incense
        and pepper.[138]
Go, but if any reader asks you the name of your author,
    reply that you can't remember my name.[139]   10

: XXXVI :

Caballus fame periens de Lelpho
Lusco domino conqueritur

Si qua tuus queritur, cupidissime Lelphe, caballus,
    da veniam: macies cogit et alta fames.
"Pulcher equus certe, velox pinguisque fuissem:
    pectora quam sint et fortia et ampla vide
5   aptaque sint videas quam cetera membra peraeque.
    Quod natura dedit, sumpsit avara manus.
Ah, quotiens faleris tectus fera bella subissem!
    Ah, quotiens cursus praestitus esset honos!
Rodo nihil, rodit sed nostras inedia vires:
10   non etiam nostris dentibus herba datur!
Vix mihi dat noster paleas aliquando dominus
    (barbariem metro barbarus ille dedit).
Turpe quidem dictu, sed cogit turpia fari
    turpis herus: proprio stercore pascor ego.
15   Stercore pascor enim, sed stercore pascimur ambo:
    nam tu, ne comedas, non, vir avare, cacas,
neve bibas etiam non meiere, Lelphe, videris.
    Extitit, ut perhibent, dira Celeno parens.
Sella carens lanis quae fecerit ulcera dorso,
20   Lusce, vides; caudae vulnera, Lusce, vides.
Cur equitans aspris calcaribus ilia tundis,
    si vix sat plane debilis ire queam?

: XXXVI :

A Nag Dying of Hunger Complains about
His Master Lelfo Loschi[140]

If your nag complains about anything, greedy Lelfo,
    forgive it, thinness and deep hunger force it.
"I surely would have been a beautiful horse, fast and fat,
    (see how strong and broad my chest is,
and you may see how my other members are just as fit).   5
    What nature gave, a greedy hand took away.
Ah, how often decked out in trappings I would have entered
      savage wars!
    How often the prize for the race would have been offered!
I gnaw nothing, but hunger gnaws away my strength.
    Not even grass is given to my teeth.   10
Scarcely ever does my master give th' straw t' me.[141]
    (That barbarian causes barbarity in the meter.)
A foul thing to say, but a foul master
    causes one to say foul things: I am fed my own dung.
Yes, I am fed dung, but we both are fed on dung,   15
    for you, you miser, so that you don't have to eat, you don't
      shit,
and you don't even seem to pee, Lelfo, so that you don't have
    to drink.[142]
    Your mother was, they say, the awful Celaeno.[143]
The saddle with no woolen blanket that makes sores on my
    back,
    you see it, Loschi. You see the wounds on my tail.   20
When you ride why do you pound my loins with cruel spurs,
    since I'm plainly weak and barely able to walk?

Cur agilis vis dem, crudelis, in aera saltus,
    tibia si nequeat lassa movere pedem?
25 Ipse quidem collo mallem vectare quadrigas,
    degere quam miseri sub ditione viri;
ocius affectem pistrino, Lelphe, dicari,
    sub te funestam quam tolerare famem.
Vera quis haec credat, nisi credunt vera molares?
30   Ferrea sunt longa frena comesa fame.
Ordea cornipedi dulcis datur esca caballo,
    sorbuit hos nunquam sed mea bucca cibos.
Vera loquar, verum quis possit credere ventrem
    dumtaxat vento vivere posse meum?
35 Est, mihi vae misero!, macies incognita toto
    corpore et in fractis artubus ossa sonant.
Sim licet informis simque aridus, hoc mage malim
    quam Lelphus vacui pectoris esse velim.
Est Lelphus rationis inops et mentis egenus,
40   corpus ei, ut sus trux, efferitate riget.
Quum loquitur, boat ut bos, et flat putor ab ore,
    ut dubius perstes culus an os loquitur!
Quum ridet, fauces inhiant ut asellus hiascens,
    fit mihi de risu nausea saepe suo!
45 Plura equidem quererer, quoniam sunt plura, sed, heu heu,
    lingua loqui plus nunc debilitata nequit!
Iam morior: sotii, stabulum, praesepe, valete.
    Me miserum, videor debilitate mori!
Vos procul ite, ferae, procul hinc vos ite, volucres:

Why do you want me to give agile leaps in the air,
  when my exhausted shins cannot move my feet?
Personally I'd rather pull a four-horse chariot with my neck   25
  than live under the rule[144] of a cheap man.
I would sooner aspire to be sentenced to the mill, Lelfo,[145]
  than to endure murderous hunger under you.
Who would believe these things are true, except that my teeth
    believe they're true![146]
  Iron bits have been eaten through in my long hunger.   30
Sweet barley is given as feed to the horny-hoofed nag,[147]
  but my mouth has never sucked those foods.
I'll speak the truth, but who would believe that my belly
  could live on wind alone?
Woe is me,[148] there is unprecedented thinness   35
  over my whole body and the bones rattle in my broken
    joints.
Granted I'm ugly and dried out, but I'd far prefer[149] to be that
  than to be empty-hearted Lelfo.
Lelfo is devoid of reason, wanting sense;[150]
  his body, like a wild boar, bristles with savagery.[151]   40
When he speaks he moos like a cow and rottenness breathes
    from his mouth,
  so that you remain unsure whether his ass or his mouth is
    speaking.[152]
When he laughs, his throat gapes like a gaping mule.
  Nausea often comes over me at his laugh.[153]
I would complain about more things,[154] for there are lots   45
    more, but, alas, alas,
  my wearied tongue[155] can speak no more.
Now I'm dying. Friends, stable, manger, farewell.
  Woe is me, I think I'm dying of my weakness.
Go far away, wild animals![156] Go far away from here, birds of
  the air!

50   quo ruitis? Modo vos pellis et ossa manent!
        Plaudite; nam Lelphum Luscum mandetis avarum:
        ille crucis poenas, furcifer ille, dabit!"

: XXXVII :

Ad libellum ut Florentinum lupanar adeat

Si domini monitus parvi facis, i, fuge: verum
    Florentina petas moenia, parve liber.
Est locus in media, quem tu pete, festus in urbe,
    quove locum possis gnoscere signa dabo:
5   alta Reparatae scitare palatia divae
        aut posce agnigeri splendida templa dei;
hic fueris, dextram teneas paulumque profectus
        siste vetusque petas, fesse libelle, forum.
Hic prope meta viae est: hic est geniale lupanar,
10   qui sua signa suo spirat odore locus.
Hunc ineas, ex me lenasque lupasque saluta,
        a quibus in molli suscipiere sinu:

Where are you rushing to?[157] Only skin and bone await   50
    you.
Raise a cheer, for you will chew on the miserly Lelfo Loschi.
    That gallowsbird will pay the penalty on the cross!"

: XXXVII :

To His Book, That It May Go to the Brothel in Florence[158]

If you think so little of your master's advice, then go ahead—
    run away.[159]
    But seek out the walls of Florence, little book.[160]
There's a cheerful place[161] in the middle of town which you
    should seek,
    and I'll give you signs so you can recognize it.[162]
Inquire after the high palace of the divine Reparata[163]   5
    or ask for the shining temple of the divine Lamb Bearer.[164]
Once you are here,[165] turn right, and after going a little
    further,
    stop, and look for the Old Market, tired little book.[166]
Here is almost the end of your road. Here is the congenial
    whorehouse,[167]
    a place which will breathe out its own signs with its   10
    stench.[168]
Enter here, and say hello from me to the madams and the
    whores,
    in whose tender bosoms you will be taken.

occurret tibi flava Helene dulcisque Mathildis,
    docta agitare suas illa vel illa nates;
15   te viset Iannecta, sua comitata catella
    (blanda canis dominae est, est hera blanda viris);
mox veniet nudis ac pictis Clodia mammis,
    Clodia, blanditiis grata puella suis;
Galla tuo peni vel cunno (nam tibi uterque est)
20   iniiciet nullo tacta rubore manus,
Annaque Theutonico tibi se dabit obvia cantu
    (dum canit Anna recens afflat ab ore merum);
te quoque conveniet crissatrix maxima Pitho,
    quicum deliciae fornicis, Ursa, venit,
25   teque salutatum transmittet Thaida vicus
    proximus, occiso de bove nomen habens.
Denique tam celebri scortorum quicquid in urbe est
    te petet, adventu laeta caterva tuo.
Hic obscena loqui simul et patrare licebit,
30   nec tinget voltus ulla repulsa tuos.
Hic—quod et ipse potes, quod et ipse diutius optas—
    quantum vis futues et futuere, liber!

Blonde Helen and sweet Mathilde will run up to you,
  both of them experts in shaking their buttocks.[169]
Giannetta will come to see you, accompanied by her puppy   15
  (the dog fawns on her mistress; her mistress fawns on
    men).
Soon Clodia will come, her breasts bare and painted,
  Clodia, a girl sure to please with her blandishments.[170]
On your cock or your cunt (for you have both)
  Galla untouched by a blush will put her hands.[171]   20
Anna will meet you and give herself to you with a German
    song
  (as Anna sings she exhales the new wine on her breath);
and Pitho the great hip-wiggler[172] will greet you
  and with her comes Ursa, the darling of the brothel.[173]
The nearby neighborhood, the one named for the slaughtered   25
    cow,[174]
  sends Thais to greet you.[175]
In short, whatever whores are in this famous city
  will seek you out, a crowd happy at your arrival.
Here it's allowed to speak and perform dirty things,
  and no rejection will make your face blush.   30
Here, what you can do and what you've long wanted to do,
  you will fuck and be fucked as much as you want, book.

: XXXVIII :

Ad Cosmum virum clarissimum de libri fine et dedicatione

Cosme, vale, vatum spes et tutela novorum:
    iamque suos fines Hermaphroditus habet.
Cum nequeat maius (nam turbant otia curae),
    hoc tibi, quodcumque est, devovet auctor opus.

HERMAPHRODITI LIBELLUS SECUNDUS ET ULTIMUS
EXPLICIT FELICITER. AD COSMUM VIRUM CLARISSIMUM
EX MEDICORUM PROGENIE ILLUSTRI.

Antonius Panhormita Poggio Florentino viro
claro plurimam salutem.

1   Epistolae tuae, quae veterem sane et antiquum illum eloquentiae
Romanae morem prae ceteris, mea sententia, exprimunt, ad me ut
iusseras perlatae sunt. Eas tametsi auctorem obticuisses abs te ta-
men pro singulari quadam earum elegantia profectas animadverte-
rim. Habent enim epistolae tuae nescioquid excelsum, suave, acre,
opulentum, grave, atque ea quidem insigniter, ut qui tuas illas esse
dubitarit, auctorem quoque praeter te non inveniat oportebit.

: XXXVIII :

To the Nobleman Cosimo: On the End
of His Book and the Dedication[176]

Cosimo, farewell, hope of poets and protector of the new
    ones.
  Now the Hermaphrodite has reached its end.
Since he can do no more (for cares disturb his leisure),
    the author dedicates this work to you, for whatever it's
    worth.

HERE ENDS AUSPICIOUSLY THE SECOND AND
FINAL BOOK OF THE HERMAPHRODITE. DEDICATED
TO THE NOBLE COSIMO OF THE ILLUSTRIOUS
FAMILY DE' MEDICI.

Beccadelli Replies to Poggio[177]

Antonio of Palermo to the distinguished
Poggio of Florence, greetings.

Your letter, which expresses that old and ancient manner of Ro- 1
man eloquence above all others (in my opinion), has been brought
to me just as you asked. Even if you had been silent about the au-
thor, I should have guessed it was sent by you from a certain
unique elegance of style. Your letters have something excellent,
sweet, sharp, rich, serious, so remarkably so that anyone who
doubted that they were yours, could not discover any author other
than you.

2 Oblectarunt me itaque et affecerunt cum ob alias causas tum vel maxime quod opusculum meum tibi non iniocundum extitisse significas nec non Antonii Lusci, poetae non obscuri, iudicio laudatum probatumque. Qua quidem ex re mihi atque meo libello plurimum gratulari licet: mihi quidem quia locupletissimos hos mihi laudatores compererim, qui pro eorum singulari eloquentia queant ex fumo fulgorem exhibere atque ipsum, si modo velint, Thersitem vel quemvis alium abiectissimae conditionis virum illustri laude perspicuum reddere; libello autem quia in doctissimorum hominum manus tandem pervenerit, quos certus equidem eram minime reprehensuros fore lasciviam eius, quippe cum plurimos norint viros doctos, graves, sanctos, et Graecos et nostros, talia scriptitasse, atque inter manus adhuc versari Catullum, Albium Tibullum, Propertium, Iunium Iuvenalem, Marcum Valerium Martialem, et prius Publium Virgilium, Publium Nasonem, poetas egregios et Latinos, qui plerumque verba adeo nuda proferunt et dictu foeda ut haud scias scaenane magis an lupanari digna sint.

3 Ego, vir humanissime, tot summos oratores, tot summos viros memoriae proditum comperio se hoc generis studio et oblectasse et exercuisse, ut ignorem mediusfidius qui se non oblectarint et exercuerint. Nam ipsum philosophorum principem, Platonem (non quidem Christianum hominem, sed qui deum non ignoraverit, imo unum deum servaverit, ceteros vero angelos vel daemones dixerit), constat versus, et quidem petulantes, fecisse in Astera, in Alexim, in Phaedrum pueros, item et de Dione Syracusano, et generaliter eius non nisi versus molles et amatorios extitisse: e quibus hos tantum hoc loci commemorem, quamvis aliquanto licentius liberiusque ex Graeco in Latinum conversos; tu Platonem lepidissimum poetam audi; audi, inquam, Platonem poetam lepidissimum:

It delighted and moved me for many reasons, not least because   2
you signified that my little work had been not unpleasing to you
and that it had been praised and approved in the judgment of An-
tonio Loschi, a not unknown poet.[178] For which reason I and my
book can greatly rejoice. I, because I have found for myself the
most authoritative praisers, men who are able, because of their
unique eloquence, to bring "lightning out of smoke,"[179] and could
make Thersites[180] or anyone else from the lowest class conspicuous
by their lustrous praise; and my book, because it has finally come
into the hands of men of the greatest learning, who I am sure will
by no means condemn its playfulness, especially since they know
that many learned, serious, and venerable men, both Greek and
our own Latins, have written such things, and that Catullus,
Tibullus, Propertius, Juvenal, Martial, and before them Vergil,
Ovid, still circulate among us,[181] exceptional Latin poets who of-
ten exhibit words so blunt and indecent to utter that you scarcely
know whether they're more suitable to the stage or the brothel.

I find, my literary friend, that there is a tradition that so many   3
orators and men of the highest rank have enjoyed and practiced
the cultivation of this type of literature that I swear I don't know
who hasn't enjoyed and practiced it! Everyone agrees that the very
prince of philosophers, Plato—admittedly not a Christian, but a
man who was not ignorant of God, who in fact served the one
God, for he said the others were angels or demons[182]—wrote
verses, and seductive ones too, to boys: Aster, Alexis, Phaedrus, as
well as about Dio of Syracuse, and (generally speaking) none of
his poetry has survived except for his tender and erotic verse.[183]
Of these I'd mention only one at this point, although it's a little
freely and loosely translated from the Greek. Listen to Plato, the
most charming poet. Listen, I say, to Plato, the most charming
poet:

Dum semiulco savio
meum puellum savior
dulcemque florem spiritus
duco, ex aperto tramite
anima aegra et sautia
cucurrit ad labia mihi
rictumque oris pervium
et labra pueri mollia
rimata itineri transitus
ut transiliret nititur.
Tum si morae quid plusculae
fuisset, in coetu osculi,
amoris igni percita,
transisset et me linqueret
et (mira prorsum res) moneret
ut ad me fierem mortuus,
ad puerum interviverem.

4   Solonem quoque et unum ex septem sapientibus habitum et severum virum et verum philosophum fuisse nemo est qui nesciat; attamen eum similiter versus lascivissimos edidisse palam est; item Diogenem cinicum, Zenonem stoicum, Theium, Lacedaemonium, Callimachum, in quibus vel praecipue numeranda est Sapho Lesbia, cuius versus, qui etiam latini extant, ad Phaonem Siciliensem amatorem suum adeo impudici, adeo procaces, alioquin ad eo elegantes sunt, ut cuique legenti pruriginem excitent, etiam ipsi Nestori Priamoque. Enimvero, ut Horatius in Poeticis Institutionibus scriptum reliquit, semper poetis atque pictoribus concessum fuit quidlibet audere licere: cum vero lasciviam delegerint, ea lex poetis est, et verissima illa quidem, quam Catullus dixit:

As I kiss my boy
with a half-open kiss
and I draw the sweet flower
of his breath,
down that open road
my soul, sick and wounded
ran to my lips
and the passage of my mouth
and to the soft parted lips of the boy
in its journey it crossed
and tried to jump across.
Then if there had been even the slightest
bit more of delay in the coming together of lips
stirred by the fire of love,
it would have crossed and left me
and — a wonder — would teach
that I had become dead to myself
but lived within the boy.

Solon as well — no one is unaware that he is held to be one of   4
the Seven Sages, a serious man and a true philosopher. And yet
it's well known that he created similarly playful verses.[184] So too
Diogenes the Cynic, Zeno the Stoic, Theius, Lacedaemonius,
Callimachus, among whom perhaps the first to be counted is
Sappho of Lesbos, whose verses to her lover Phaon of Sicily,
which exist in a Latin version, are so immodest, so provocative,
and yet so elegant that they stir the loins of anyone who reads
them, even in Nestor or Priam themselves.[185] Indeed as Horace
left written testimony in his *Principles of Poetry* the license has al-
ways been granted to poets and painters to be a little daring.[186]
Even when they love playfulness, this is the law for poets, the very
true law that Catullus spoke about:

Nam castum esse decet pium poetam
ipsum, versiculos nihil necesse est,
qui tum denique habent salem ac leporem
si sint molliculi ac parum pudici
et quod pruriat incitare possint.

Quod et Valerius Martialis eruditissime simul ac facetissime pro-
bat in haec verba:

Sed hi libelli
tamquam coniugibus suis mariti
non possunt sine mentula placere.

5   Ego itaque tantorum virorum exemplo nitor, maiorum prae-
cepta custodio, denique aliquid struere studeo quod sit in suo ge-
nere perfectum, fremat licet Hodus nescioquis ex ultima vulgi
faece, alioquin vir malevolus et qui nihil furiosi habet praeter cere-
brum, falsoque putet me proinde parum pudicum, quia versiculi
mei molles atque ludicri sunt, quasi, ut cetera bona, ita illud
quoque nescierit, quod scilicet eo iocundiores futuri sunt huius-
modi versus quo minori cum severitate compositi atque eo sanc-
tiores iudicandi quo apertiores sunt.

6   Qua in re si meo testimonio satis non fidat, Madaurensi cui-
dam magnae auctoritatis viro non potest non assentiri, qui non
ineleganter ait Platonis versus "tanto pudicitius compositi quanto
simplicius professi. Dissimulare" enim "et occultare peccantis,
profiteri et promulgare ludentis est" et sane perquam ridiculum est
eos impuros interpretari qui spurcis verbis utantur quom res exi-
git, quippe qui medendi scientia morbos curant, ii, quom obscenis
partibus medicamenta adhibere volunt, obscenis vocabulis id ex-
plicent opus est: an idcirco eos vita obscenos arbitrabere? Scimus
Voconium poetam summa castimonia praeditum fuisse, et tamen
eum parem lasciviam exercuisse satis indicat epigramma quod di-

For it's right that a proper poet be pure,
himself, but there's no need for his verses to be,
which only can have wit and charm,
if they are a little on the lax side and scarcely modest
and can stir up what makes you itch.[187]

This opinion Martial approved of most learnedly and at the same time most wittily in these words:

But my little books
like husbands with their wives
can't please without a cock.[188]

So I rely on the example of such great men as these, I hold to the precepts of our ancestors; in sum, I am trying to build something that is perfect of its kind, let Oddo rage as he will,[189] that nobody from the utter dregs of the rabble, as well as a mean-spirited man and one who has no frenzy except in his brain, and so falsely thinks that I am "scarcely modest" because my verses are lax and fun, as if he were as ignorant of this as he is of other good things, that verses of this sort will be pleasanter to the extent that they are composed with less seriousness, and should be judged venerable to the extent that they are more forthright.

In this matter, if he doesn't trust my testimony, he cannot but concur with a certain citizen of Madaura, a man of great authority,[190] who said of Plato's verses that "the more directly they were expressed, the more modestly they were composed," and that "to conceal and hide is the mark of the sinner, but to speak openly and to publish is the mark of the wit." It is completely ridiculous to judge verses to be impure because they used dirty words when the subject matter requires. For example, those who cure the sick using the science of medicine, when they need to apply medicines to the indecent parts of the body must explain it in indecent vocabulary. And yet would you think them indecent in life? We

vus Adrianus ita in eius sepulchro inscripsit: "Lascivus versu, mente pudicus eras."

7   Rursus quis ambigit Annaeum Senecam Christum novisse et apostoli Pauli amicum fuisse et in cathalogo sanctorum positum? Ceterum, si quid Plinio Secundo credimus, non seria modo, verum etiam lusus ac sales descripsit. Praeterea floret hac in nostra tempestate sacerdos quidam non minus continens quam disertus atque eloquens habitus, cuius, ut vulgo loquar, praedicationibus saepenumero ipse affui, et, nisi surdus omnino sum, ita eum nudis ac deturpatis affatibus interdum excandescentem in frequentissimum populum exaudivi, ut non dicam in templo, sed ne in foro quidem adesse crediderim: an ideo illum turpem iudicabis quia turpia turpiter, idest foedioribus verbis, castiget? Minime, hercle! Mihi quidem, si nescis, eadem mens est et intentio, nec refert si per lusus ac iocos id agam: namque eo modo et nos agere posse maiores nostri instituerunt et instituta perpetuo observarunt et sane omnes. Nam si veterum scriptorum monumentis fides praestanda est, quicumque perlegitur aut rerum, aut verborum simul et rerum, lascivia praelusit: quorum ex nostris perpaucos nominabo (nam si singulos exequi velim, equidem scribam Horestem alterum, et in tergo scriptum necdum finitum, necesse est). Igitur, ut Plinii verbis utar, "verear ne me non satis deceat quod decuit Marcum Tullium, Caium Calvum, Asinium Pollionem Messallamque et Hortensium ac Marcum Brutum, Lucium Syllamque ac Scaevolam, Servium Sulpitium, Varronem, Torquatum, immo Torquatos, Caium Maevium, Lentulum Getulicum, Verginium Ruffum," Cornelium Nepotem et denique ipsum Plinium? Et, quos paene praeterieram, Hennium Acciumque? "Et si non sufficiunt exempla

know that the poet Voconius was famed for his great chastity, and yet he exercised an equal playfulness as made clear by an epigram of the Emperor Hadrian inscribed on his tomb: "Playful in your verse, you were modest in your heart."[191]

Again, who doubts that Annaeus Seneca knew Christ and was a friend of the Apostle Paul and has been placed in the catalog of the saints?[192] And yet, if we are to believe Pliny the Younger, he wrote not just serious things but also things that were playful and witty.[193] Furthermore, in our own day there flourishes a certain priest, considered to be as self-controlled as he is learned and eloquent, whose sermons (to use the vernacular term) I have attended many times.[194] I would have to be completely deaf not to have heard him on occasion getting so heated up against the packed audience, with such bare and shameful expressions, that I had difficulty believing I wasn't in a market square, much less a church. And would you call him base because he attacked base things basely, that is, with foul words? Good heavens, of course not! In case you don't know, I have the same mind and intention, and it doesn't matter if I do it by means of fun and games. Our ancestors gave us the tradition of being able to do things in this way and nearly everyone has kept that tradition ever since. For if there is any trust to be put in the writings of the ancients, all those we read now made a trial rehearsal with these risqué matters, in their lives or in life and literature together. I shall name just a few of them from among our own Latin writers — if I wanted to list them all, I'd be writing another *Orestes* and have to continue writing on the back of the pages.[195] So to use the words of Pliny: "Should I be afraid that it might not be quite suitable for me, what was suitable for Cicero, Calvus, Pollio, Messalla, Hortensius, Brutus, Sulla, Scaevola, Sulpicius, Varro, Torquatus (or rather the Torquati), Maevius, Lentulus, Verginius Rufus," plus Cornelius Nepos and finally Pliny himself? And those I almost skipped, Ennius and Accius.[196] "And if examples of men in private life are

privata, divum Iulium, divum Augustum, divum Nervam, Tiberium Caesarem" atque alios sane innumerabiles? Ego vero, tot tantorumque virorum exemplo ac auctoritate fretus, non est quod verear hisce carminibus iocari, ludere, ridere, tum irasci, amare, flere et denique remitti posse: mire quidem his opusculis animus remittitur, refovetur et ad maiora succenditur. Verum enimvero epigrammata, quia brevia, licet arguta, sunt et quibus non copia, sed acumine certamus, potest inotiosus quisque perficere. Seria vero, quia continua et longa sunt, sane nisi otiosus securusque non potest: quo fit ut, etsi maxime id concupiscam, serias res tamen reponere non queam impresentiarum; distringor equidem mille atque iterum mille occupationibus, quibus nullo pacto carere nunc possum. Si vero his — quod deus optimus maximus sinat! — aliquando extricer:

> condere victuras tentem per saecula curas
> et nomen flammis eripuisse meum!

8   Sed quid ego haec tecum, qui itidem quod ego sentis, qui pro tua eruditione facile concedis me, sed cum tot tantisque viris, errare potuisse? Nam cum neque Hodum neque reliquum vulgus tanti fecerim ut suae maledicentiae ad sese responderem, tecum id agere consilii fuit, quasi apud te, virum doctissimum et qui vulgi imperitiam satis exploratam habes, quererer de eius in me meosque mores opinione, falsa praesertim. Sed iam multa satis superque satis.

9   Redeo igitur ad epistolam tuam, ut ornatissimam atque officii plenam, ita mihi admodum gratam et iocundam: in qua quidem nihil legi, nihil vidi, quin aequo animo, quin laeta fronte accepe-

not enough, what about the divine Julius Caesar, the divine Augustus, the divine Nerva, Tiberius" and countless others? Relying on the example of so many important men, there is no reason for me to fear to joke, play, laugh in my poems, and then in turn to be angry, love, weep, and finally to be able to relax. It is wonderful how much my spirit is relaxed, rewarmed, inspired to greater things by this little work. Epigrams, since they are short, must be pointed, and in them we fight "not with massed troops but a spearhead."[197] Anyone can compose them even when busy. But as for serious works, because they are unbroken and lengthy, no one who is not at leisure and free from care can complete them. That is the reason why, no matter how much I wanted to, I cannot undertake a serious work at the present. I'm distracted by a thousand and one calls on my time, which I am completely unable to get out of. If ever I can extricate myself from them—and may God Best and Greatest grant it—

> I shall attempt to lay down works that will live through the
>   ages
> and snatch my name from the flames.[198]

But why do I go on about these things with you, who feel just 8 as I do, who in keeping with your erudition grant freely that I, in company with so many illustrious men, can go astray? Even though I don't care enough for Oddo and the rest of the common crowd to respond to their backbiting, I decided[199] to do this with you, as though I were laying a complaint before you, a most learned man and one well acquainted with the ignorance of the crowd, about Oddo's opinion of me and my morals, all quite false. But that's quite enough about that.

So I return to your letter, so very ornate and filled with cour- 9 tesy, and so all the more pleasing and amusing to me, in which I have read nothing, seen nothing that I cannot accept with a calm spirit and unwrinkled brow, except for its brevity. So be sure to

rim, praeter brevitatem. Proinde cura ut deinceps ad me longior fias, quod tute perhumaniter polliceris, ut intelligas nihil mihi brevius videri quam Poggii epistolae longissimae.

10 Postremo me totum dedas viro claro Antonio Lusco, compoetae meo, et vel tu soluto vel ille vincto pede aliquid litterarum ad me exarate.

11 Vale, decus nostrum, et me, ut facis, ama: ego enim te diligo, te observo, te admiror, et quidem quam maxime possum. Iterum vale, nec me fraudes, oro, voluptate ac vice tuarum epistolarum, quae, ut initio dixi, prae ceteris gratae, iocundae et vere Romanae mihi visae sunt. Ex Bononia quam cursim.

12 Scribam posthac ad acerrimum et pereloquentem virum Nicolaum de Malpiglis, si modo festinantis atque alacris huius nuntii ratio permiserit. Sin minus, quam primum per alium. Tu tamen, in omnem eventum, ex me illi salve dicas, desiderium, sitis et corculum Antonii Panhormitae.

Avetote.

Si bene commemini scripsi tibi, Cosme, libellum
    cui turpis titulus Hermaphroditus erat.
Hic faeces varias Veneris moresque profanos,
    quos natura fugit, me docuisse piget.
5 Immortale mihi sperabam surgere nomen,
    si possem Vestae frangere templa deae.

make a longer one for me, which you will very kindly promise me, when you realise that nothing seems briefer to me than the longest letter from Poggio.

Finally, remember me kindly to that famous man Antonio 10
Loschi, my fellow poet, and either you pen me some letter in prose or he in verse.

Farewell, glory of our people, and love me, as you do. For I 11
cherish you, I respect, I admire you, all as much as possible. Again farewell, and do not deprive me, I beg you, of the pleasure and the exchange of your letters, which, as I said at the beginning, seem to me more pleasing, amusing, and truly Roman than any others.

Bologna, in haste.

I will write next to that most witty and eloquent man, Niccolò 12
Malpigli, if the plans of this hasty and speedy messenger allow.[200] If not, by the next available one. In any case, give him my greetings, you who are the desire, longing, and dear heart[201] of Antonio Panormita.

Goodbye. [April 1426].

Beccadelli's Recantation[202]
[c. 1435]

If I remember well, Cosimo, I dedicated to you a book
    with the foul title of *The Hermaphrodite*.
I am now ashamed that I taught various filthy acts and
    impious ways of Venus, which nature shuns.
I was hoping to raise up an immortal name for myself, 5
    by seeing if I could smash the temple of the goddess Vesta.

Te quoque, quem sanctum coluit Florentia civem,
    non puduit sociis commemorare meis,
sic quoque non Rhodi famam nomenque celebre
10   Parnasi: at corvo non maculatur olor.
Iam tantis si indigna viris cecinisse nefandum est:
    parcite: proh noxam conspicor ipse meam.

I was not ashamed to brag to my friends even about you,
    the man whom Florence honors as a revered citizen,
and likewise with the glory of Rhodes[203] and the famous name
    of Parnassus, but the swan is not soiled by contact with the   10
        crow.
It is wrong now to have sung of things unworthy of such great
        men.
    Forgive me. Alas, I myself now recognize my offense.

Antonius Panormita Guarino Veronensi s. p. d.

1 Etsi acceperam Hermaphroditon meum plurimorum iudicio probatum, laudatumque magnifice, nihilomagis tamen animo movebar, quod satis sciebam partim exuberantia quadam amoris erga me, partim novitate quam veritate magis illorum profecta iudicia esse, praeterea qui "sub vulpe," ut aiunt, "latentes" meque et opusculum meum divinis laudibus et plus quam liceret cumularint, cuius generis bipedes levissimos quidem illos, quia adulatione et callida assentatione se insinuant, vehementer odi, a quibus eo animum semper alienum habui quo ipsi a veritate. Ceterum cum te virum simplicem verum apertum et qui in manibus quodammodo mentem geras, idem de me meoque libello sentientem animadvertam, non modo non moveri non possum, sed, ut fatear mollitiem meam, gaudio non prodi distrahive, cum presertim antehac nulla mecum amicitia nulla familiaritate fueris devinctus unde potius quam ex re ipsa iudicasses.

2 O felicem meum Hermaphroditon vocalissimum tibi hunc buccinatorem sortitum, o fortunatam libelli lasciviam! Iam modo ab invidorum ac vulgi sagittis tuta es septemplice Aiacis umbone, id est Guarini auctoritate. Sed quamquam tua haec de me sententia mihi iocunda sit, vereor tamen ne modum excedat plurisque me existimes quam ipse sim. Quamobrem te quaeso, mi Guarine, ho-

APPENDIX
ASSOCIATED LETTERS AND POEMS

: I :

Beccadelli's reply to Guarino's letter[1]

Antonio Panormita to Guarino da Verona, greetings

Even though I have heard that my *Hermaphrodite* has been approved by the judgment of many men and praised to the skies, nonetheless I am deeply moved, especially since I knew full well that their judgment was formed partly by a certain exuberance of their love for me and partly by the work's novelty more than by the truth. Furthermore, as to those who "lurk under the fox's hide," as they say,[2] and pile divine praises on me and my little work more than is proper — and of this species I especially hate those fickle bipeds who insinuate themselves through adulation and clever flattery — I have always had a spirit that differs as much from them as they differ from the truth. But when I learn that you, an open, straightforward and honest man and one who wears his heart on his sleeve,[3] has the same opinion about me and my book, not only can I not be unmoved, but (to confess my weakness), I am betrayed and distracted with joy, especially since you were not bound to me by any previous friendship or relationship on which you would base your judgment rather than on the work itself.

How lucky you are, my *Hermaphrodite*, to have found so vocal a trumpeter! How fortunate, indecent little book! Now at last you are safe from the arrows of the envious and the vulgar under the seven-layered shield of Ajax, that is, under Guarino's authority.

nora mensuram, nam cum in omnibus rebus mensura adhibenda sit, tum maxime puto cum aliquem laudare studemus. Solon Atheniensis, unus e septem sapientibus habitus, legem apud Graecos dederat de decipientibus, qua cum his actio erat qui alios in laudibus cuiuspiam decipiebant.

3   Iohanni vero Lamolae viro docto et emendato et vere ex Guarini ludo litterario profecto discipulo gratias et ingentis habeo, propterea quod insciente me quidem Hermaphroditon ad te dimiserit meum measque partis ultro sustinuerit, nam cum tibi illum ut exhiberem accingerer, praevenit me vir diligentissimus.

4   Plura tecum agere animo insidebat sed abs te vel invitus avocor ad auditorium iurisconsulti nostri. Illinc autem versus quod supererat tibi plenius explicabo, quod quemadmodum ex epistulis tuis colligo non parva cum voluptate leges.

Ex Bononia, quam cursim.

: II :

Poggius pl. sal. dicit Antonio Panormitae V. C.

1   Pluribus verbis quam necesse erat defendis libellum tuum apud hominem non solum non accusantem eum, sed defendentem. Mihi enim satis probatur opus tuum iis limitibus, quos antea tibi perscripsi, quos si servaris, praestabo me tibi etiam militem pugnatorem in subsidiis tuis.

2   Perplacuit mihi tum verborum suavitas, tum gravitas sententiarum. Testimonia insuper quae affers ad causae tuae defensionem

But even though your opinion of me was pleasing, I am afraid that it goes over the limit and you think me more valuable than I am. Wherefore I beg you, dear Guarino, for measure in honor, for measure ought to be observed in all things, but especially I think when we seek to praise someone. Solon of Athens, considered one of the Seven Wise Men, passed a law among the Greeks about those who would deceive. Under this law, an action would lie with those who deceived others in praise of someone.[4]

I give thanks, great thanks to Giovanni Lamola, that learned 3 and refined man, and truly a disciple of Guarino's literary school, for having (quite without my knowledge) sent my *Hermaphrodite* to you and taking my part voluntarily, for when I was girding my loins to show it to you, that thoughtful man beat me to it.

I had it in mind to write to you at greater length, but I am 4 called away unwillingly to a lecture by my law professor. I will discuss the rest more fully when I've got back from that, something that I gather from your letters you'll read with no little pleasure.

Bologna. In haste. [February 1426].

: II :

Poggio's reply to Beccadelli's letter[5]

Poggio gives greetings to the distinguished Antonio Panormita

You defend your little book with more words than are necessary 1 against someone who not only is not attacking it but actually defending it. I quite approve of your work, within the limits I wrote to you about previously, and if you keep within them I shall continue to serve as your soldier, a fighter in your reserves.

The sweetness of your words pleased me, as well as the serious- 2 ness of your thoughts. In addition, the witnesses that you offer in

tam sunt gravia, tam veneratione et fide digna, ut religiosum sit eis nolle assentiri, et impudentiae singularis; si tamen in tuam sententiam loquantur. Sed vide ne longe a te dissentiant.

3   Ego quidem, qui Academicorum more nil audeo affirmare, vereor, ne plurimi eorum, si singulatim citentur coram aequo iudice, vel pudore sileant eius causa, qui eos in causam suam adduxerit, vel si dicere testimonium cogantur, aperte et palam causam tuam deserant, religioni potius eorum ac veritati consulentes quam opinioni tuae; teque summopere reprehendant, qui continentissimos, ac prudentissimos viros non solum a vitae, sed verborum quoque turpitudine abhorrentes, in obscenae vilisque causae defensionem rogaris.

4   Nam quis tibi vel parum doctus concedat (ut missos faciam Graecos, quibus ad libertatem dicendi, fingendique quae vellent summa fuit tum levitas tum licentia), quis inquam concedat tibi virum sanctissimum castissimumque M. Tullium, virum omni virtutum laude cumulatum, cuius non solum facta, sed dicta omni petulantia caruere, isto dicendi genere et turpiloquio usum? Lege vitam suam, lege mores, lege aemulos atque obtrectatores eius, nil tale invenies ne ab invidis quidem et malevolis obiectum. Quis M. Varronem tibi credat adesse, virum gravem, maturum, cuius nomen etiam quamdam prae se fert maiestatis venerationem? Brutum vero ex Stoicorum schola, cuius vita fuit virtutis exemplar: si quis roget sententiam suam, vereor ne vel solus illa stoica severitate causam tuam funditus evertat, et sibi a te grandem iniuriam fieri clamet, qui eum levem et lusorium in quadam vili scena inter actores ponas et mimos. Quid loquar de Servio Sulpitio, viro suae

defense of your case are so serious, so worthy of veneration and trust that it would be almost sacrilegious and a mark of singular impudence to be unwilling to agree with them, provided they follow your interpretation. But make sure they're not greatly at variance with you.

Personally speaking, I follow the custom of the Academic 3 school of philosophy in refusing to swear to anything,[6] and I'm afraid the majority of your witnesses, if arrayed one by one before an impartial judge, would keep silent out of modesty for the sake of someone who had hailed them into court in his defense; or if forced to testify, they would openly and publicly desert your case, having more regard for their own scruples and the truth than for your opinion. They would vigorously condemn you for having summoned men of the greatest self-control and intelligence, men who shrank from indecency in life as well as words, to the defense of an obscene and frivolous case.

No one, however poorly educated, would yield to you on this 4 point. I pass over the Greeks, who were frivolous and licentious with the freedom to say and make up whatever they wanted. Who, I repeat, would grant that that most holy and chaste man, Cicero, a man loaded with praise for all manner of virtues, a man whose life as well as words were free from any filth, used that manner of speech and smutty talk? Read his life, read his works, read his rivals and detractors—you will find no such charge even from those who envied or hated him.[7] Who would believe that Varro was on your side, a serious, mature man, whose very name carries with it a certain venerable majesty?[8] And Brutus, a follower of the Stoics whose life was a model of virtue, if he were asked his opinion, I'm afraid that with his stoic severity he would turn your case on its head all by himself, and would claim that you did him a great injury by making him appear light and frivolous, as if you were casting him among the actors and pantomime artists in some cheap play. What I am to say about Servius Sulpicius, the most

aetatis gravissimo, quem numeras inter scriptores lascivos? Quid item permultos reliquos, lumina linguae Latinae, qui solam honestatem in bonis ponendam duxere? Quos omnes si in tuam aciem collocaris, apertissime in adversariorum castra migrabunt. Neque enim est aliud hos viros in tuis praesidiis ponere, quam virginem vestalem prostituere in vulgus summo cum dedecore.

5   Neque si quid aliquando temporis aut loci causa forte luserunt, hoc scribendi petulans et lascivum genus probabunt. Non eadem licentia est philosophis quae oratoribus; non oratoribus quae poetis, quos tu omnes tanquam ex eadem officina affers ad tui operis excusationem: probant philosophi; persuadent oratores; oblectant poetae: tu non solum poetas, sed oratores, sed philosophos, ad lasciviam redigis: neque eos, quibus voluptas sola in bonis numeratur, hoc est Epicureos, quod forsan tibi concedi possit, sed Stoicos, et eos, qui solam honestatem summum bonum posuere; qui non solum bene vivendi, sed etiam honeste loquendi praecepta tradiderunt.

6   Etiam pictores quibus omnia licent, item ut poetis, cum nudam mulierem pinxere, tamen obscena corporis membra aliquo contexere velamento, ducem naturam imitati, quae eas partes quae haberent aliquid turpitudinis, procul e conspectu seposuit. Fuerunt tamen nonnulli, qui lasciva scripserunt, sed ita ut procul abessent a verborum lascivia; qua si qui liberius usi sunt, non ideo sunt laudandi quia instar aliorum scripsere. Invenies enim perplures luxuriosos, invidos, raptores, sicarios quam honestos viros; neque tamen quisquam est adeo perversis moribus, quin se malit bonorum similem quam malorum. Alexandrum magnum et item Marcum Antonium accepimus ebrietate nimia laborasse; at hoc

serious writer of his age, whom you count among the indecent writers? And what of all the others, leading lights of the Latin language, who thought that virtue was to be accounted the only good? If you try to range them on your side, all of them will openly defect to the enemy camp. Calling these men to your defense is no different than prostituting a Vestal Virgin among a crowd of men — an act of the greatest indecency.

And if they were perhaps occasionally a little playful in keeping 5 with the time or place, they will not thereby give their seal of approval to this filthy and indecent way of speaking. Philosophers do not have the same freedom of speech as orators, and orators don't have the same freedom as poets, all of whom you summon to the defense of your work as though they all formed part of the same school. Philosophers prove; orators persuade; poets delight. But you're reducing not just poets, but orators and philosophers too to mere indecency. And not just those philosophers who count pleasure as the only good, that is the Epicureans, which could perhaps be granted to you, but the Stoics and those who reckon virtue the highest good, and who have passed down precepts not only for moral living but for honest speaking.

Even painters, who along with poets, are allowed everything, 6 when they paint a naked woman, nevertheless cover up the obscene parts of the body with a veil of some kind, imitating the example of nature, which placed the parts of body that have something shameful about them well out of sight.[9] There were admittedly some who wrote about indecent things, but in a way that kept them well away from indecent language. And if some of them used indecent language rather too freely, they are not to be praised because they wrote in imitation of others — you will find many more libertines and malevolent people, more robbers and murderers than honest men. But no one's morals are so perverse that he wouldn't prefer to be like the good than the bad. We learn that Alexander the Great and Mark Antony suffered from excessive

turpissimum vitium aequabant plurimae et magnae virtutes. Si quis igitur ex nostris homunculis excusaret ebrietatem suam talium virorum exemplo, nonne esset ridendus? Multa illos ingentes viros decuere quae nos dedecent. Si quid aliquando Catoni licuit, cuius legitur saepe mero caluisse virtus, aut Platoni aut Socrati summae sapientiae et auctoritatis viris, non itidem licet nobis, nulla auctoritate, sapientia, gloria, virtute praeditis. Scripsit adolescens comoediam Plato, in ea posuit versiculos quos refers, qui ita lascivi sunt, ut salva honestate et audiri possint et referri. Dixit in puerum, quod tum neque moribus neque legibus prohibebatur: hoc et multi fecere, tum ex Graecis, tum ex nostris, sed tamen ut scurrilitate vacarent.

7   Diversa sunt iocandi genera, aliud liberum hominem, aliud servum decet; aliud facetum, aliud scurram. Quod autem Plinii verbis uteris, vide ut ea rite interpreteris et ex eius sententia. Iocis et salibus omnes isti usi sunt, quos enarras: ab obscoenitate verborum tantum abfuerunt quantum semoti fuerunt a turpitudine vitae. Valerius Martialis tamen omnibus est apertior in epigrammatibus suis, res turpes narrans quandoque turpius, qui si quos ex superioribus est imitatus, non est tamen ideo probatus quod aliorum lasciviam expressit potius quam suam.

8   Sed nonne ego sum homo ridiculus, ut ait Terentianus Mitio, qui adversus illum causam dicam, cui veneram advocatus? Ego tecum sentio, et tibi ea licuisse opinor, si tamen tibi finem statueris: hoc vero est quod volo persuadere tibi, imitandos potius esse graves poetas quam leves; severos quam lascivos; honestos quam impudicos. Conveniant verba moribus nostris atque id est satius quam dare adversariis aliquam ansam ad obloquendum. Non sum autem ex eorum sententia qui vitam hominum aestimant ex versi-

drinking; but they offset one terrible vice with many great virtues. If one of our little men of today were to excuse his drunkenness by the example of these great men, wouldn't he be laughed at? Many things were fitting for those giants that are unfit for us. If a certain allowance was occasionally made for Cato, whose virtue, we read, often grew warm with wine,[10] or to Plato or Socrates, men of the greatest wisdom and authority, the same is not permitted to us, who are endowed with no such authority, wisdom, glory or virtue. Plato as a youth wrote a comedy, in which he set the verses to which you refer, which are indeed indecent, but one can still hear and repeat them with one's virtue intact.[11] He spoke about a boy, a thing which was then forbidden neither by custom or law.[12] Many others did the same, both Greeks and Romans, but in a way that avoided indecency.

There are different types of jokes: one sort may be suitable for a free man, another for a slave; one for a wit, another for a jester.[13] When you use Pliny's words, make sure that you interpret them correctly and with his meaning. All those you mentioned used jokes and wit, but they avoided obscenity in their words just as they shunned vice in their lives. Admittedly Martial is more open than the rest in his epigrams. He tells shameful stories sometimes in very shameful language. If he imitated those of the previous generations, he is not on that account to be praised, because he depicted other people's indecency rather than his own.

But aren't I being ridiculous, as Micio says in Terence's *Brothers*, by "making the case against the man I came to defend"?[14] I agree with you and think you are allowed these things, provided that you set yourself a limit. That's what I'm hoping to persuade you of: that you need to imitate the serious poets rather than the frivolous; the decent rather than the indecent; the honest rather than the immodest. Let our words match our lives. That is better than giving our enemies a handle to attack us with. I am not one of those who think that they can deduce a man's life from his verses.

bus. Non solum enim id puerile est, sed ridiculum et leve, dicta potius et verba inspicere quam vitae consuetudinem et rationem. Iocamur saepe verbis, utimur facetiis et salibus quae si eadem redderemus gesta corporis, diceremur merito insani.

9   Itaque sive Odus nescio quis, odio certe dignus, sive quivis alter, qui lasciviam vitae arguit ex petulantia verborurm, errat procul dubio et iniquus est rerum aestimator, quos tu despicias ac contemnas licet, fretus potius conscientia recte factorum quam motus aemulorum maledicentia. Neque enim a malivolis laudari cupis sed a doctis; neque eorum iudicium magni faciendum est, qui stultitiane magis an malevolentia laborent, incertum est. Nam ut existimatio eorum qui te bonum putarent, si malus esses, nihil tibi prodest ad bene vivendum; ita iudicium perversum eorum, qui vitam turpem iudicant, cum sit honesta, nil possunt demere quo virtus a te queat auferri, quam tu sequere, et una cum vitae temperantia adhibe moderationem verborum. Hoc et utillimum tibi et amicis tuis et praesertim mihi erit gratissimum.

Romae.

: III :

Antonius Panormita Bartholomaeo pontifici s. p. d.

1   Non poteram equidem gratiore aut iucundiore nuntio affici, vir humanissime, quam eo, quo proxime mihi ab Ioannis Lamolae docti in primis adolescentis et emendati litteris allatus est, siquidem enuntiat, quod ego magni semper aestimavi, quodque mirifice concupivi, me tuam gratiam inivisse iam. Cum enim saepenumero tuum suave ingenium, doctrinam, animi virtutes, a maximis spec-

Not only is it childish, but ridiculous and frivolous, to consider someone's words and speech rather than his way of life. We all play around with words, we use jokes and witty remarks, things that if we were to act out physically, we should quite rightly be regarded as insane.

So some Oddo or other (definitely worthy of odium),[15] or anyone else who deduces an indecent life from dirty words, is plainly wrong and a poor judge of things, and you may despise and disdain him, relying on your own consciousness of having done things right rather than being upset by the gossip of your enemies. For you desire not to be praised by ill-wishers but by the learned. Whether these people are motivated by stupidity or by malice, no weight should be given to their opinion. Just as the opinion of those who think you good even if you are bad does not help you to live right, so the perverse judgment of those who think your life is wicked when it is actually upright can take nothing from you that would strip you of your virtue. So follow the path of virtue, and to temperance of life add moderation of language. This will be most useful to you and to your friends, and specially pleasing to me.

Rome. [April/May 1426].

: III :

Antonio Panormita to Archbishop Bartolomeo Della Capra[16]

I could not have been moved, kind sir, by any happier or more pleasant news than that brought to me just now in a letter of Giovanni Lamola, that most learned and faultless of young men. For he announced something that I've always valued highly and greatly desired: that I have entered into your favor. I have often heard your sweet nature, your learning, and your spiritual excel-

tatisque viris celebrari laudibus audirem, mirum in modum me ipse alliciebas, perfringebas, irrepebas denique in sensus meos, fiebatque ut te, tametsi numquam videram, tam ardenter diligerem quam te illi vehementer laudarent probarentque. Fatebor in amore mollitiem meam: numquam benevolentiae impetum continere potui, si modo cuiuspiam fieret aliqua virtutis aut probitatis significatio. Natura quidem omnes in amore proclives sumus, eorum praesertim qui prae se ferunt aliquam probitatis lucem.

2   Quorsum haec? Ut intelligas me iampridem in te tuosque mores affectum incensumque: in praesentia vero quoniam et abs te multa caritate diligi me audio, adeo prae laetitia distractus, adeo distensus sum, ut si ungula uel leviter me contingas, facile me totum dirimas, aperias. Quis me felicem et beatum non putet? Quis me vera et praecipua laude dignum non existimet, quis me perspectum et abunde iudicatum non habeat, qui tam praeclaro, tam magno, tam gravi, tam denique litterato viro placuisse et amicum fuisse cognouerit? Qua ex re si quando musis habui gratias, nunc maxime et habeo et ago peringentes certe, quae me voti compotem effecerunt. Qua quidem in re illud pro virili semper adnitar ut perpetua sit amicitia quam musae ipsae conciliarunt. Et sane cum alioqui haud facile amicitia ad postremos cineres perduret, eam tamen quam musae devinxerunt, a musis didici perpetuam simul et memorabilem esse solere. Sed de amore hactenus.

3   Nunc ad Lamolam nostrum redeo. Is me per epistolas rogat et quidem tuo nomine, ut Hermaphroditum meum ad te propediem mittam. Ait enim incredibilem tibi sitim incessisse videndi eius et lectitandi versus meos. Ego cum primum subsisterem, siquidem res admodum lasciva est et adolescentis opus, dein certa ratione decrevi quicquid id esset pro tuo iussu dimittere, ut si quid tuis

lence praised to the skies by the most important and well-regarded men, and so you have wondrously entranced me, broken down my defenses, and crept into my senses. And so it has come about that, even though I have never seen you, I love you as ardently as those men enthusiastically praise and approve you. I confess my weakness in love; I have never been able to contain the rush of affection. Provided that there's some sign of someone's virtue or morality, we are all naturally inclined to love, especially to love those who exhibit any light of morality.

What is the point of all this? Simply to let you know that I   2
have long been passionately devoted to you and your character; and now when I hear that I am loved by you with great affection, I am so wild with happiness, so puffed up, that if you were to touch me lightly with a fingernail, you'd easily split me and open me completely. Who wouldn't think me happy and blessed, worthy of genuine and abundant praise, who wouldn't think me thoroughly tried and tested, when he learns that I have pleased and become a friend to such a renowned, important, serious and (most especially) erudite a man? On that account, if ever I have thanked the Muses, now more than ever I give them the greatest thanks for having granted my wish. In this matter, as far as it lies within my power,[17] I shall strive to see that a friendship which the Muses have created lasts for ever. And though in other cases friendship endures to the final ashes[18] only with difficulty, I have nevertheless learned from the Muses that one that they have bound together is likely to last forever and be memorable. But that's enough on the subject of love.

Let me return to our friend Lamola. In his letter he asked me   3
on your behalf to send you my *Hermaphrodite* at once — he says that an incredible thirst for seeing it and reading my verses has seized you. Though I hesitated at first, since the matter is somewhat indelicate and a work of youth, I then made up my mind and decided that, such as it was, I would send it to you at your bid-

moribus tuaque aetate alienum offenderes, esset quod tibi potius imputares, qui id exegeris, quam mihi qui ut tuae voluntati obtemperarem exhibuerim.

4   Mitto igitur tibi meum Hermaphroditum, libellum quidem lascivum, sed ea lascivia, qua summi oratores, sanctissimi poetae, gravissimi philosophi, viri continentes et Christiani denique praelusere. Et sane:

> castum esse decet pium poetam
> ipsum, versiculos nihil necesse est,

quod tu pro tua eruditione plenissime nosti. Quare hoc apud te prolixius tractare esset, quod aiunt, Minervam edocere. Istud autem simplicius et amicitius feceris si quod de eo dicturus es aliis, id ipsum egeris apud me, ut quid de me sperandum sit, ex tuo magno acrique iudicio deprehendam atque constituam.

5   Vale meum decus, tibique meam musam habe, eamque desidiae indormientem quandoque excita.

Ex Bononia, quam raptim. Kal. Decembr.

: IV :

Antonius Panormita dulcissimo Iohanni Lamolae p. s.

1   Si vales gaudeo, nam cum tibi bene est, id quidem mihi dividitur. Accepi proximis diebus ex te litteras sane officii et diligentiae plenas, quibus satis superque docuisti quod mecum saepiuscule egeras vivo sermone, scilicet te neque in amore neque in omni re diligentia a quoquam superari posse, non etiam ab ipso Scipione. Ego cum iam nunc rem re ipsa plane videre videor, te maxime laudo, te admiror, te deosculor mihique plurimum gratulor, qui eo benivolo

ding, so that if you come across something not in keeping with your morals or your time of life, you would lay the blame on yourself for having demanded it, rather than on me for having shown it to you in obedience to your wishes.

And so I am sending you my *Hermaphrodite*, an indecent book   4 to be sure, but with the sort of indecency in which the greatest orators, the most holy poets, the most serious philosophers, men of self-restraint, and indeed Christians have indulged themselves. And indeed,

It's right that a proper poet be pure himself
But there's no need for his verses to be,

something that with your learning you must know full well.[19] And so to treat this matter any further to you would be, as they say, "to teach Minerva".[20] But you will be acting in a more straightforward and friendly manner if you tell me directly what you are going to say about it to others, so that I can learn and determine from your powerful and acute judgment what hopes I may have for myself.

Farewell, honored sir, and take my muse for yourself, and rouse   5 her from her sleep and indolence from time to time.[21]

Bologna, in haste. 1 December [1426].

: IV :

Antonio Panormita to his dear friend Giovanni Lamola[22]

If you're well, I'm happy, because when things are good for you, I   1 share it. A few days ago I received from you a letter full of kindness and solicitude, in which you showed me more than sufficiently what you have so often shown me in face to face conversation, namely that you cannot be outdone in attentiveness to matters of friendship — or anything else — by anyone, not even by Scipio himself.[23] And now that I seem to see clearly your action in

fortunatus sum, quippe qui id semper et enixe studeat quo pacto
suos amicos et familiares exornet inlustret praedicet atque omni-
bus gratos atque familiares efficiat.

2   Sane non poteras me potiori aut cariori munere adficere, non si
quidem ipsius Croesi divitias mihi dono dederis, quam amicitia
atque familiaritate Bartholomaei archiepiscopi, viri non incele-
bris neque inlitterati. Huius, ut nosti, coniunctionem vehementer
atque diutissime desideravi. Acceperam equidem clarissima multo-
rum voce virum hunc, de quo loquimur, esse magnum et prope
singularem, quem et omnes pro egregiis atque eximiis eius virtuti-
bus et amare et observare deberent. Itaque illum, quamquam vide-
ram numquam, nescio quomodo prolixe diligebam contraque ab
eo amari exardebam cupiditate incredibili.

3   Nunc vero cum id tuo munere sim adsecutus, quos complexus
quae oscula quos versus quas laudes denique quas tibi gratias de-
beo? Certe immortales. Illud autem recte quidem et amice facis
mihique admodum gratum, quod me measque res ita promittis
atque obligas quasi tuas. Nam, ut Euripides ait, τὰ τῶν φίλων
κοινά. Et quidem memini me legisse Pythagoram solitum dicere
nihil nobis privatum, omnia communia esse debere. Perge igitur,
ut facis, optime adolescens, me meaque omnia iure tuo polliceare;
ego quidem tuis omnibus de me pollicitationibus promissionibus
obligationibus spondeo me ultro ac sponte fore satisfacturum;
quin et si me glaebae cuiuspiam adscripseris, id quoque me confes-
tim impleturum existima.

4   Ecce quoad ocius quivi Hermaphroditum isti Principi mitto
doleoque ipsum animum, quo ut nihil in homine divinius ita nihil
mihi carius est, avelli emittique non posse: eum profecto dono mi-
sissem Principi una cum libello. Ceterum vereor et quidem immo-
dice ne, cum Hermaphroditus noster sese Principis bibliothecae

action, I greatly praise you, I admire you, kiss you, and congratulate myself over and over for having been blessed with a kind friend who is always eagerly searching for ways to praise, show off, and promote his friends and acquaintances, and to make them welcome and acquainted with everyone.

You really couldn't have given me a more desirable or dearer   2
gift, not if you had granted me the wealth of Croesus himself, than the friendship and acquaintance of Archbishop Bartolomeo, a man not without fame and learning. As you know, I have long and eagerly desired an association with him. I had gathered from the clear report of many people that the man we are speaking is a great man and nearly unique, a man that everyone should love and admire for his great and exceptional virtues. And so, although I have never seen him, I somehow loved him wholeheartedly and burned with an incredible desire to be loved in turn.

And now that I've achieved this, thanks to your gift, what em-   3
braces, what kisses, what verses, what praises, in short, what thanks do I owe you? Undying gratitude, to be sure. You act rightly and as a friend should, and give me great pleasure when you promote and pledge me and my affairs as if they were your own. For as Euripides says, "Friends have all things in common." And I recall reading that Pythagoras was in the habit of saying, "There is nothing private between us, all ought to be in common."[24] So continue to do what you are doing, best of youths, and use your authority to give undertakings on behalf of me and all my works. And I pledge willingly and voluntarily that I will fulfill all your guarantees, promises, and obligations. Not only that, but if you were to bind me to be someone's serf, consider it done at once.[25]

So look: I'm sending *The Hermaphrodite* as fast as I can[26] to the   4
prince[27] and I am grieved that my very soul — and just as there is nothing more divine in man, so there is nothing dearer to me — cannot be torn out and sent to him; in truth I would have sent it

quasi nitidissimis pavonibus immiscere desideraverit, sibi id accidat quod et graculo accidisse pueri didicimus. Proinde eum promone, eum cohibe; est quidem audax natura sibique plusquam satis est, quod abominor, indulget atque suas partes quam maxime potes tutare contra vulgi imperitiam. Scio equidem fore ne umquam plebeculae gratificetur id libelli, quo magis ac magis sapientibus atque humanissimis viris collibeat gratusque sit.

5   Quod superest ne addubites velim, enimvero animi non diffidemus, modo Maecenates compereris. Nam ut versu dicere consuevi:

Mecum sunt musae, mecum formosus Apollo est,

crescitque in me furor nescioquis fortasse divinus. Vereor ne satis arroganter dixerim, quamquam, ut apud Platonem legi, poetis concessum est furere.

6   Postremo ut iubes Guarino, Aurispae, Ambrosio monacho, Tuscanellae nostroque Aretino et reliquis familiaribus nostris tuam abitionem tuaeque vitae rationem per epistolas commodum renuntiabo faxoque, ni fallor, uti summam rationem te ad hoc consilium compulisse persuasum habeant. Tuque etiam officio tuo ne deesto, de repente illis epistolas dato, tute tuum casum exprimito; etenim vehementer in eorum ad me epistolis admirati sunt, quam ob rem ad illos silueris tamdiu meque etiam inculpant measque litteras carpunt, quae te quoque iamdudum obticuerint.

Ex Bononia, quam cursim. Kal. Decembris

to the prelate as a present along with the book. But I'm afraid, in fact terribly afraid, that since my *Hermaphrodite* has longed to mingle in the prince's library as though with the most elegant peacocks, he may suffer the same fate that we learned as boys happened to the jackdaw.[28] So warn him, stop him! He is bold by nature, and indulges himself far too much—something I hate. Take his part as much as you can against the ignorant crowd. I know that this little book will never please the crowd, and for that reason it will please and be all the more welcome to the wise and cultivated.

Please have no fear for the future, for we will not lose heart, 5 provided you find Maecenases.[29] Just like the verse I used to recite:

The Muses are with me, handsome Apollo is with me.[30]

And some madness, perhaps divine, rises in me. I'm afraid I'm speaking too arrogantly, though I've read in Plato that poets have the license to go mad.[31]

Finally, as you ask, I'll pass on right away the news of your de- 6 parture and how you're doing in letters to Guarino, Aurispa, Brother Ambrogio,[32] Toscanella,[33] our friend Bruni,[34] and all our acquaintances, and I'll be sure (unless I slip up) to persuade them that you were forced to adopt this plan for the best of reasons.[35] But you too must not fail in your duty, so send them letters at once and explain your situation yourself. In their letters to me they are very surprised that you have been silent so long, and they blame me and criticize my letters for also having been silent about you for so long.

From Bologna, in haste. 1 December [1426].

: V :

Antonius Panormita suo Iacobo Genuensi
viro docto et eloquenti s. d.

1 Facis ut amicum decet et frugi virum, Iacobe Genuensis, quippe
qui me contendis aram ex cloaca cotidie facere et ex tenui quodam
homullulo Croesum regem. Sic enim ex Lamolae nostri viri tersis-
simi litteris accepimus. Tu vero pergas, age sis, siquidem qui alios
ornare studet, is non ornatus esse non potest; alioquin grato ac
memori viro beneficium confers <et> quo me[1] divite non eris pau-
per. Haec hactenus.

2 Nunc abs te peto et, si pateris, oro: fac ne Cambius noster vir
amplissimus Hermaphroditum a me petere pergat; nam ut nosti
res affatim turpis est et sanctissimi viri lectione non digna. Is ta-
men sum qui petenti iubentique Cambio vel ipsa viscera exhi-
beam. Tu fac, ut dixi, ne ulterius nostras ineptias poscat. Cura te
molliter, Iacobe suavissime, meque perseveranter ama.

Vale mea rosa.

: V :

Antonio Panormita to the learned and eloquent
Giacomo Bracelli of Genoa[36]

You act like a friend and an honest man should, Giacomo of 1
Genoa, in maintaining that I am "making an altar out of a sewer
every day,"[37] and a King Croesus out of a poor little man. At least
that is what I gather from our friend Lamola's very polished letter.
Don't stop, come on, please: if someone strives to praise others, he
cannot remain unpraised himself. Besides, you confer a benefit on
a grateful and mindful man, and you shall not be poor where I am
rich.[38] But enough of that.

Now, I ask and by your leave implore this of you: make sure 2
that our grand friend Cambio Zambeccari does not continue to
ask me for *The Hermaphrodite*. For as you know it's a dirty business
and not suitable for such a devout man to read. However, if
Cambio really wanted me to and asked for it, I'd be ready to show
him my very guts. So make sure, as I say, that he doesn't ask for
my trifles any more. Take good care of yourself, my sweetest
Giacomo, and love me steadfastly.

Farewell, my rose. [1426/27].

: VI :

Meretrices Papienses ad Mediolanum
de laudibus Antonii Panormitae

Plaudite, lenones, meretrices, plaudite: vester
    quam bene membrosus Hermaphroditus adest!
Ut mulier clunes agitat, superincubat ut vir,
    arrigit et futuit, vult futuique simul.
5   Quam magnos culleos libret si scire cupido est,
    tam parvos dicam quam gerit ipse caput.
Et si quam grandem extendit sub pectine penem
    aut muli aut asini forma virilis erit,
nec minor est cunnus quam sit sibi mentula, ut intro
10   late cum culleis ipse Priapus eat.
Nec solum futuit vulvas, aut accipit inguen
    cunno, ast et teneros irrumat ipse mares.
Tam bene paedicat puerum quod nulla marisca
    podice succrescit: tam bene trudit opus.
15   Non tamen id peragit faciat quin merda galerum
    cum retrahit penem Siculus iste suum!
Ipse Panormita est qui se velit esse poetam,
    qui femora et penes tam bene cantat ovans.
Currite, lascivi iuvenes puerique petulci,
20   et quae vis futui, curre puella cito.
Tollite! Iam nostras leges vitiavit et artes.
    Quid referam leges? Inficit omne solum.
Moenia nostra secus serpit: qui vitreus olim
    amnis erat, maculis nunc scatet ipse novis;

: VI :

The prostitutes of Pavia write to Milan
in praise of Antonio Panormita[39]
[mid-1429]

Applaud, pimps! Whores, applaud! Your
   well-endowed Hermaphroditus is here.
Like a woman he wriggles his butt, like a man he lies on top.
   He gets it up and fucks — and he wants to be fucked too.
If you want to know how much his mighty balls weigh,   5
   I'll tell you they're as big as the head he carries.
Or how long his penis sticks down from its groin?
   It's the size of a mule's or a virile donkey's.
His cunt is no smaller than his cock, so that Priapus
   can go wide inside balls and all.   10
Nor does he just fuck pussies or take prick
   in the cunt, he also mouth-fucks soft males.
He butt-fucks boys so well that no piles[40]
   grow in their assholes: so well does he ram the job home.
Yet he doesn't do it without the shit making a cap for his cock   15
   when the Sicilian pulls it out.
This is Panormita, who wants to be a poet,
   who rejoices as he sings so well of pussy and prick.
Come running lustful youths, and rutting boys,
   and any girl who wants to be fucked, run quickly.   20
Take him![41] He has violated our laws and arts.
   Why mention laws? He infects the very ground.
He slithers around our walls. What once was a glassy river
   now gushes out with new stains.

25   nec satis est toti sordes sparsisse Ticino,
       nunc urbem anguigeram commaculare cupit.
    Tollite! Nec pigeat! Turba uenit ipse pudica:
       nam paedicones scortaque sancta trahit.
    Dic tales socios qualem iam diximus illum:
30   sic merda est ano quam bene iuncta suo.
    O felicem urbem tantam, cui fortia facta
       deerat qui caneret! Plaude, poeta venit.
    Non erat in tota calamum qui verteret urbe:
       qui exornet proceres Hermaphroditus adest.
35   Tollite in urbe virum, sed non Quiriti atque Iulitae
       in sacris procul hinc quisque profanus erit.
    Auspiciis mediis monstrum hoc auferte, neque aras
       polluat, et vestri sit mala stella ducis.
    Ipse lupis lenisque simul sua carmina ructet
40   et paediconum facta nefanda probet.
    Tollite in urbe virum qui non spectacula cernat
       principis anguigeri proelia nonque iocos.
    Sint cunnis sua bella feris; sint bella Priapis
       et cum podicibus certet adusque velit.
45   Inde locis meritis putridum deferte cadaver,
       membraque iam tumulo condite viva suo.
    Collum quaeque suum meretrix supponat, et ante
       stent paedicones, lumina quisque ferat.
    Ursa, Nichina, Helene plorent dulcisque Mathildis
50   defleat et mammis Clodia pulchra suis;
    dilanient crines Zaneta et Galla Pythoque,
       sed scindat vestes ebria semper Io.

Not content with having scattered his filth all over Pavia,   25
   he now desires to defile the city that bears the snake as
      well.[42]
Take him and don't regret it; he comes with a modest crowd.[43]
   For he drags along buggers and holy whores.
You may say his friends are just like I said he is:[44]
   they stick like shit perfectly to his asshole.   30
O great and fortunate city, which has lacked someone
   to sing its mighty deeds! Applaud! The poet is coming.
There was no one in the entire city who could wield a pen.
   Hermaphroditus is here to praise princes.
Take the man in the city, but in the church of Sts. Quirico   35
      and Giulitta
   no profane person will keep away from the sacrifices.[45]
Remove this monster from your rites, and let him not
   pollute the altars and be a disastrous omen to your Duke.
Let him puke up his songs for whores and pimps,
   let him praise the unspeakable deeds of buggers.   40
Take in the city the man who does not see the spectacles,
   the battles, and the jokes of the prince who bears the snake.
Let his wars be with wild cunts. Let his wars be with
      Priapuses,
   and let him battle with assholes as much as he wants.
Drag his putrid cadaver away from worthy places,   45
   and bury his living members in his own tomb.
Let each of his whores set up her own monument, and in
      front
   let the buggers stand guard, and bear torches.
Let Ursa, Nichina, Helena, and sweet Mathilde weep for him,
   and Clodia with her pretty titties.   50
Let Giannetta and Galla and Pytho tear out their hair,
   but let Io, who's always drunk, rip her clothing.[46]

"Te nostrum sepelit," clament, "geniale lupanar;
    quam bene sic moreris, quam bene membra iacent."
55   Scripsimus et titulos sunt sculptaque verba sepulchro,
    sic quisque ut mores possit habere suos.
Infamis Siculus iacet hoc Antonius antro
    qui in Venerem et Bacchum spintria totus erat.
Nunc se Vergilio, nunc sese aequabat Homero,
60   nec lac Pieridum, sed bibit ille merum.
Hic cecinit cunnos, cecinit cum podice penes,
    paedico exsuperans atque futuator erat.
Clauditur extrema nostra hac ex urbe cloaca,
    quam bene conveniens moribus ipse locus.
65   Pro ture hic fumant meretricum stercora, sanguis
    menstruus exundat perpetuoque fluit.
Huc coitus tandem manant centone retorto,
    faex quoque bracarum contumulata sapit.
Non deerunt bombi ructus vomitusque lutosi,
70   quae cacet aut meiat iam lupa semper erit.
Tolle ergo inferias, quae sint tibi sacra quotannis,
    nec nasum obtures, androgynose, tuum.

: VII :

Antonius Panormita Antonio Raudensi
salutem plurimam dicit.

1   Etsi facile multi existimant te quosdam in me versus edidisse—
obscenos quidem illos atque petulantes—ego vel solus adhuc id
mihi persuadere non possum. Primum professioni tuae atque reli-

"Your 'congenial whorehouse'," let them cry, "will bury you.
    How fittingly you will die here and how fittingly your
        member will lie!"
We have written an epitaph and the words are carved on his   55
    tombstone,
    so that everyone can know his morals.[47]
The infamous Sicilian, Antonio, lies in this cave,
    who was a complete pervert for Venus and Bacchus.[48]
He compared himself now to Vergil, now to Homer,
    he didn't drink the water of the Muses but pure wine.   60
He sang cunts, he sang cock in asshole,
    he was an outstanding bugger and fucker.
The sewer on the outer edge of our city hides him,
    a fitting place for his morals.
Instead of incense, the smoke comes from whores' shit;   65
    menstrual blood floods out and flows in an endless stream.
From here sex trickles from the pulled-back blanket,[49]
    and shit piled up in pants gives off its smell.
Nor will there be any lack of farts, burps, and mucky vomit,
    and a whore to shit or piss will always be there.   70
Celebrate his funeral, an annual festival for you,
    and don't hold your nose, you half-man, half-woman!

: VII :

Antonio Panormita to Antonio da Rho,
greetings[50]
[1431]

Even though many have reached the easy conclusion that you   1
wrote certain verses against me — obscene and lewd ones at that —
I alone still cannot persuade myself of it. First, it scarcely befits

gioni minime id congruit hominem exterum, nocentem nemini, honeste agentem, compoetam atque benivolum tuum maledictis provocare, eum[2] praesertim cui tantum tribueras, ut alias tuo carmine nihil de me dicere dubitaris:

> Antoni mi, nunc decus et lux una Latini
> eloquii, succurre precor

et huius generis multa.

2   Deinde non ea rerum ignorantia atque inscitia damnatus es, qui vel meo ingenio vel doctrinae, quae minima est, invidere debueras, cum praesertim si quid in me sit vel ingenii vel doctrinae, id omne divo nostro Principi, quem et tu colis, devotum dedicatumque sit, exploratum habeas. Quamquam hi versus qui nuper in me compositi sunt, rauci, claudi, pingues atque adeo pueriles sunt, ut ex tua vena proficiscantur nequaquam crediderim. Alioquin vana profecto est spes omnis, quam de te maximam Princeps concepit, nam ut poetae cuiusdam versus est:

> Non erit obscuris laudandus versibus Hector

addas et "pertritis."

3   Praererea ut te auctorem illius maledicentiae non putem, iterum suadet quod is (quicumque fuerit) non quidem poeta sed versificator, non versificator sed ne quidem syllabicator, non in me solum sed in Hermaphroditum meum etiam invectus est. Et tu pro eruditione tua satis nosti id nobis arte poetica concessum esse, iocos et sales praeludere, "nam," ut eleganter Catullus ait,

> castum esse decet pium poetam
> ipsum, versiculos nihil necesse est.

4   Et extat in manibus Publii Vergilii *Priapeia*, opus permaxime lascivum, ceterum poeta ipse pro morum sobrietate "Parthenias"

your profession as a monk or your religion to hurl insults at a man who is an outsider, hurting no one, living his life honestly, a fellow poet, and one who wishes you well. Especially when you once paid him the compliment of not hesitating to say of me (elsewhere in your poetry):

> My Antonio, the glory and only light of Latin
> eloquence, I pray you, come to the rescue . . .

and many other things of this sort.

Secondly, you have not been faulted for such a level of igno- 2 rance or lack of awareness that it caused you to envy my talent or learning (small as it is), especially when you know full well that if there is any talent or learning in me, it is all devoted and dedicated to our Prince, to whom you too pay court. Yet, these verses which were lately composed against me are so hoarse, limping, clumsy, and childish, that I could never believe that they came from your vein of talent. Otherwise, the great hopes that our Prince has formed of you are totally in vain, for as a certain poet's line has it:

> It will not do for Hector to be praised by unknown verses,[51]

to which you might add "and hackneyed."

Further, this persuaded me to think that you could not have 3 been the author of this slander, the fact that he—whoever he was—was not even a poet but a versifier, not even a versifier but barely a syllabifier, and he atttacked not only me but my *Hermaph-rodite*. You in your erudition know full well that poetic licence allows us to play around with jokes and witticisms, "for," as Catullus elegantly put it,

> it's right that a proper poet be pure
> himself, but there's no need for his verses to be.[52]

We have in our hands the *Priapea* by Vergil, an extremely inde- 4 cent work, yet the poet was called "Virginia" for the chasteness of

appellatus est. Plato autem, vir ipse summa doctrina pari sancti-
monia praeditus, hisce etiam salibus oblectatus est, cumque inter-
rogaretur quid lascive ita admodum scriberet respondisse fertur:
poetarum est furere. Et generaliter poetam adhuc neminem audivi,
neminem legi, quin verborum aut sententiarum saltem lascivia non
fuerit oblectatus: extat Valerius Martialis; extat Catullus; extat
Iuvenalis; extant omnes qui foedioribus verbis utuntur cum res
exigit.

5   Quamquam id nostrum opusculum a tenera usque aetate
fuerit compositum, ubi et iocandi et peccandi licentia maior est,
nunc autem verum fateri liceat; alia aetas atque alii mores mihi
sunt et studia prorsus diversa; neque Hermaphroditus cuipiam
magis quam mihi ipsi odio est, et editionis simul et lectionis auc-
torem in primis taedet pigetque, non quod illa aetate ludendo deli-
querim, sed quod haec mea aetas ab omni lascivia atque voluptate
prorsus abhorret et severos mores et severum dicendi genus expos-
tulat.

6   Verum enimvero, si vita suppetat, cordi est expurgare nequi-
tiam illam — si modo nequitia est quod poetae omnes factita-
runt — severo ac gravi quodam orationis stilo, non sine summa et
sempiterna fortassis optimi maximi nostri Principis laude ac glo-
ria, ut si quis deinceps sit qui mihi meisque Musis invideat, non
mihi, quippe qui invidia nescio quo pacto carere non possim, sed
domino nostro Caesari invidisse se intellegat. Mihi quidem sub-
laudari licet, quod undequaque sim livore circumventus. Et pro-
fecto res male se habet cum quis sine invidia poetam evasisse sibi
persuadet. Vergilium ipsum nostrorum facile principem ob ae-

his ways.[53] Plato himself, a man endowed with the greatest learning and equal probity of life, enjoyed this sort of wit, and when he was asked why he wrote so very indecently he is said to have replied: "It is the part of poets to be insane."[54] And in general, I have yet to read or hear of a poet who was not delighted by a little indecency of word or expression. There's Martial; there's Catullus; there's Juvenal; there are all those who used somewhat coarse language when the subject matter demanded it.

Although my little work was composed when I was still of a   5
tender age, when one has greater license to joke and sin, now I have to tell the truth: I am at a different time of life and have other habits and quite different interests. No one dislikes *The Hermaphrodite* more than I do, and the author is the first to be bored by and regret both the publication and the reading of it — not because I did anything wrong by playing around at that age but because the age I am now instantly revolts against any indecency and sensuality and calls for serious habits and a serious manner of expression.

But of course if life allows, I have a desire to expiate that sin —   6
if indeed what all poets practice is sin — with a certain serious and sober style of speaking, possibly bringing the highest and eternal glory and praise to our great and good Prince, so that if anyone hereafter envies me and my Muses, he may know that he envies not me — for somehow or other I'm unable to escape envy — but our lord Caesar. I may be permitted some second-hand praise, since I am surrounded on all sides by jealousy. And indeed things are bad when someone thinks that he can become a poet without envy. Vergil, so the story goes, by far the greatest of our poets, because of rivals and critics (the lowest race of humans)

mulos atque obtrectatores, genus hominum perditissimum, urbe
Roma semel atque iterum decessisse et Caietae se continuisse tra-
ditum est: verum eo magis Maecenati suo gratus atque iocundus
quo poetam sciret livore non carere. Argumentum quidem prae-
stantiae est invidia et immortalitatis coniectura. Omittam hoc loco
poetas ceteros, nam Homerum deum illum poetarum, Terentium,
Nasonem atque omnes egregios poetas quis nescit livoris dente se-
penumero dilaniatos? Sane Musarum comes invidia.

7   Sed ad te revertor, sanctissime sacerdos, qui si ut perhibetur
tute es qui turpes atque obscenos illos in me versus nuper edideris,
quid est, quaeso, quod a spurcissimis verbis ne tu quidem absti-
nueris, non quidem adulescens sed grandior natu, non profanus
sed religiosus, non ludendi animo sed iniquitate adductus? Non
possum non illud Iuvenalis exclamare:

En animum et mentem cum qua dii nocte loquuntur.

8   Rursum cum a nostro sapientissimo Duce tibi iamdudum
iniunctum esset ut Lucanum in linguam maternam converteres, in
quo maiorum suorum industriam, solertiam, fortitudinem legeret,
probaret, imitaretur, tu Suetonium Tranquillum traducere ma-
luisti, ubi adulteria, stupra, incestus, et alia huiusmodi plerumque
leguntur, ut si qua insit rosa, sine urtica tum legi non queat: rem
profecto neque divi Francisci professione qua obstringeris neque
nostri Principis lectione dignam.

9   Amplius cum haec ad te scripsissem ab Antonio Cremona, viro
officiosissimo, mihi renuntiatum est quosdam nescio quos in te
versus nuperrime descriptos teque me procul dubio auctorem exis-
timare; ea, ut arbitror, ratione quia tua mens in quem deliquerit
laboret opus est. Ceterum satis adhuc non gnosti "musas Siceli-

more than once left Rome and moved to Gaeta.[55] Yet he was all the more pleasing and agreeable to his friend, Maecenas, since he knew that a poet cannot escape jealousy. Indeed envy is a proof of excellence and an indication of immortality. Here I will pass over the other poets, for who does not know that Homer, the god of poets, Terence, Ovid and all the exceptional poets were often savaged by the tooth of jealousy? Truly envy is the comrade of the Muses.[56]

But to return to you, most sacred priest. If you are, as rumor 7 has it, the one who recently circulated those foul and obscene verses against me, then how is it, I ask you, that *you* did not abstain from dirty words, you who are not a youth but of mature years, not a layman but a monk, not motivated by a spirit of playfulness but by malevolence? I can't help quoting the line of Juvenal:

> Just look at the mind and spirit that the gods talk to at night![57]

Again, when you were ordered by our most wise Duke[58] to 8 translate Lucan into our mother tongue so that he could read about the industry, talent, and bravery of his ancestors, you chose rather to translate Suetonius, where one can read about adultery, rape, incest, and many other things of that sort, so that though there is a rose, it cannot be gathered without the nettle:[59] a matter worthy neither of your profession to St. Francis by which you are bound nor of our Prince's reading.

After I had written the above to you at length, that obliging 9 man Antonio Cremona told me that some verses or other had recently been written against you, and that you of course took me to be the author, I imagine because your mind must be distressed about someone you have maligned. But you still haven't got to know those "Sicilian muses" who are apt to "sing on somewhat

das," quae "paulo maiora" canere solent et aperto quidem, non fur-
tim, non clam more latronum atque proditorum. Si quando autem
gratias tibi relaturus ero, nihil me hercle addubitabo tibi bellum
indicere atque aliquid adversum te scribere quod ex officina mea et
ex Sicilia illa poetarum matre profectum nemo ambigat, nemo
nesciat. Illud mihi satis abunde est maledicentiae causam dedisse.

10   Sed ut epistulae finem faciam, quod clarissima multorum voce
tum vel maxima a consacerdotibus tuis audio, te scilicet illius im-
pudentiae auctorem extitisse, id a te potius accipere concupisco.
Tu, fare ingenue, fare apertius, ut quid ipse facturus sim aliquando
deliberem. Ea quidem mihi natura est: neminem offendo nisi la-
cessitus iniuria.

Vale.

: VIII :

Antonii Panormitae
in invidos

Quid curem Rodus cum nostra poemata culpet,
    si mea Maecenas carmina docte probas?
Quid curem, quod me cimex Laurentius odit,
    si me Crottiades unus et alter amat?
5   Quid curem carpat vitam Cato Saccus Iacchus,
    si Ferrufino iudice vita proba est?
Quid curem quod me livor sectetur ubique,
    si semper virtus invidiosa fuit?

more important matters," and openly, not furtively, not secretly like thieves and traitors.[60] If ever I return the favor, by Hercules, I will not hesitate to declare war on you and write something against you which no one will doubt or fail to see came from my workshop and from Sicily, the mother of poets. It is quite enough for me to have given cause for slander.

But to put an end to this letter: what I hear very clearly from 10 the report of many people—most of all, of your fellow priests— namely, that you are the author of that piece of impudence, I should prefer to hear directly from you. So speak freely. Speak openly, so that I can plan what I am going to do. That is my nature: I hurt no one unless I am first provoked by injury.[61]

Farewell. [1431].

: VIII :

Antonio Panormita
against the envious[62]
[c. 1431]

What care I if Rho blames my poems,
   if you, learned Maecenas, approve my songs?
What care I if that louse Lorenzo hates me,
   if both the sons of Crotti love me?
What care I if the drunkard Catone Sacco picks at my life,   5
   if my life is innocent in Feruffini's judgment?
What care I if jealousy follows me everywhere,
   if virtue is always the object of envy?

Curandum placeas tantum doctisque bonisque:
10   summa quidem laus est displicuisse malis.

: IX :

Antonii Panormitae de Hyla

Venit Hylas, sed dormit Hylas, dormitque bibitque.
    Endymion somno, corpore verus Hylas.

: X :

Antonii Panormitae ad Ergotelen

Cum nequeat nummos, mittit tibi carmina vates.
    Tu tamen argento carmina pluris habe.
Eripiunt quemvis a mortis dente Camoenae:
    carmine vivit Itys, carmine vivit Hylas.
5   Fortunate puer, quem dilexere poetae.
    Grate puer vati, non moriere puer,

Just make sure to please only the learned and good:
   the highest praise is to displease the evil.   10

TWO POEMS TO BOYS INCLUDED IN
POEMATUM ET PROSARUM LIBER
[c. 1431]

: IX :

Antonio Panormita on Hylas[63]

Hylas arrived, but Hylas is sleeping; he sleeps and drinks.
   An Endymion in sleep, a true Hylas in body.

: X :

Antonio Panormita to Ergoteles[64]

Since the poet can't send you money,[65] he sends you songs,
   yet you should value songs more than silver.
The Muses snatch anyone from the jaws of death
   Itys lives in song, Hylas lives in song.
Lucky boy, whom poets cherish.   5
   Boy pleasing to poets, you will not die, boy.

et te sanctus amat vates, ut teque perennet
    conatur, modo tu cur amet ille stude.
Ergo vale, Ergoteles, cari spes una parentis,
10   spes patria,[3] hercle puer, sed gravitate senex.[4]

: XI :

Eiusdem ad puerum formosum

Est tibi forma decens quam nec pharetratus Apollo
    spernat et ipse sibi Bacchus inesse velit.
Es[5] quoque tam pulchro teneroque in corpore praestans;
    quod rarum est, virtus mensque pudica manet.
5   Sic ergo crediderim frendentes dentibus apros
    saltibus Hippolytum figere Cecropiis.
Sic erat Arcadiae cum gloria Parthenopaeus
    audaci in Thebas sumpserat arma manu.

: XII :

Eiusdem ad puerum formosissimum

Belle puer, nostris penitus defixe medullis,
    lilia qui superas exsuperasque rosas.

The holy poet loves you, and strives to make you live forever,
    provided that you give him a reason why he should love
    you.
So farewell, Ergoteles, the only hope of a loving parent,
    as a boy, your father's hope, by god, but in dignity you're   10
    ripe in years.

TWO UNCOLLECTED POEMS BY BECCADELLI

: XI :

To a handsome boy[66]

You have a handsome appearance,[67] nor would quiver-bearing
    Apollo
    reject it and Bacchus himself would wish he had it.[68]
You are also outstanding for so beautiful and tender a body;
    what is rare,[69] virtue and a pure mind remain.
Just so, I believe, was Hippolytus when he speared   5
    boars with their gnashing tusks in the Cecropian woods.[70]
Thus was the glory of Arcadia, Parthenopaeus,
    when he took up arms against Thebes with daring hand.[71]

: XII :

To a most handsome boy[72]

Beautiful boy, fixed deeply in my marrow,
    you surpass the lilies and more than surpass the roses.

: XIII :

Maffei Vegii ad Andream Pisanum

Pulcra Panormigeni perlegi scripta poetae
    qui canit imparibus sexus utrosque modis.
Non potui non hunc laudare, non oscula dulci,
    dulcior Andrea, dulcia ferre operi.
5   At nostrum in vatem si sit qui turpiter audet,
    qui moveat dentes ore calente truces,
pone animo antiquos illustres laude poetas,
    qui similes pulcre composuere sales.
Quid cecinit Naso? Quid blandi musa Propertii?
10   Lesbia tu, Sappho, tuque, Tibulle, places.
Clarus Callimachus. Placuerunt scripta Catulli.
    Hi tamen et flammas et cecinere iocos.
Quidque, ut praeteream reliquos, Maro, gloria vatum,
    quid cecinit? Lusus scripsit et ille leves,
15   mox sese ad segetes pascuaque et arma recepit.
    Si dicit pecudes, an Maro pastor erat?
Multa canunt docti, quae non fecere, poetae,
    quae sua non novit dextera, multa canunt.
Verum illud sapere est et dignum laude perenni.
20   Quae non viderunt lumina, Musa uidet.
Sic igitur Plautus miraeque Terentius artis
    essent convivae, leno et uterque foret?
Atque alii quorum sine fine est copia magna
    quos studii et famae scribere iussit amor.

A POEM IN DEFENSE OF *THE HERMAPHRODITE*

: XIII :

Maffeo Vegio to Andrea of Pisa[73]
[c. 1432]

I've read completely the beautiful writings of the poet from
    Palermo
  who sings of both sexes in unequal measures.[74]
I can't keep from praising him, from giving sweet kisses
  to this sweet work, Andrea sweeter still.
But if there is someone who foully attacks our poet,[75]   5
  who gnashes his cruel teeth in his hot mouth,
call to mind the ancient poets famed in praise,
  who beautifully composed similar sallies of wit.
What did Ovid sing? What the muse of charming Propertius?
  And you Sappho of Lesbos, and you Tibullus are pleasing.   10
Callimachus is famous. Catullus's writings have pleased.
  Yet these all sang of the flames of love and of jokes.
And, to skip the rest, what about Vergil, the glory of poets?
  What did he sing? He too wrote about frivolous games,
and then turned himself to crops, and pastures, and arms.[76]   15
  Though he sang of pastures, was Vergil a shepherd?[77]
Learned poets have sung many things they have not done.
  Many things their right hand knows not, they sing.
Truly that is to be wise and worthy of eternal praise.
  Things the eyes see not, the Muse sees.   20
Following that logic, Plautus and Terence with their great art
  would be drunkards and both would be pimps.
And there is an unending supply of others
  whom love of study and fame has compelled to write.

25   Haec satis, Andrea, nunc ad maledicta revertor
        quae cecinit foedis[6] invida lingua modis.
    Clara Panhormitae vivent praeconia vatis;
        quive nefas ausus voce furente cadet.
    Ille cadet, tenuesque furor vanescet in auras
30   et stabit nostri nobile vatis opus.

⁚ XIV ⁚

    Qui sine labe meam maculasti carmine vitam
        si legis hoc carmen, crimine liber ero.[7]
    Da, precor, intentas nostris sermonibus aures,
        da faciles animos, corda benigna mihi.
5   Musa Syracusio cantu si laeserit hostes,
        iuro tibi nullum crimen inesse sibi.
    Causa sui iusta est, iustissima sumpsimus arma
        iustus et armavit corpora nostra dolor.
    Nec mihi lis coepta est <sed ipse>[8] irritor in arma
10   inque caput nostrum mille ruere manus.
    Mille sagittarunt durae mea terga sagittae,
        obseditque meam gens inimica domum,
    undique erant hostes, clamor resonabat in auras.
        Vix poteram clausa liber abire domo.
15   Quid facerem? Dic ipse meos qui crimine versus
        inficis et nostris hostibus addis opem.

Enough of this, Andrea; I now return to the slanders   25
    which an envious tongue has sung in foul verses.
The loud fanfares for the poet Panormita will live.
    The man who with furious words dared this crime will fall.
He will fall and his fury will vanish into thin air,
    but the noble work of our poet will abide!   30

: XIV :

[A Further Defense by Beccadelli][78]

You, who never made a mistake, have defiled my life with a
        poem:
    If you read this poem, I will be free from the crime.
Pray give attentive ears to our speech,
    Give me well-disposed minds and a kind heart.
If my Muse in her Syracusan song has wounded my enemies,   5
    I swear to you there's no crime in it.
Its cause is just; we have taken up most righteous arms,
    and righteous anger has armed our body.
I didn't begin the law suit, but I was provoked to arms,
    and a thousand hands have fallen on our head.   10
A thousand cruel arrows have arrowed my back[79]
    and a hostile race besieged my house.
Everywhere there were enemies, the noise of battle re-echoed
        in the winds.
    I was barely able get away free from my locked house.
What was I to do? Tell me, you who charge my verses with   15
        crime
    and give aid to my enemies?

Vin patiar nostras everti funditus aedes?
    Hostibus ipse meis reserare fores?
Vin patiar nostros violari turpiter agros,
20   vin sine caede meam presserit hostis humum?
Opto ego sim potius rabidis[9] lacerandus ab ursis,
    viscera nostra prius torva leaena voret.
Opto prius lanient corpus sine fine volucres,
    quam tantum tantum dedecus ipse feram.
25   Iuppiter in patrem sumpsit crudeliter arma,
    fertur ob hoc Latiis is latuisse iugis.
Mutua Thebani senserunt vulnera fratres;
    hinc subit Stygias alter et alter aquas.
Sic furor armavit geminas in caede sorores.
30   Saeva parens puerum vulnere truncat Itim.
Ergo ego perpetiar vilem sine pectore turbam
    quae mihi stat nullo sanguinis arta[10] gradu?
Non patiar! Stat firma animo sententia mortem
    intrepidum assiduos ante subire dies.
35   Hi referunt vitam similem sermonibus esse,
    hos vincam falso clarius ore loqui.
Excidium Troiae quamvis depinxit Homerus,
    aequavit numquam Pergama magna solo.
Musa canit pecudes, pecudes nec pavit in agris,
40   Virgilii totos non moritura dies.
Si docuit curvis tellurem scindere aratris,
    non tamen attrivit curvus arator humum.
Si cecinit pugnas, non pugnam sensit in armis,
    huic sua militia grata poesis erat.

Do you want me to endure my home being overturned?
   Do you want me to open my doors to the enemy?
Do you want me to endure my fields being foully violated?
   Do you want the enemy to tread my earth without facing   20
      slaughter?
I would rather wish to be torn apart by rabid bears,
   that a savage lioness might devour my guts.
I would rather that vultures tear at my body without respite,
   than bear such great, such great disgrace.
Jupiter cruelly took up arms against his father: 25
   it is said that for that reason he hidden lies in the hills of
      Latium.[80]
The Theban brothers felt mutual wounds,
   from which each succumbed to the waters of the Styx.[81]
Just so madness armed the twin sisters in slaughter:
   a savage mother cut down her son Itys with a wound.[82]   30
So shall I endure the cheap and brainless crowd[83]
   which stands in no relation of blood to me?
I shall not endure it! The resolution stands firm in my mind
   intrepidly to endure death rather than endless days.
These people say that my life is like my words;   35
   I shall prove clearly that they speak with a false tongue.
Although Homer depicted the fall of Troy,
   he never razed great Troy to the ground.
Vergil's muse, which will never die,
   sang of herds, but did not feed the herds in the fields,   40
Though he taught how to split the earth with the curved plow,
   he was not a bent plowman breaking up the soil.
Though he sang of battles, he never experienced battle in
      arms;[84]
   the service he liked was poetry.

45   Si tuba Lucani cantarit Caesaris arma,
      belli acies numquam duxit in arma manus.
   Naso licet varias variarit carmine formas
      dulcisono[11] vati pristina forma fuit.
   Si licet obscenos vexarim carmine mores,
50   non tamen obscena vita putanda mea est.
   His super exemplis stabili speculabere mente,
      quisquis eris nostrum qui lacerabis opus?
   Postmodo desistes convicia tanta referre,
      post licet errorem confiteare tuum.

: XV :

Epitaphium Antonii Panormitae

   Insula, Scyllaeis contermina flatibus, undis
      clauditur Ioniis, nomine Trinacria,
   terra Syracusis olim regnata tyrannis,
      luxuriae vetitae perfidiaeque ferax;
5   Cyclopes utero saevosque enixa gigantes
      et quicquid superest corpore feta mali,
   quam mare, ne sanctam posset pervertere terram,
      fluctibus immensis frangit ab Hesperia.
   Haec me foeda tulit tellus. Ego ab urbe Panormi
10   ortus et indignus nominis haud Siculi,

Though Lucan's trumpet sang the arms of Caesar,   45
    never did the line of battle make him put his hand to his
      sword.
Although Ovid variegated various forms in his poems,
    that sweet-sounding poet's own form was what it had been.
Although I have upbraided obscene habits in my poems,
    nevertheless my life should not be thought obscene.   50
Whoever you are who will attack our work,
    will you calmly contemplate the above examples?
Thereafter, you will cease to bring such charges.
    Then you can confess your error.

ADDITIONAL POEMS AGAINST *THE HERMAPHRODITE*
AND BECCADELLI

: XV :

[Pier Candido Decembrio]
The epitaph of Antonio Panormita[85]
[c. 1432]

The island bordered by Scylla's breezes is enclosed
    by the Ionian waves, Trinacria by name,
a land once ruled by the tyrants of Syracuse,
    fertile in forbidden luxury and betrayal.
From its womb its pregnant body[86] gave birth to the Cyclopes   5
    and the savage giants and whatever other evils there are.
The sea, lest it should corrupt the sacred land,
    broke it off from Hesperia with vast waves.
This foul earth bore me. I am a native of the city of Palermo
    and not unworthy of the name Sicilian,   10

Italicam colui terram, mensisque superbis
    pontificum assuetus, bracchus erilis eram,
cumque sacerdotum[12] colerem mensasque torosque,
    indignos cecini religione sonos.

15   Nam veterum insanus vatum mirator et ipse
    vates, me summis vatibus esse parem
rebar. At atra Venus, patriae moresque sinistri
    mentem traxerunt in scelus omne meam.
Lemniades Thraciosque optans aequare poetas,
20   sentinam excolui carminibus Latiis.

Vulvas et coleos, penes, culosque natesque
    stercoraque et merdam turpiter ore canens,
ne foret intactum quicquam, sum versibus ausus
    sacrilegis almi rumpere iura thori,
25   et Venerem in sanctam vocem vectare protervam,
    dissuadere viris legitimasque faces.

Quoque fides dictis sceleratis altior esset,
    firmavi exemplo foetida dicta meo.
Audax et petulans animo, moechusque, gulosus,
30   ipse fui iuvenis, prostibulumque domus
et foedi comites scelerataque turba clientum,
    fama cuncta mihi cara fuere magis.

Ah! Quanto melius me si genuisset agrestem[13]
    natura aut asinum vel nihil ipse forem!
35   Humana effigie gestabam corpus, et intus
    humani generis pessimus hostis eram.

Nomen terra meum nunc execratur, et ibit
    spiritus in Stygias non rediturus aquas,
aeternasque feram poenas pro talibus ausis

I have lived in the land of Italy, grown used to
    bishops' proud banquets. I was my master's bloodhound[87]
and though I cultivated the tables and dining couches of
      priests,
    yet I sang songs unworthy of religion.
For I am a mad imitator of the ancient poets, and a poet   15
      myself.
    I thought that I was the equal of the greatest poets.
But black Venus and the evil habits of my fatherland
    drove my mind toward every sin.
Hoping to equal the Lemnian women and Thracian poets,[88]
    I produced bilge water in Latin poems.   20
Cunts and balls, penises, assholes and butts,
    shit and crap, singing all this foully from my mouth,
so that nothing would be undefiled, I dared in sacrilegious
    verses to break the laws of the life-giving marriage bed,
and carry forth perverted Venus into holy song,   25
    and to dissuade men from legitimate marriage.[89]
And to have my lyre sink deeper than mere infamous
      language,
    I confirmed my filthy words in action.
I was bold and impetuous in spirit, adulterer, glutton,[90]
    even as a youth; a home turned into a brothel,[91]   30
foul comrades and a criminal crowd of clients,
    all these were dearer to me than my reputation.
How much better if nature had made me a rustic
    or an ass or if I had never been born.
My body bore a human appearance,   35
    yet within I was humankind's worst enemy.
Now earth curses my name, and my soul
    will go to the waters of the Styx, never to return.
I will pay eternal penalties for such recklessness

40   caelicolis meritum suppliciumque dabo.
Tu modo, posteritas, nostro lege carmina digna
    nomine, et exemplum sit mea vita tuum,
quam parvo aeternum liceat sibi quaerere nomen
    gentibus et taetro quis modus est sceleri.

⁘ XVI ⁘

In Antonium Panormitam, Vegio vati clarissimo, pro obscenitate Hermaphroditi

Arca vetus stabat variis repleta libellis,
    quos inter Siculus Hermaphroditus erat.
Haec rima tenui parvoque foramine fracta est,
    ut vix vel minimum reptile adiret opus.
5   Mus adit et Siculum partes in mille libellum
    dilanians[14] salvis exiit inde meis.
Ut vidi admirans, non haec sine numine divum
    eveniunt; volui consuluisse Deum.
"Verbula depereunt, quae sint sine pondere, quae sint[15]
10   digna lupanari verbula," Phoebus ait.
"Irrita nimirum vatis monimenta Sicani,
    hoc se volt falso nomine adire polos.
Non sunt digna viro, non sunt ea digna poetis,
    quidquid habent est quod plena cloaca iacit."

and I will have well-deserved punishment from the gods.   40
But you, posterity, read songs worthy of my
    name, and let my life be an example to you
of how cheaply one may seek eternal fame for oneself
    among people, and what limits there are to foul crime.[92]

: XVI :

[Porcellio Pandoni]
Against Antonio Panormita to the noble poet Maffeo Vegio
on the obscenity of The Hermaphrodite[93]
[c. 1432]

An old chest stood filled with various books
    among which was the Sicilian *Hermaphrodite.*
It had a slight fracture with a gap so tiny
    that the smallest reptile could scarcely get into the thing.[94]
A mouse entered and tore the Sicilian book into a thousand   5
        pieces,
    but it left with my books undamaged.
I marveled as I saw this, for these things do not happen
    without the presence of the gods. I decided to consult the
        god.
"Mere words vanish, if they are without weight, if they are
    mere words fit for a brothel," said Phoebus.   10
"No wonder then if the monuments of the Sicilian 'poet' are
        in vain,
    — he hopes to go to heaven under this false title.
They are not worthy of a man, not worthy of a poet,
    what they have is what a full sewer spews forth."

15   Digna quidem vox est, vates[16] celeberrime, Phoebo.
      Regula lenonum est et gravitate caret.
   Est illinc podex, tentigo, mentula, cunnus,[17]
      et paedicones Hermaphroditus habet.
   Illa cacat violas, opobalsama micticat illa,
20   Alda cacat violas, pulchra Corinna rosas.
   Illinc et meretrix structa est iuvenisque petulcus,
      illa movere latus, ille movere nates.[18]
   Hic futuit futuique cupit, nunc ille uel illa
      materia ad inguen, dive Priape, tuum.
25   Estne in podicibus gravitas, probitasve decusve?
      Et femur et colei quid gravitatis habent?
   Dicet: "Sic quondam prisci lusere poetae,
      inque Priapeis luserat ante Maro.
   Cur non Virgilio liceat conferre Panormum?
30   Hosque olim vates Attica Musa docet.
   Quis sibi delicias, quis blandimenta iocosve
      abnuat et lusus illecebrasque, sales?
   Callimachum tenui certus superare cothurno est;
      Maeonius Siculo cede poeta deo.
35   Virgilium superat, neque non mirabere doctos
      inter lenones et superare Iovem.
   Cedite, Pierides, novus insurrexit Apollo,
      hunc genitum summo credimus esse deo.
   Ah quanto est satius sanctas ediscere leges;
40   coepisti, abruptum consolidetur opus.
   Nam neque te Aoniis aluit pia turba sub antris,
      nec te Cirrhaeo vertice Phoebus amat.
   Immo leves Bromius choreis attollere saltus,
      cymbala te docuit Inda movere manu.

The utterance, most celebrated of poets, was worthy of   15
    Phoebus.
  His standards are those of a pimp and he lacks seriousness.
Therein is asshole, erection, cock, cunt,
    and *The Hermaphrodite* has buggers.
One woman shits violets, another pisses balsam
    (Alda shits violets; lovely Corinna, roses).[95]   20
Therein the whore is taught and the rutting boy:
    she how to move her flanks; he, his buttocks.
He fucks and wants to be fucked;[96] now boy or girl
    is material for your member, divine Priapus.[97]
Is there any dignity in assholes, or decency or seemliness?   25
    What dignity have pussy and balls?
He will say: "But that's how the poets of old played around.
    Even Vergil once played around in the *Priapea!*
Why shouldn't Panormita be compared to Vergil?
    The Attic Muse once taught these things."   30
Who forbids him delights, sweet nothings, or jokes,
    and pleasantries and enticements, wit?[98]
He is sure to outdo Callimachus with his delicate style.[99]
    Let Homer, the Maeonian poet, yield to the Sicilian god.[100]
He outdoes Vergil, and among the learned pimps   35
    you'll be amazed that he conquers Jove himself.[101]
Give way, Muses, a new Apollo has arisen.
    We believe he was born of God on high.
Ah, how much better it is to study holy law!
    You made a start; now consolidate the work you left off.[102]   40
Because no pious throng of Muses nourished you in the
    Aonian caves,[103]
    nor does Apollo on Cirrha's peak love you.[104]
No, it was Bacchus who taught you to lift light steps in dance,
    to wield the Indian cymbals with your hand.

45 Fabula narratur totum celebranda per orbem,
       instar habet Siculi carminis, instar habet:
    pisciculos pelago cernit de colle lacerta,
       quis a natura scire natare datum est.
    "Et nos sollicitis pedibus velocius," inquit,
50   ibimus," e scopulo se cito mergit aquis.
    Nat quantum miseranda potest; mox fessa sub undas
       fert caput et trepidans, non peritura, perit.
    Terruerant animos clypei galeaeque sudesque;
       num terrent animos carmina blanda tuos?
55 Scripsimus armatas convexo umbone phalanges,
       scripsimus anguigeri martia gesta ducis,
    cumque triumphali quondam Capitolia curru
       scripsimus et Fauni corpora nuda dei.
    Carmina mille dedi dudum de prole Columnae
60   Pontifici sacro, carmina mille dedi.
    At quandoque Venus, quandoque Cupidinis arma,
       interdum digitis Flora notata meis.
    Multa tuae dedimus, quae mallem incondita, laudi;
       servabam, quam tu fallis, amicitiam.
65 Damnasti fugiens, quod me praesente probaras,
       et pugnant dictis dicta priora tuis.
    Langusti certa est de me sententia vatis,
       cui male dixisti ruptus ob invidiam.
    Haud tecum sentit, quisquis mea carmina legit,
70   haud tecum sentit Bornius ille tuus.

There's a tale told, famous throughout the world:[105]   45
   it is the model of this Sicilian poetry, the very model.
From a hill, a lizard looked down on the little fish in the sea—
   they know how to swim by nature.
"With my busy feet, I'll go even faster," he said
   and immediately dived from the cliff into the water.   50
He swam, as much as the poor thing could, but soon
     exhausted
   his head sank under the waves, and fearful, though he
     didn't have to die, died.
Helmets and shields and stakes have terrified some souls;
   do soothing songs really terrify yours?
We have written about phalanxes armed with the rounded   55
     shield boss,[106]
   we have written about martial deeds of the Duke whose
     arms bear the snake.
And long ago we wrote about the Capitoline games and the
     triumphal chariot
   and naked body of the god Faunus.
I have long since produced a thousand songs for the holy pope
   of the Colonna family, a thousand songs I produced.[107]   60
But sometimes Venus and sometimes Cupid's arms,
   and Flora now and then, have all been written up by my
     hand.[108]
And I produced many things in praise of you, things I wish
     had been left undone.
   I kept the friendship that you betray.
You fled and condemned what you had praised to my face.   65
   Your earlier words contradict what you say now.
The poet Languschi has a firm opinion of me,[109]
   the man you have insulted, bursting with envy.[110]
No one who reads my poems agrees with you,
   not even your friend Bornio agrees with you.[111]   70

Nimirum est hominis, qui se velit esse poetam,
    fingere; finxisti; di tibi digna duint.
Quidquid habent, viridi vates dignissime lauro,
    eloquio firmes et gravitate tua.

: XVII :

Persuasio ad lecturam

Egregii pueri et castae properate puellae.
    Non est haec Sicula carta notata manu.
Mentula, cunnus abest. Non incubat Ursa Priapo.
    Paedicat nemo, non movet Alda latus.
5   Hic nullus podex, hic nullum tenditur inguen.
    Assyrios flores femina nulla cacat.
Ista legas, Cosme, digna haec sunt carmina Cosmo.
    Conveniunt meritis laurea serta tuis.
Quisquis adhuc tristes obliquas maestus ocellos,
10   disticon hoc summum sit tibi supplicium.

Of course a man who wishes to be a poet makes things up,
   as you have. May the gods give you worthy subjects.
O poet worthy of the green laurel, whatever they give
   you must build up with your eloquence and dignity.[112]

: XVII :

[Porcellio Pandoni]
An encouragement to read his works[113]
[c. 1432]

Hasten hither noble boys and chaste girls,[114]
   This is no page marked by a Sicilian hand.
Prick and cunt, there are none. Ursa does not lie on top of
     Priapus.[115]
   No one buttfucks, Alda does not wiggle her flanks,[116]
Here there is no asshole, no member gets erect here,   5
   no woman shits Assyrian flowers.[117]
You may read these poems, Cosimo; these poems are suitable
     for Cosimo,
   These entwined laurels suit your virtues.
You who still avert your sad gaze in grief,
   this couplet will be your final punishment.[118]   10

: XVIII :

Ad castos pueros et puellas[19]

Egregii pueri et castae properate puellae,
   non est haec Sicula carta notata manu.
Mentula, cunnus abest. Nullum hic tenditur inguen,
   nullaque cum Musis iura Priapus habet.
5   Non hic furta Jovis metuunt, non Pana puellae,
   nec Venus imperium habet nec pharetratus habet.
Ista legant doctique senes, pueri atque[20] puellae,
   religio in quibus est aequaque iustitia.
Hic vatum viridi lustrantur tempora lauro.
10   Aliger hic puer est, hic vaga fama ducum.
Delicias si quando legis, lususque iocosque,
   nimirum; hos lusus luserat ante Maro.
Interdum Aeacides rutilis secessit ab armis,
   clavaque in Herculea non fuit usque manu.
15   Me lege, siquis amas doctos sanctosque poetas,
   et pereas siquis rumperis invidia.

: XVIII :

[Porcellio Pandoni]
For chaste boys and girls[119]
[c. 1432]

Hasten hither noble boys and chaste girls,
  this is no page marked by a Sicilian hand.
Prick and cunt, there are none, no member gets erect here,[120]
  and Priapus has no claim on the Muses.
Here girls do not fear Pan or the tricks of Jove;   5
  Here Venus holds no sway, nor her quiver-bearing boy.[121]
Learned old men, boys, and girls may read these lines[122]
  in which there is religion and justice for all.
Here the poet's brows are bound with green laurel.[123]
    Here is the winged boy and the changeable fortunes of   10
      leaders.[124]
If occasionally you read delights and pleasantries and jokes,[125]
  no surprise. Vergil played the same games once.
Achilles occasionally withdrew from bloody arms,
  and the club was not always in Hercules's hand.
Read me if you love learned and sacred poets.   15
    And anyone who's about to burst with envy, may you go
      hang.

: XIX :

Vallae

Procerum pectis pueri tingisque capillum,
    uxoris solitus dilaniare comas.
Cur facis hoc, Bechatelle? Quod hic, non illa sit uxor.
    Paedico speciem non mulieris amat.

: XX :

Vallae

Censorem veritus tonso, Bechatelle, puello,
    (censor enim rerum est tela parata tenens)
corda metu pulsante, tamen mulieris amantem
    te facis, exclamans: "depereo, proh iam,
5   depereo, proh iam!" Sed abest tibi pusio nusquam,
    pusio qui modo vir, qui modo fit mulier;
pusio quem puerum dum credimus esse, puella est,
    pusio, quem puerum crede, puellus erit.
Ecquis, io, nequam vel vir vel femina nescit
10   Quas potius partes e muliere petas?
Odit te, odit Hylam illa tuum, nam dispare causa
    femineum invisum sentit uterque genus.

TWO EPIGRAMS AGAINST BECCADELLI[126]

: XIX :

Lorenzo Valla
[c. 1442–43]

You comb and touch the boy's long hair
    but you always tear out your wife's.
Why do you do this, Beccadelli? Because he, not she is your
    wife.
    A bugger does not like a woman's form.

: XX :

Lorenzo Valla

In fear of the judge, now that your boy's been shaving[127]
    (for there is a judge of these affairs, holding the weapons
      ready),
with heart beating in fear, you yet make yourself out to be a
    lover of women,[128] exclaiming, "Alas, I die for love,
alas, I die for love." Yet your boy never leaves your side,   5
    your boy who becomes now a man, now a woman.
The boy, who when we think he's a boy, is a girl,[129]
    the boy—believe that he's a just a boy—will be a boy-
      toy.[130]
Ah, what depraved person, man or woman, does not know
    what part of a female you prefer to have?   10
She hates you, she hates your Hylas,[131] for each *feels*,
    for different reasons, how you hate the female sex.

Vis, non vis fieri, haud mirum, Bechatellule, adulter,
    nec mas est tibi mas, nec mulier mulier.
15   Viderit Oedipus, qui nescis esse maritus,
    esse queas moechus, an magis esse bechus.
Viderit hoc censor, cui vis dare verba; sed ille
    verbera post, gemina de ratione, dabit.

: XXI :

Ioannis Ioviani Pontani
ad Balbum sodalem
de munere libelli editi per Antonium Panhormitam

Delicias Siculi mitto tibi, Balbe, poetae,
    quas modo ab Aoniis rettulit ille iugis,
quas sacra Calliope blanda dictavit in aure,
    dum lepidis calamos aptat in articulis.
5   Sed tibi miranti, releges dum saepe, caveto
    ne liber is stupidis decidat e manibus:
Ille gerit gemmas, illi sunt inclyta dona,
    blandaque in auratis gratia carminibus;
illum Pimpleo nymphae compsere sub antro,
10   et minio titulum Cynthius excoluit,
illum pampinea limatum pumice fronde
    deque suis hederis Euchius inuoluit;

You want, you don't want, no wonder, to be an adulterer, little
    Beccadelli;
    male isn't male to you, nor female female.
Since you don't know how to be a husband, it would take an   15
    Oedipus to see
    whether you can be an adulterer rather than a cuckold.[132]
But the judge will see it. You're trying to give *him* the slip but
    he'll
    give *you* the slap, and a double dose of it.[133]

: XXI :

Giovanni Pontano
to his friend Balbi
on the gift of a book published by Antonio Panormita[134]
[1452]

The delights of the Sicilian poet, Balbus, I am sending to
    you,[135]
    which he has just brought back from the Aonian
    mountains,[136]
which sweet Calliope dictated into his holy ear,[137]
    as he fitted the pen to his clever fingers.
But as you read and reread it often in wonder, take care   5
    lest the book fall from your amazed hands.
It bears gems, it has in it illustrious gifts,
    and sweet grace in its golden songs.
The nymphs adorned it in their cave by Pimpla,[138]
    and Apollo wrote the title in red.   10
Polished with a vine leaf for pumice,[139]
    Bacchus wrapped with his own ivy.

quem, canerent gelidae Musae dum vertice Cirrhae,
    aspersitque sua Cypria tunc venere.
15 Sacra Panhormigenae facimus cum carmina vati,
    in nostros calamos currite, caelicolae;
scilicet et tanti non est cantanda poetae
    gloria vel superis vel sine teste Iove.
O nimium dilecte Iovi, cui solis ab aula
20   in laudes currunt agmina sancta deum,
cui Phoebus nitidis pendentem barbiton armis
    sepositumque diu temperat ore melos,
cui Venus et castam dederat pro coniuge Lauram,
    cuius ab ingenii Pallas honore rubet:
25 et quamvis superat forma praestante puellas,
    nobilitate tamen non erit ulla prior,
tantum cara suo quantum non ulla marito,
    quantum non lepido parvula neptis avo.
Sed castos Caesar nuper diiunxit amantes:
30   ah pereant reges ipsaque regna simul!
Quaenam, Alfonse, tibi fuerat iam tanta voluptas
    legatum hunc Venetis mittere pisciculis?
Per te Laura iacet duro deserta cubili
    et queritur longos non properare dies,
35 et te conviciis tota iam distulit urbe,
    quae Venus et castus dicere cogit Hymen.
Quid faceres, Caesar, ni te tua cura teneret,
    atque amor ardentes subderet usque faces?
Gaude, Laura, tuis coniux flectetur ocellis,
40   spernet et irati Caesaris imperium;
plus illi poteris uno prodesse labello,
    laedere quam Caesar, quam vel obesse deus.
Heu, heu solabor alios periturus amantes,
    cum me solari non queat ipsa Venus!

And while the Muses sang on cool Cirrha's peak,[140]
    the Cyprian goddess sprinkled it with her own desire.
As we perform the rites of the poet born at Palermo,   15
    run into our pens, gods of heaven.
For, of course, the glory of so great a poet cannot be sung
    without those above, without Jove as witness.
O thou, too beloved of Jove, in whose praise
    the holy armies of the gods rush from the halls of the Sun,   20
for whom Phoebus tunes the lyre hanging amid shining arms
with the song too long absent from his mouth, to whom
       Venus has given chaste Laura for a wife.[141]
    Pallas blushes at the honor done to Laura's talent.[142]
and although she surpasses other girls with her outstanding   25
      beauty
    yet there never will be a girl greater in nobility,
nor any so dear to her husband,
    as dear as a tiny granddaughter is to her grandfather.[143]
But now Caesar has parted the chaste lovers.
    Ah perish kings, and their kingdoms with them![144]   30
Why, Alfonso, did you have such a desire to send
    this ambassador to the Venetian fishes?[145]
Because of you, Laura lies deserted in her cruel bed,
    and complains that the long days will not hurry,
and defames you through all the city with reproaches   35
    which Venus and chaste Hymen force her to say.
What would you do, Caesar, if your love did not hold you,
    and love put out his burning torches utterly?
Rejoice, Laura, your tears have affected your husband,
    and he spurns the commands of angry Caesar.   40
You will be able to aid him more with one little kiss
    than Caesar can harm him or a god obstruct.
Alas, alas, I console other lovers while I'm dying for love,
    when Venus herself cannot console me.

45   Quando erit illa dies, tibi quae me, Cinnama, reddet
       pendeboque tuis, lux mea, brachiolis?
      Quando erit, ut liceat cara saturasse figura
       lumina, et in tenero me implicuisse sinu?
      Quando erit, ut possim tecum consumere noctem,
50   servatumque diu carpere basiolum?
      Tunc extrema mihi veniat iam deprecor hora,
       namque erit hoc nullus sanctior interitus.

: XXII :

Bartholomaei Facii
De viris illustribus

Antonius Panormita

Antonius Panormita in hoc genere clarus habetur. Allectus ab adolescentia poeticae atque oratoriae suavitate, omissis legibus, illarum rerum studiis incubuit. In utro magis excelluerit, non facile iudices. Res gestas omnes antiquitatis memoria tenet. Lusit in Hermaphrodito Virgilii exemplo. Eodem ferme tempore scripsit in Antonium Raudensem ab eo lacessitus libellum elegiaco versu, quem inscripsit Rhodum, et item poematum ac prosarum libros duos. Epigrammata quoque multa, et epistolas versu pulcherrimas edidit. Elegiam, quae perdiu iacuerat, rursus in lucem excitavit. A

When will be the day that returns me to you, Cinnama,   45
    when will I hold you in my arms, my light?[146]
When will it be that I am allowed to satisfy my eyes
    with your dear figure, and fold myself in your tender
        bosom?
When will it be that I can spend the night with you
    and take those long hoarded kisses?   50
Then I shall pray that my final hour may come,
    for there will be no holier death than that.

FOUR OPINIONS OF BECCADELLI[147]

: XXII :

Bartolomeo Facio
On Famous Men[148]
[c. 1456]

Antonius Panormita

Antonio of Palermo is considered famous in this genre. From his
youth he was drawn by the sweetness of oratory and poetry. He
abandoned the law and devoted himself to those studies. It is not
easy to judge in which of the two he was more accomplished. He
knows all the deeds of antiquity by heart. In his *Hermaphrodite*, he
made light verse after the example of Vergil. At about the same
time, having been attacked by Antonio da Rho, he wrote a book of
elegiac poetry which he entitled *Rhodus*, as well as two books of
poetry and prose. He also produced many epigrams and very
beautiful letters in verse. Elegy, which had long lain in darkness,
he restored to the light of day. When the Emperor Sigismund

Sigismundo imperatore in Italiam profecto poeta comprobatus laurea corona veteri more repetito donatus est.

Non temere alius quispiam aliena in dicendo vitia aut virtutes acrius animadvertit, quod ei aliquando a Leonardo Arretino doctissimo viro in praecipuam laudem tributum est. Alphonsi regis, qui eo doctore perdiu usus est, atque utitur, dicta factaque memoratu digna quatuor libris explicuit. Permagnum librorum numerum ex omni bonarum artium facultate congessit. Legationibus ac summis honoribus regis functus, quibuscumque viris doctis et probis potest, enixissime semper favit, ac favet.

: XXIII :

Pauli Cortesii
De hominibus doctis dialogus

In aliquo igitur numero fuit Antonius Panormita homo doctus et iuris bene peritus. Diligenter etiam satis loquutus est et, ut esset paulo politior, elegantiam sermonis Plautinam volebat imitari; sed ab eo aberat illa orationis integritas ac sententiosa concinnitas; itaque sunt epistolae eius languidiores. Fuit tamen perargutus poeta et illis temporibus non contemptus: nam is primus versus ad mensuram quandam numerosumque sonum revocavit (antea enim fractis concisisque numeris parum admodum versus a plebeis rhythmis differebant) quamquam eius fere tota poesis est obscena.

came into Italy, he was acclaimed poet laureate and given the laurel crown in a recreation of the ancient ceremony.

No one else is quicker to notice another's mistakes in diction, or his virtues, something that Leonardo Bruni, that most learned man, once attributed to him as a matter of the highest praise. He set out in four books the deeds and sayings worthy of memory of King Alfonso, who has long relied on his learning and continues to do so. He has accumulated a great number of books across the whole range of the humanities. He has served on embassies and in the most important royal offices. He has helped (and will always help) any learned or virtuous man as vigorously as he can.

: XXIII :

Paolo Cortesi
On Learned Men[149]
[c. 1490]

Among this number was Antonio of Palermo, a learned man and well educated in law. His speech was fairly careful, and to give it a little extra polish he decided to imitate the elegance of Plautus's language. But he lacked Plautus's purity of style and harmoniousness of meaning. As a result his letters are a little tedious. He was, however, a very witty poet and not bad for those times. For he was the first to recall poetry to regular meter and a rhythmical pronunciation (for previously with its faulty and choppy meters poetry had scarcely differed from ordinary speech patterns), despite the fact that nearly the entirety of his poetry is obscene.

: XXIV :

Pauli Iovii
Elogia virorum literis illustrium

Antonius Panormita Siculus Bononiae equestri familia natus, qui
a Pontano alumno elegantiarum pater appellatur, clare genus suum
ab ultimis Britannis, Becadellaque familia Bononiae celebri repete-
bat, praeclaro genti insignium argumento, quod iisdem militari in
scuto depictis alatis viperis utererur.

Sed maiorem profecto sibi e laude optimorum studiorum nobi-
litatem comparasse videri potest. Moribus enim ac litteris praes-
tantibus exornatus, quum Philippo Mediolanensium principi ferti-
lis ingenii industriam obtulisset, tanta liberalitate susceptus est ut
principem noscendae historiae cupidum, familiariter doceret et
publice octingentis annui aureis elegantiores literas profitetetur.
(Hic est ille Philippus, qui summam clementiae fructum generosis
optatum regibus gloriosissime decerpsit, cum Alfonsum regem
navali praelio captum non emiserit modo, sed auctum copiis ac
opibus in regnum restituerit.) Verum eo gravissimis bellis oc-
cupato, Panhormita Alfonso adhaesit, secretioris scrinii magister
et studiorum expeditionumqae omnium terra marique perpetuus
comes.

Scripsit epistolas candidiore stylo sed maxime iucundo, victoris
regis triumphum, et de factis dictisque optimi eius regis aureum
libellum, quem Pius pontifex exemplis paribus intertextis nobi-
liorem reddisse videtur.

: XXIV :

Paolo Giovio
Memorials of Men Distinguished in Literature[150]
[1546]

Antonio Panormita, a Sicilian, was descended from a knightly family of Bologna, whom his pupil, Pontano, called "the Father of Elegance."[151] He traced his genealogy back to the "furthest Britons"[152] and the famous Beccadelli family of Bologna, using as proof that family's coat of arms, which used the same winged vipers that were depicted on his shield.[153]

But one might in fact think that he won a greater nobility from the praise given to his outstanding studies. Adorned as he was with excellent manners and literary talent, when he offered the industry of his fertile genius to Duke Filippo of Milan, he was received with such generosity that he gave the duke, who was eager to learn history, private lessons, and delivered public lectures on classical literature at a salary of 800 gold florins a year. (This was the Duke Filippo who most gloriously plucked the highest fruit of clemency, desired by all noble kings, when he not merely released King Alfonso, whom he had captured in a naval battle, but also restored him to his kingdom, with troops and money besides.) But when Filippo became involved in major wars, Panormita joined Alfonso, as overseer of the private dispatch box and became his constant companion in his studies and on all his expeditions by land or sea.

He wrote *Letters* in a rather frank but highly enjoyable style, a *Triumph* of the victorious king, and the golden book of the *Deeds and Sayings* of that excellent king. Pope Pius is thought to have made it better still by inserting additional anecdotes of the same sort.

Sed cum Valla demum ad exercendum maledicentiae dentem naturae acerbitate paratissimo simultatem concepit: eo quidem eventu ut mutuis veluti confixi telis, foede admodum inimicis risum excitarent.

Senex uxorem duxit Arcellam sibi magnopere dilectam, liberosque suscepit, quorum honesta soboles Neapoli visitur. Postremo aeger vitaeque diffidens, in supremo morbo hoc carmen composuit, quod tumulo inscriberetur.

Quaerite Pierides alium, qui ploret amores,
    Quaerite, qui regum fortia facta canat.
Me pater ille ingens hominum sator atque redemptor
    Evocat, et sedes donat adire pias.

: XXV :

Lilii Gregorii Gyraldi Ferrariensis
Duo dialogi de poetis nostrorum temporum

Antonius vero Panhormita lascivioris quidem carminis conditor, dulcis tamen et facetus: legi eius aetatis quorundam epistolas, quibus Hermaphroditus illius multis laudibus commendatur, sed quare nescio. Dicam ego vobis sane quid sentio: nec is mihi poeta bonus nec bonus orator; quae enim soluto et pedestri sermone eius scripta legi luxuriantis magis quam bonae frugis referta videntur, ut impudicas et prostitutas eius Musas mittam. Panhormitam tamen quidam excellentes viri elegantiae parentem appellaverunt.

Hic etsi Siculus ex Bononia tamen originem duxisse ex nobili familia praedicatur; acer Laurentii Vallae inimicus fuit et contra

In the end, he picked a quarrel with Valla, who because of the bitterness of his nature was all too ready to bare his teeth in invective. The result was that they ran one another through with matching weapons, so to say, and became an utterly shameful laughing stock to their enemies.

In old age he married Arcella, whom he loved deeply, and had children by her; their noble descendants are still to be found in Naples. At the last, sick and not expecting to live, in his final illness he composed this poem, which is carved on his tomb:

> Seek another, Muses, to weep over love affairs,
> Seek another to sing the mighty deeds of kings.
> The great Father, the sower and savior of man,
> calls me back and grants me entrance to his holy home.[154]

: XXV :

Lilio Gregorio Giraldi
On the Poets of Our Time[155]
[1551; written c. 1549]

Antonio Panormita was the founder of the dirty poem, though a sweet and witty man. I have read certain letters from his time in which his Hermaphroditus is recommended with great praise, but why I don't know. I'll tell you honestly what I think. In my opinion he was neither a good orator nor a good poet. What I have read of his prose works seem to me to be stuffed with fruit that is more overripe than good and I dismiss his poetry as immodest and prostituted. Admittedly, a number of excellent men called him the father of elegance.

Though a Sicilian he is said to have come from a noble family of Bologna. He was a fierce enemy of Lorenzo Valla, and Valla of

Laurentius illius. Senex diem obiit hocque sibi moriens epita-
phium arrogantiae plenum condidisse legi.

> Quaerite Pierides alium, qui ploret amores,
>   Quaerite, qui regum fortia facta canat.
> Me pater ille ingens hominum sator atque redemptor
>   Evocat, et sedes donat adire pias.

him. He died an old man and I have read that as he was dying he
composed this epitaph full of arrogance:

> Seek another, Muses, to weep over love affairs,
>   Seek another to sing the mighty deeds of kings.
> The great Father, the sower and savior of man,
>   calls me back and grants me entrance to his holy home.

Note on the Texts

꽃⟨?⟩꽃

Donatella Coppini's 1990 edition, pp. xiii–ccxl, gathered, sifted, and classified the very large number of manuscripts of the text of *The Hermaphrodite* with such thoroughness that it seems unlikely the work will ever need to be done again. Vast and intricate though the tradition is, it can be reduced in its essentials to a small number of "redactional phases," of the most primitive of which we have only isolated witnesses. There are no autograph manuscripts of the collection as a whole or of individual poems. The first "publication," in the sense of circulation beyond a small group of like-minded friends, is effectively represented by the manuscript of dedication, L = Biblioteca Medicea Laurenziana, plut. 34.54. L was written for Cosimo de' Medici by a professional scribe, Giacomo Curlo of Genoa, who wrote several other manuscripts for him; this one presumably at the request of Beccadelli, and presumably in 1426, some short time after the collection was finished. The definitive redaction is that found in another Medicean manuscript written by Curlo somewhat later, Laur. plut. 33.22 (F). This manuscript, regarded by Coppini as representing the "author's final intention," is distinguished, like its congeners and descendants, by the addition of three letters to the collection: Guarino's before Book I, Poggio's after Book I, and Beccadelli's reply to the latter placed after Book II. In practice, F supplied the copy-text for Coppini's edition, though with copious report of variants elsewhere, and for the most part I have followed her critical text, except for restoring to their canonical positions the letters she placed in appendix.

As for the appendix to the present edition, it gathers contemporary texts (not in Coppini's edition or in manuscripts of *The Hermaphrodite*) to illustrate the immediate and often fierce response to the appearance of collection, a propaganda battle in which Beccadelli's insertion of the three letters into his book was the first move. Here too are later and more tranquil judgments on the character and talents of its author. The source of each, in early or modern editions, is given in the Notes to the Translation.

Notes to the Texts

꿍ᵛ꿍

1. Sabbadini's addition: see Notes to the Translation.

BOOK II

1. tui *MSS, Coppini.*

APPENDIX: ASSOCIATED LETTERS AND POEMS

1. <et> quo me *scripsi* : quone *MS,* quove *Sabbadini.* See Notes on Translation.

2. eum *Sabbadini* : cum *Rutherford* (both with manuscript support, but *cum* cannot cohere with the following *cui*).

3. patria<e> (*i.e.* patrię) *Sommer,* but the meaning is presumably literal: "hope of the father", with an echo of the previous line.

4. 9–10 are omitted in *N* and *C.*

5. es *scripsi* : nec *N.*

6. foedis *scripsi* : fidis *Cinquini-Valentini* (the verses are foul, not faithful).

7. crimine *scripsi* : carmine *Cinquini-Valentini, Sommer.*

8. *Addidi* : the text as printed is unmetrical and the manuscript has a gap in the middle.

9. *Scripsi* : rapidis *Cinquini-Valentini, Sommer.*

10. *Scripsi* : acta *Cinquini-Valentini, Sommer.*

11. dulcisono *Cinquini-Valentini* : dulcissimo *Sommer.*

12. sacerdotum (*with Rutherford's* α *MSS*) : sacerdotem (*Rutherford, with the* β *MSS*).

13. agrestem : horestem (= Orestem). *See Coppini 1985: 334 n. 5, regarding the* Orestem *transmitted by Rutherford's β MSS (printed by him and Cinquini-Valentini) as a corruption of the true reading in Ambros. D. 112 inf.*

14. dilanias *Sommer* : dilanians *Gaspary.*

15. sunt . . . sunt *Bottari* : sunt . . . sint *Gaspary Sommer.*

16. Veggi *Sommer* : vates *Bottari Gaspary.*

17. *17–26 are omitted by Bottari, Gaspary. These lines were understandably left out by the first editors.*

18. illa . . . illa *Sommer* : illa . . . ille *Coppini.*

19. Ad *scripsi* : In *F (the poem is not "against" chastity).*

20. pueri atque *scripsi* : facilesque *F (see notes on translation ad loc.).*

Notes to the Translation

꽃∫?꽃

1. Guarino da Verona (1374–1460), lived in Constantinople from 1403 to 1408, where he learned Greek from Manuel Chrysoloras and collected manuscripts. He was one of the most influential of humanist teachers. Giovanni Lamola (c. 1405–49) was a pupil of Guarino and an important discoverer of manuscripts.

2. Guarino rings changes on the conceit of the hermaphrodite, son of Hermes (in Latin Mercurius) and Aphrodite (in Latin Venus, whose quality is *venustas*); the god Mercury stands for personified eloquence, as in the work of Martianus Capella, *De nuptiis Philologiae et Mercurii* ("The Marriage of Philology and Mercury"), alluded to here.

3. Apelles (fl. 322 BC) was considered the greatest Greek painter, who painted many nudes, including the Aphrodite Anadyomene (Venus Arising from the Sea); Pliny *HN* 35.79–97. Fabius, surnamed Pictor, was one of the first painters at Rome: Pliny *HN* 35.19.

4. Cf. Aristotle *Poetics*, 1448b10–12.

5. One of the few places where I am forced to disagree with Coppini's text. Sabbadini in his edition of Guarino's letters (1915: 1, 505 no. 346; 3, 197) added the necessary words, omitted by haplography. I can find no parallel for the transmitted text's *flente rideo* "I laugh when he weeps," and the context is clearly one of imaginative sympathy, not mockery. The words recall Horace *Ars Poetica* 101–2: "Ut ridentibus adrident, ita flentibus afflent / humani voltus" ("just as human faces smile at those who smile, so they weep with those who weep") and (perhaps somewhat daringly) Romans 12:15: "gaudere cum gaudentibus, flere cum flentibus" ("Rejoice with those who rejoice and weep with those who weep"). Coppini (1990, p. clxxxvi, n. 90) notes that the emendation is "probabilissimo," but does not include it in her text: "The reading of all the codices . . . is perhaps justifiable in relation to the irony of certain apparently

serious passages in Panormita (see, for example, 2.9) but one should note that the [scribal] mistake is very likely." This has important consequences, since there exists an expanded version of this letter (Sabbadini 1915–19: I, 702) which exists in a single manuscript copy (Bergamo, Biblioteca Civica Angelo Mai, MA 613 [olim Λ II 32], a collection of humanist letters, including ones purporting to be by Plutarch to Trajan, Plato, King Philip to Aristotle, and Pontius Pilate). Sabbadini raises the possibility that this is a new redaction of the letter, where Guarino attempts to qualify his earlier praise for Beccadelli, only to reject the idea: "The letter of Guarino has lost, through the copyists' error, the two words *fleo, ridente* (l. 16) which are missing in the augmented edition as well and which I firmly believe have been securely supplied. But if Guarino had rewritten his own letter, wouldn't he have noticed the lacuna?" He concludes that the letter was rewritten by some of Guarino's students "as an exercise." I would add the possibility that the purpose was less an exercise than an attempt at saving Guarino's reputation by making his praise of Beccadelli more cautious. There is a decisive reason for not attributing the rewrite to Guarino. In his 1435 recantation he quotes his own letter, but without the interpolation (Sabbadini 1915–19: II, 210). The new version also misquotes Catullus (*cum* for *tum, pruriam incitari* for *pruriat incitare*), mistakes not in any of the copies of the original letter, but those may be copyists' errors.

6. Catullus, like Guarino from Verona.

7. Possibly referring to the Lenten sermons of San Bernardino (see Introduction).

8. Catullus 16.5–9, which Beccadelli quotes again in his letter to Poggio (after Book II), to Bartolomeo della Capra (Appendix, III.4), and to Antonio da Rho (Appendix, VII.3).

9. In the *Life of St. Paul the Hermit* 3. The reader will be relieved to know that the saint bites off his own tongue rather than submit.

10. Theocritus, fl. 270 BC, the brilliant Hellenistic poet who created the pastoral. Guarino may have chosen him not only as a Sicilian like Beccadelli, but also with a nod to his pederastic poems.

11. A joke that Guarino is proselytizing for Epicureanism.

NOTE: The text and translation of the expanded parts of the letter follows. I have placed the added material in italics.

Guarinus Veronensis suavissimo Iohanni Lamolae
plurimam salutem dicit.

Posteaquam alteras ad te descripseram, tuae et graves et ornatae redditae mihi sunt, quae eo accumulatiores venerunt, quo etiam comitem habuerunt libellum *Panormitae nostri* vere Ἑρμαφρόδιτον. Adeo prudenter et polite *et pro re* conscriptus est, ut sane Mercurio iuncta Venustas videatur, quod et ipsum Graece sapit vocabulum. Mirari profecto licet suavissimam carminis harmoniam, dicendi facilitatem, inelaborata verba et inoffensum compositionis cursum; nec idcirco minus carmen ipsum probarim et ingenium quia iocos, lasciviam et petulcum aliquid sapiat: an ideo minus laudabis Apellem, Fabium ceterosve pictores quia nudas et apertas pinxerunt in corpore particulas natura latere volentes? Quid si vermes, angues, mures, scorpiones, ranas, muscas fastidiosasque bestiolas expresserint? Num ipsam admiraberis et extolles artem artificisque solertiam? Ego mediusfidius hominem probo, ingenium miror et ludente delector, flente <fleo, ridente> rideo, lupanari medio scortantem laudo versum.

Si poeticum per se decorum consideres, plus valet apud me conterranei mei vatis non illepidi auctoritas quam imperitorum clamor, quos nil nisi lacrimae, ieiunia, psalmi delectare potest, immemores quod aliud in *vivendi ratione et morum probitate*, aliud in oratione spectari convenit. Ut autem ad meum conterraneum revertar, ille hunc in modum ait:

Nam castum esse decet pium poetam
ipsum, versiculos nihil necesse est,
qui tum denique habent salem ac leporem
si sint molliculi ac parum pudici
et quod pruriat incitare possint.

A qua quidem sententia et noster Hieronymus non abhorret, homo castimonia et integritate praeditus in primis, qui, cum in meretricis sermonem incidisset, quantam lascivienti ac vere scortanti calamo, *salva vitae sanctitate*, permisit usurpare licentiam!: "Quo cum, recedentibus cunctis, meretrix speciosa venisset, coepit delicatis stringere colla complexibus, et, quod dictu quoque scelus est, manibus attrectare virilia, ut, corpore in libidinem concitato, se victrix impudica superiaceret." Quis leno impudens flagitio magis linguam involveret? Habeo mille et quidem locupletissimos testes, graves, continentes et Christianos homines, qui spurcissimo uti sermone nihil expaverunt, cum res *et sermonis ratio reique turpitudo explananda* postulabat: sed in re certa supervacuum est testes citare minime necessarios.

4   Laudo igitur non modo ἐποποιίαν sed et poetam nostrum, ita enim appellare velim.

> Musarum decus, Antoni, per saecula salve!
> Theocriton, antiquum Siculae telluris alumnum,
> effingis, prisca revocans dulcedine vatem.
> Sicelidas Latio per te dabit Aetna Camenas.

Ceterum animadvertes, Iohannes optime, ne ideo me vel auctore vel exhortatore materiam ipsam et carminis argumentum probari putes, sicuti carmen ipsum pro decoro laudaverim. Magis autem magisque velim ut ad res viro dignas et virtutis opera stilus ipse vertatur et quasi "relictis nucibus" sumpta virili toga dignitati laudi et honori serviat, vel Catullo praeceptore: "Nam castum esse decet pium poetam ipsum." Haec aetas alios exigit mores; tempus fuit iocandi, tempus instat seria loquendi serioque vivendi. Suade amico utrique communi id Virgilianum iam servet illud: "Claudite iam rivos pueri, sat prata biberunt"; et qui inscribit ad Cosmam, cosmi idest ornamenti rationem teneat. Nil nisi grande talis ingenii pollicetur acumen. Danda est opera ut quemadmodum scribendi praeceptio, sic et scriptoris mores vitaque probentur plusque poeta quam poema ad imitandum alliciat.

5   Vale, mi Iohannes . . .

> Guarino da Verona sends greetings to his
> dearest Giovanni Lamola.

1   After I had written a second letter to you, I received your serious and elegant letter, which arrived all the more richly laden in that it had as its companion a book *by our friend from Palermo*, truly a Hermaphrodite! It is written with such skill and polish *and in keeping with the subject* that it certainly seems to be Mercury united with Elegance, as the Greek word itself suggests. One may admire its sweet harmony of song, its ease of

diction, its elaborate word choice, and the unimpeded flow of its composition. And so I would not approve less of the poem itself and the author's talent just because it smacks of jokes, playfulness, and something a little wanton. Would you therefore praise Apelles, Fabius, and other painters the less because they painted naked and open to view those parts of the body which by nature prefer to be hidden? What if they painted worms, snakes, mice, scorpions, frogs, flies, and disgusting vermin? Wouldn't you admire and praise their art and the skill of the artist? I in truth praise the man *as a writer*, admire his talent, delight when his verse plays around, when he cries <I cry, when he laughs> I laugh, praise it when it goes whoring in the middle of a brothel.

If you consider poetic decorum as such, the authority of my fellow country-   2
man, a not inelegant poet, carries more weight with me than the shouting of the ignorant, who can delight in nothing but tears, fasting, and psalms, and who forget that things ought to be looked at differently *in one's way of life and the probity of one's morals* than in speech. And to return to my countryman, he spoke to this effect:

> For it's right that a proper poet be pure
> himself, but there's no need for his verses to be,
> which can only have wit and charm
> if they are a little on the lax side and not too modest
> and can stir up what makes you itch.

This was an opinion that even our own St. Jerome did not disagree with,   3
a man of the most exceptional chastity and rectitude, who, when he chances to be speaking about a courtesan, what license does he allow his playful, even whorish pen to use — *though the sanctity of his life was intact*: "After everyone had left him, a beautiful courtesan came to him, and began to stroke his neck with sensuous embraces, and (though it is a sin even to mention it) to fondle his manhood with her hands, so that, once his body was roused to lust, the lewd woman might be the victor and mount him." What shameless pimp would get his tongue around a more disgraceful act? I have a thousand very trustworthy authorities, serious, self-controlled and Christian men, who were not afraid to use the vilest language when the occasion — *and the nature of the discourse and the shame-*

fulness of the act to be described—demanded it. But in a case that's already been decided, it's pointless to call unnecessary witnesses.

4   So I praise not only the poetry, but our poet, as I should like to call him:

> Hail, glory of the Muses, Antonio, for ever,
> You imitate Theocritus, the ancient son of the land of Sicily,
> Recalling the poet with the sweetness of old.
> Etna will give Sicilian Muses to Latium through you.

But you should be sure, dear Giovanni, not to think, just because I praised the poem itself for its elegance, that on that account I approve of the matter and argument of the poem, either as an instigator or encourager. How I wish that his pen would turn to matters worthy of a man and to virtuous works, that it would throw away its childish toys [Persius I.10], take on the toga of manhood and devote itself to dignified, praiseworthy and honorable subjects in line with that very precept of Catullus, 'it's right that a proper poet be pure himself'. This time of life requires different manners—there was a time for fooling about, now the time for talking seriously and living seriously presses on us. Persuade our mutual friend to follow that line of Vergil, "Stop up the streams now, boys, the meadows have drunk enough" [Ecl. 3.111]. And one who dedicates a book to Cosimo, should take account of cosmos, that is to say, of decency. Nothing but great things are promised by such a sharp talent. An effort must be made that, just as with the precepts of writing, so the morals and life of the writer should meet with approval, and the poet prove more tempting to imitate than the poem. . . .

The rest is identical.

BOOK I

1. Cf. Martial 1.4.

2. *Si vacat:* cf. Ov. *Pont.* 1.1.3, 3.3.1.

3. *quicquid id est:* cf. Ov. *Pont.* 1.1.29; Cat. 1.8–9.

4. *placido lumine:* cf. Hor. *Odes* 4.3.2.

5. Hippolytus, son of Theseus king of Thebes, and a devotee of Diana, who rejected the confession of love from his step-mother Phaedra, most famously in Euripides's *Hippolytus*. Less a model of chastity than of mi-

sogyny. For Hippolytus as a proverbially tough audience, cf. Ov. *Am.* 2.4.32; Martial 14.203; *Priap.* 19.5–6.

6. For the trope, cf. Guarino's letter above, citing Cat. 16.

7. The misuse of *suus* is typical of Beccadelli, and of medieval and humanist Latin in general before Lorenzo Valla clarified the use of reflexives.

8. *nec et:* not a classical usage (much less repeated).

9. For similar warnings, cf. Ov. *Am.* 2.1.3–4, *Ars* 1.31–34, 3.57–58; Martial 3.68. 3.69, 11.15–16. See *Herm.* 2.2 below.

10. The Flemish prostitute celebrated in 2.30.

11. *Ursa:* "She bear." A recurring character. See 1.5, 1.8, 1.21, 1.27.6. 2.7, 2.8, 2.9, 2.10.

12. Latin *femur* disappeared from Italian to be replaced by *coscia*, except as the anatomical term for 'thigh bone'. Though Beccadelli could have learned its regular Latin meaning, he seems to employ it primarily in the sense 'cunt', 'pussy', 'crotch' or the like. So Tuscan *feme*, defined by Florio (1611, 183) as "the upper and forepart of the thigh. Also the privy parts of a woman"; cf. *femora*. For *femur* in Christian Latin to mean metonymically 'generative organs' (male and female) see, e.g., Jerome, *Ep.* 65.10.2, Vulgate Num. 5.21. Isidore of Seville (11.24) derives the word *femina* from *femur* "since there the appearance of the sex is distinguished from the man." (*Femina vero a partibus femorum dicta, ubi sexus species a viro distinguitur*), and vice versa (11.106). Beccadelli uses *femur* to mean male sex organs at 2.7.3.

13. A boy's anus was preferable to a woman's in the opinion of Martial 11.43, 12.96.

14. *veges*, a 'barrel', post-classical.

15. Cf. Ov. *Am.* 2.2.11–12: *vir quoque non sapiens; quid enim servare laboret, / unde nihil, quamvis non tueare, perit?* ("Her husband, too, is not wise. Why does he work at preserving that from which nothing is lost, whether you guard it or not?"). Also *Priap.* 3.1–2: *Obscure poteram tibi dicere: "da mihi, quod tu / des licet assidue, nil tamen inde perit."* ("I could tell you a riddle: 'Give me what you could give constantly and yet not lose any of it'.")

16. *mis* for *meas*. The mss of Plautus write *mis* for *meis* dat. and abl. (i.e. monosyllabic in synizesis) at *Poen.* 1189 and *Trin.* 822, which Beccadelli has extended to *meas*.

17. Chiron, the centaur, was the teacher of Achilles.

18. Beccadelli follows the convention of Aeschylus's *Myrmidons* in making Achilles, now grown up, the dominant partner of Patroclus; see Plato, *Symp.* 180a, Martial 11.43.10.

19. Hercules's love for Hylas was famous: Verg. *Georg.* 3.6; Prop. 1.20. Ap. Rh. 1.1207–19 tells how Hercules killed Hylas's father and took the boy. Martial 11.43.5 is clear and clever: *Incurvabat Hylan posito Tirynthius arcu* ("Hercules put down his bow and bent Hylas instead"); *percisus* is almost the *vox propria* for anal intercourse: Martial 4.48.1 and 4; 6.3.14, 7.62.1, 12.35.2, *Priap.* 13.1, 15.6. See Adams 1990: 146.

20. *Tentigo*, 'swelling', in the title used by Juv. 6.129 of Messalina's uterine hard-on. Beccadelli uses it for the clitoris itself. Cf. Martial 6.36 for a big nose matching a big penis.

21. Beccadelli writes from Bologna. A Cornutus is the dedicatee of Persius's satires. The name Cornutus, however, for an Italian, would have had the comic overtones of one has been cuckolded (e.g. Florio 1611: 125 s.v.), but the general sense of 15–21 seems to contradict this.

22. Thalia, the muse of comedy.

23. Whether a particular Frenchman or the French in general is unclear. In *Herm.* 1.14.5–6, the French and Germans are said to be especially given to sex with boys. The syntax here is a little convoluted. *pene potens* 'powerful with the cock' is built to such phrases and compounds as *armipotens* 'mighty in arms'. *agit*, then, seems to be used absolutely. The *quaeque* clauses are construed first with subjunctives (*quaeque velit*) and then with indicatives (*quodcunque . . . est; quicquid . . . venit*).

24. *cruscula* 'little legs': Plaut. *Cist.* 408, where it is not a compliment. Beccadelli uses this rarity again in *Herm.* 2.24.4 where he contrasts it with *cunnum* 'cunt' (see note *ad loc.*). He apparently takes it to mean boys' thighs and I have translated it as such.

25. Beccadelli apparently now turns to Cornutus to complain that his friend is monopolizing the women. The transition is less than clear.

26. Cf. Juv. 3.109–112:

> Praeterea sanctum nihil illi et ab inguine tutum,
> non matrona laris, non filia virgo, nec ipse
> sponsus levis adhuc, non filius ante pudicus.
> Horum si nihil est, aviam resupinat amici.

("Besides nothing is sacred to him or safe from his crotch not the mother of family, not the virgin daughter, not even her still smooth-faced fiancé, not the son chaste till now. If there's none of them, he lays his friend's grandmother on her back.")

27. Beccadelli's meaning is clear, even if his expression is not. O'Connor's version (2001: 36), "Your wants extend to the city's whole supply of holes that ladies piss from, / while he desires all the holes through which boys shit," pretty much captures the gist.

28. It is hard to know what Beccadelli meant by *vices*; "sexual positions," as in *Herm.* 2.30.20, does not really seem to fit.

29. Sparrows were proverbial for their randiness.

30. Mattia Lupi da San Gimignano (1380–1468), Beccadelli's former teacher, author of the poem *Annales Geminianenses* in ten books, tracing the history of San Gimignano down to the 1460s. See Traversari 1903, Davies 1984, Fioravanti 1999.

31. *id monstri*: a periphrasis for *monstrum*.

32. The unequal metrical feet of the elegiac couplet. Cf. Claudian *Carm. min.* 13:

> In podagrum qui carmina sua non stare dicebat
> Quae tibi cum pedibus ratio? Quid carmina culpas?
> Scandere qui nescis, versiculos laceras?
> "Claudicat hic versus; haec" inquit "syllaba nutat";
> atque nihil prorsus stare putat podager.

("On a Gouty Man, Who Said That the Author's Verses Did Not Scan. What have you to do with feet? Why do you criticize my songs? You don't know how to scan [climb], and you attack my verses? 'This verse limps,' he says, 'that syllable is off'; and a gouty man thinks nothing at all stands.")

33. Cf. *Priap.* 60. Mamurianus comes from Martial 1.92.2, who there is a pederast.

34. A slight reworking of Martial 3.26. For another poem against Lentulus, see *Herm.* 2.20. Here apparently a taste for boys (active sodomy) is not incompatible with being passively sodomized.

35. Beccadelli seems to assume that boys (6) will offer not only anal but oral sex, something not in keeping with ancient views, where oral sex (as the more degrading) was rather expected from women.

36. *Brito:* used in medieval Latin for both Britons and Bretons, in the Renaissance more commonly for the latter (see Girolamo Baldi, *Carmina* 4.81 where *Brito* is distinguished from *Anglus*). Forberg (1908: 20–2), Gagliardi (1980: 43), Sommer (1997: 51) and O'Connor (2001: 38: "a Brit or a blockhead") assume that the British were more likely to be considered laggards in love; Ottoline (1922: 22), Tognelli (1968: 59), and Cossart (1984: 30) translate as Breton.

bardo: Mercier (1791) and Coppini (1990) capitalize *Bardus*, as does Thurn (2002: 307), who takes this as referring to Bardi, a town in Emilia. However, the usual meaning of 'thick', 'stupid' is that used here. The vice of pederasty is said to be endemic to all the major Italian cities, but a novelty in Brittany, France, and Germany.

37. This aetiological story is also told (without the reference to pederasty) in MS Paris lat. 8568, fol. 84r, before a selection of Petrarch's *Epistolae Familiares.* One notices that the story does not actually answer the question, but is rather merely an extended metaphor (sex with boys is as sweet as honey).

38. *obaudio,* a post-classical formation for *oboedio* 'obey'. The word was occasionally misused to mean the opposite: 'not to hear', so Alanus, *Anticlaudianus* 6.94. The *Dictionary of Medieval Latin from British Sources* s.v. cites this sense from Gerald of Wales.

39. *subnitor*: the compound is post-classical, usually in the meaning 'be subordinate to, to rely on'.

40. For *inclino*, see Juv. 9.26; Adams 1990: 192.

41. Cf. Martial 10.60 and *Herm.* 2.16 below.

42. Cf. Auson. 19.7, Juv. 2.4–7.

43. The name Alda (Alde) is that of the beautiful sister of Oliver in the *Chanson de Roland*, and the Italian tradition derived from it. However, it may be intended to recall the heroine of *Alda*, the twelfth-century comedy by Guillaume de Blois (Guilelmus Blesensis) who having once been tricked into sex, cannot get enough (see Introduction).

44. *suis* misused for *eius*. The scribes of A and V₁ tried to correct this to *tuis*.

45. The manuscript (R, 74v = Florence, Biblioteca Riccardiana, cod. 636) containing an early version of this poem in a letter dated 9/10 December [1424] identifies "Coridon" as Antonio Roselli (1381–1466), Beccadelli's friend, at that time a professor of law at the University of Siena. See Corso 1953: 145; Coppini 1990: lxxxvi–lxxxix. For Roselli, see Belloni 1986: 143–9.

46. Cf. Verg. *Ecl.* 2.1. Corydon is the classical form of the name.

47. Cf. Cat. 23.12.

48. Cf. *Priap.* 32.9.

49. Cf. Cat. 97.7–8.

50. Cf. Cat. 97.1–4.

51. *Figo* is normally construed with *in* + ablative, not dative, and the use of the reflexive is again incorrect.

52. Unlike the usual classicizing names, the common Italian name Oddo has been thought to point to a specific individual. Thurn (2002: 308) suggests Petrus Odus Montopolitanus (*Pietro Oddo da Montopoli*, ed., Maria Teresa Acquaro Graziosi, 1970), who, however was not born till at least 1420 and possibly as late as 1425 (Donati 2000: 31); or a certain "Gilbert Oux," whom I have not been able to find elsewhere; Thurn calls him a teacher of Pomponius Laetus (which is true of Petrus Odus).

However, the name may be meant to recall *odi* 'I hate'. Two manuscripts (*P* and *U*, descendants of a lost exemplar *m*) read *Nicolaum* for *Hodum* in the title to 2.11. This probably represents a scribal attempt at identification, since none of the other mss in this branch share the gloss, nor is it found here in 1.20. Nicolaus is perhaps the contemporary scholar Niccolò Niccoli (c. 1364–1437), who may have been chosen simply because he was a famous quarreler. For Oddo, see also *Herm.* 2.11; Appendix, II.9 (Poggio's reply to this letter).

53. The adjective is from Martial 4.14.13–14 (also an apology for light verse): "Sic forsan tener ausus est Catullus / magno mittere Passerem Maroni" ("Even so perhaps tender Catullus dared to send his Sparrow to the great Vergil"), with a fine disregard for chronology.

54. *verpe*: cf. Cat. 47.4. In classical Latin, *verpus* means "with the glans of the penis exposed," because of an erection and applied humorously to Jews because of circumcision; see Adams 1990: 12–14. The word continued to be used in Italian (see Florio 1611: 595: "*Verpa, used for* Vega, *a mans yard. Verpo, he that is circumcised and hath the foreskin of his yard cut off.*"). See below on 2.6.35. Priapus here is used by metonymy for the *Priapea*, then attributed to the youthful Vergil.

55. Alluding to Martial Book 1, preface, who lists Catullus, Marsus, and Pedo as his exemplars. Cf. Pliny *Ep.* 5.3.5: *quod decuit M. Tullium . . . Torquatum, immo Torquatos*, etc., cited by Beccadelli in his letter to Poggio. Marcus is probably Cicero (or Cicero and Martial).

56. Leon Battista Alberti (1404–72), the consummate humanist, was at this point a student of law in Bologna.

57. *litterulis . . . ingenuis*. Cf. Hor. *Ep.* 2.2.7: *litterulis Graecis*.

58. *sanguine . . . cretus*. Beccadelli earlier had *sanguine . . . natus*, which he revised to the more Vergilian *cretus* (*A.* 2.74, 3.608, 4.191; also picked up by Stat. *Silv.* 5.2.17). See Coppini 1990, page c.

59. *vera simplicitate*: cf. Mart. 1.39.4.

60. *casmate*: for *chasma* in the sense 'ruin, collapse', cf. William of Canterbury, *Mir. Thom.* 2.45.

61. *subsitiens*: another post-classical compound.

62. This line and the entire poem are a variant on Juv. 10.223–24: "quot longa viros exorbeat uno / Maura die" ("as many men as tall Maura sucks off in one day").

63. Cf. Mart. 3.76. Antonio da Rho singled these lines out for his particular disgust; Rutherford 2005: 262. Beccadelli's free use of the reflexive makes it unclear whose bottom is to be titillated. Coppini 1990: 40 compares Boccaccio, *Decameron* 2.10.39, where the young wife, Bartolomea, asks her old husband, Ricciardo di Chinzica, if he's hoping "rizzare a mazzata?" ("to get it up with a beating") and to Francesco d'Altobianco degli Alberti's "Capitolo di vecchiezza," which according to Martelli's interpretation (1989: 45–46 on lines 52–54) refer to anal self-stimulation for an old man to get an erection. Closer still is Aretino, *Ragionamenti* 1 (ed. Aquilecchia 1969: 24.1–2), where a sexual jouster "spronando se stesso con le dita" ("spurring himself on with his fingers"; Rosenthal [Aretino 1971: 32] adds by way of explanation, "in his asshole"). So Cossart 1984: 33, O'Connor 2001: 42; see Turner 2003: 276. On the other hand, Aretino begins *Sonetti Lussoriosi* 2 with "Mettimi un dito in cul, caro vecchione" ("Stick a finger up my ass, dear old man"), but here the purpose (according to Aretino) is the woman's pleasure rather than stimulating an erection in the man (who is already erect).

64. Cf. Martial 1.35.

65. For *femur*, see 1.5.3 above.

66. Orietta, daughter of Francesco Benzi, died in the plague of 1424, along with her sister, commemorated in the next epigram. See Corso 1953: 150–51.

67. The death from plague of this young girl on 27 January 1424 is mentioned by Beccadelli in a letter (Vendôme cod. 112, fol. 30r; see Sabbadini 1910a). See also *Herm.* 1.32 below.

68. Alternate form of Philomela, daughter of Pandion, king of Athens, and sister of Procne. Procne's husband, Tereus, raped Philomela and cut her tongue out. Philomela wove a tapestry telling the crime and sent it to her sister. In vengeance, Procne killed Itys, her son by Tereus. Procne is turned into the swallow, Philomela into the nightingale (the roles are

sometimes reversed), Tereus into a hawk (or hoopoe). See Appendix, XIV.30 below.

69. Cf. Hor. *Odes* 1.16.1.

70. Cf. Mart. 3.71.

71. The name Hisbo may be taken from the Hispo of Juv. 2.50.

72. Cf. Ov., *Am.* 1.13.18.

73. Tiresias: the blind prophet of Thebes who warned Oedipus and others of their fates. Cf. Sen. *Oedipus* 288.

74. Santia Ballo (Xantius Ballus), a fellow Sicilian, was Beccadelli's friend in Siena and Bologna. He introduced Filelfo to *The Hermaphrodite* (Sabbadini 1891: 20–21); see Introduction.

75. *lector studiose*: cf. Martial 1.1.4.

76. The *ut* of line 5 seems still to hold sway over the subjunctives after *nosti*.

77. For this couplet cf. Ov. *Trist.* 3.14.43–44.

78. Beccadelli here seems to promise the greater, epic verses that Guarino urged him to move on to.

79. The Parcae, or Fates, spun the thread of each person's life. Clotho spins it, Lachesis allots the span, and finally Atropos ('she who cannot be turned away') cuts it. "Comes the blind Fury with th'abhorred shears / And slits the thin-spun life." (Milton, *Lycidas*, 76–77).

80. Cf. Ov. *Rem.* 511.

81. Cf. Ov. *Her.* 9.12.

82. Cf. Ov. *Am.* 1.3.1.

83. *gymnasium*: In medieval Latin the term usually denotes the university. Siena's university was already fully established by 1240. The university temporarily removed to Montalcino later in 1424 to avoid the plague (Corso 1953: 139). Lucia is thought of as acting as a patron saint of the university.

84. For the Fates, see 1.27 n. above. The *sua* probably (though incorrectly) refers to Lucia; *pensum* is not technically "thread" but a weight (amount) of wool to be spun.

85. The nine goddesses are seemingly the nine Muses, each imagined as inhabiting her own planetary sphere, but with overtones of various virgin saints.

86. *victitet:* a Plautine word, meaning properly 'to subsist on'.

87. That is, Cosimo, would prefer for such a splendid girl to be from Florence. Cf. Martial 1.39 and its brief appendage 1.40.

88. Another victim of the plague of 1424 mentioned in Beccadelli's letter (above, n. 67). Beccadelli relates how when Catherine caught the plague, she was left to die by her terrified husband, Tommaso, and her brothers and their tutor, but was nursed by a certain Francesco, who was in love with her, disregarding all danger. After her death, Francesco took her body back to Siena, built a tomb and "inscribed the tomb with these verses" (*atque hiis versibus tumulum inscripsit*). This present epigram follows in the letter, reading, however, *bella* for *scita*, in line 2. Beccadelli appears to have written the epigram as a favor for Francesco, a fellow citizen of Palermo, and then revised it for publication. See Sabbadini 1910a; Coppini 1990: lxxiv–lxxv.

89. See 1.23. The name Mamurianus comes from Martial 1.92. *Penisuggius* is a neologism.

90. *virilem . . . notam:* cf. *Priap.* 66.1.

91. The name Amilus is taken from the pederast Hamillus of Martial 7.62 and Juvenal 10.224.

92. See *Herm.* 1.18 for Alda. The basic joke is that of Martial 11.28.

93. The meaning of the opening line is unclear. Forberg (1908: 50), Cossart (1984: 39), and O'Connor (2001: 50) assumed that *porticus* was a mistake for *portator* 'litter bearer', and Tognelli (1968: 103) and Gagliardi (1980: 66) so translate it. I can find no evidence that *porticus* was ever used in that sense and it is difficult to believe that Beccadelli could have made such a mistake (or assumed that his readers would understand the text thus), especially given the common Italian words of *portico* and

portatore. Further it is hard to see how a litter bearer contributes to the scenario. Martial uses Ponticus as one of his filler names, but none of his verses aids us much here. The problem seems then to lie in the sense of *sustinet* and Coppini compares Prop. 2.23.5–6, where the lover asks *"quaenam nunc porticus illam / integit?"* (What colonnade shelters her now?). For the sense of *sustinet* 'withhold, hold back', cf. Verg. *Aen.* 11.750, and *Herm.* 1.38.24 below ('hold on to'). In fact, *sustineo* seems to be used as a convenient metrical alternative to *retineo* or *contineo*, which Beccadelli uses in the same way in 2.30.6: "tandem me placidae continuere Senae" ("Finally pleasant Siena kept me"). Thurn (2002: 27) translates "Während beim Portikus Alda, das strahlende Antlitz, sich aufhielt"; and cf. Sommer 1997: 71: "Als die an Gestalt gewichtige Alda von einer Säule gestützt ward" (apparently confusing *Säule* and *Säulenhalle*). The late and contaminated ms. *Pan* (1475) reads <R>*usticus* and this is tempting, but probably no more than a guess by the copyist, Francesco Viviano Lambertini, who understood what Beccadelli was trying to say little more than I.

insignem facie: cf. Verg. *Aen.* 9.336.

94. Cf. Ov. *Her.* 15.44: *oscula cantanti tu mihi rapta dabas.*

95. *verbo . . . uno:* cf. Ter. *Andr.* 45, Cat. 67.15.

96. *ceveo:* to wiggle the buttocks, apparently used exclusively of men (the female equivalent is *crisso*), cf. Martial 3.95, Juv. 2.21, 9.40; Adams 1990: 136–7.

97. Sanzio (Sanzo, Santio) Liguori is unidentified.

98. *domi militiae:* cf. Cic. *Man.* 48: a good reuse of a prose idiom in verse.

99. Pontano: This is Francesco Pontano, not the more famous Giovanni Gioviano Pontano (1429–1503), later Beccadelli's friend and successor at Naples. See Marletta 1942 and cf. Sabbadini 1910b: 130, 142 (referring to a later affair).

100. *si vacat . . . accipe:* cf. Ov. *Pont.* 1.1.3–4, 3.3.1; *Herm.* 1.1.1 above. Aonia is the part of Boeotia where Mt. Helicon is located, hence a conventional epithet for the Muses.

101. *dent annos:* cf. Ov. *Pont.* 2.53.

102. *dignior . . . digno:* cf. [Tib.] 3.12.10, Sulpicia [Tib.] 3.13.10. *Candida* is a favorite Catullan word: Cat. 13.4, 35.8, 68b.70, 86.1.9.

103. *anus:* the old woman is the procuress, a traditional blocking figure of New Comedy, and of daily life, hence Beccadelli's final prayer.

104. Cf. Ov. *Trist.* 2.86.

105. Cf. Ov. *Met.* 7.410.

106. The change into the third person singular is clumsy, especially in the use of *vir* in 16 to indicate Pontano, the lover, but to mean the husband in 20. It seems to be the result of Beccadelli's inserting *hic* (in two different uses) to make a short preceding syllable.

107. Tindaris: Helen, daughter of Tyndareus king of Sparta and Leda, abducted by Paris, whence the Trojan Wars.

108. The god of gardens is the well-endowed Priapus, but the thought is unclear; perhaps "may he die, unless he's the god Priapus, in which case he cannot die," that is, he keeps on living despite Pontano and Beccadelli's wish. In the more usual comic scene the rival husband is old and feeble, no match for the virile young lover. For a wish for the husband's death, cf. Ov. *Am.* 1.4.1–2.

109. Cf. Ov. *Am.* 3.5.57–58 (she is French-kissing him) and 3.14.23 (next note).

110. For the alternate sense of *femur,* see 1.22.4 above. For *sustinuisse femur,* see Ov. *Am.* 3.14.22 of the woman's part. Beccadelli has lifted the phrase without fully understanding it (since he is not praying that Pontano get Polla on top); cf. 1.5 above.

111. Cf. Hor. *Ep.* 1.19.35–36, Ov. *Am.* 2.4.21.

112. *trilinguis:* cf. Hor. *Odes* 2.19.29, 3.11.20, i.e. he will be Cerberus, a very hell-hound.

113. One manuscript (*Pa₂,* Paris lat. 6707; 1466) gives an explanation of this poem: "Note: there was a certain poet who tried to attack Antonio Panormita. He names him under the guise (*typo*) of the shitting peasant.

For the bird, you will understand the poet's talent; for the Muse, the fervor and heat of the mind; for the grove and the stream, the quiet and pleasure of writing. Crispus was a distinguished citizen of Siena named Berto, whose name he altered for reasons of circumspection." Two other manuscripts (*Be₁* and *M₂*) containing early versions of the poem have the name Bertus for Crispus, *Be₁* adding in the title "Berto Senensium cancellario." This would be Berto (di Antonio di Berto) Aldobrandini, who was first elected chancellor of Siena in 1428. The gloss, though not the identification, must postdate this. See Coppini 1990: lxxxi–lxxxii; Corso 1953: 162–64.

114. For a similar opening, cf. Ov. *Am.* 3.1.1–6.

115. *egero*: "discharge," a term more medical than crude (*OLD* 3b).

116. Cf. Juv. 14.199.

117. *tonitrua*: the neut. pl. form (though occasionally attested in classical authors, e.g., Cic. *Phil.* 5.15, *Div.* 2.42) is standard in the Vulgate, e.g. Ex. 9:20, Rev. 10:3.

118. *excutior*: cf. Verg. *Aen.* 2.302; *cessit in auras*: cf. Ov. *Met.* 14.848; Sil. 6.39. *dea*: Originally Beccadelli wrote the unmetrical Clīō.

119. Based on Juv. 3.108, a difficult line: the flattering friend is ready to applaud if the patron merely pisses straight or *si trulla inverso crepitum dedit aurea fundo* ("if the golden ladle [*trulla*] gives off a sound when its bottom is turned over"). Some have thought of a type of ancient dribble glass that would gurgle, or of a chamber pot; but *trulla* only means 'ladle' in Latin. Giorgio Valla of Piacenza in his edition of Juvenal (Venice 1486) took it to mean the rich man does a "pull my finger" trick and farts as he turns over his cup. In any case, Beccadelli simply takes *trulla* as 'a fart'. Older Italian attests the verb *trullare* (Dante *Inf.* 28.24) and both *trullo* and (less-common) *trulla* as the noun. Cf. Florio 1611: 583: "*trulla*: any broad woodden tray, or washing bowle. Also a close stoole pan. Also a filthe slut or troll"; "*trullare*: to fart or break winde behinde. Also to shite, to cacke, or skommer"; and "*trullo*: a fart. Also a trill or bum-hole. Also a close stoole pan or chamber-pot."

120. *deprecor*, usually 'beg' (from a person), rather than 'pray' and usually with a neg. *planto* is strictly 'propagate from cuttings'. Cf. Tib. 1.1.7–8.

121. *sua* again misused. The correction to *tua* is in many mss.

122. Homer, *Iliad* 9.502–12, a close translation. For this poem and its situation, see Lefèvre 2002. Although manuscripts offer different forms, Beccadelli seems to have written the nom. consistently as Ἄτης, rather than the proper Ἄτη.

123. *Nocumentum*: a post-classical coinage.

124. Giovanni Aurispa (1376–1459), a fellow Sicilian, from Noto. In 1423 he returned from Constantinople, where he had been studying Greek, with a treasure trove of Greek manuscripts. In 1424 he became professor of Greek at Bologna, where he met Beccadelli. In fact, Aurispa gave Beccadelli a manuscript of Martial, possibly the one mentioned here, which survives and contains corrections in Beccadelli's hand (Wolfenbüttel, Herzog August Bibliothek, Cod. Aug. 50.5 4°). See Hausmann 1976: 186–88; Gaisser 1993: 286 n. 92.

125. *per si*: cf. Verg. *Aen.* 2.142.

126. *damnas* (indeclinable adjective) standing for *damnatus*.

127. *decus indelebile*: cf. Ov. *Pont.* 2.8.25.

128. For the place of Poggio's letter in Beccadelli's defense, see O'Connor 1997: 996–97. Ironically, Poggio himself would later write the milder (more Boccaccio-esque) *Facetiae* (Bowen 1986: 5; composed between 1438 and 1452).

129. For Lamola, see n. 1 above.

130. Antonio Loschi of Vicenza, c. 1368–1441, protofeminist, student of Travesio at Pavia, head of the Chancery of Milan (1398–1404) under Giangaleazzo Visconti, author (inter alia) of *Inquisitio artis in orationibus Ciceronis* (c. 1399), and an *Invective against Florence*, answered by Salutati.

131. One sees here the danger to Beccadelli of a biographical reading.

132. For Vergil as the supposed author of the *Priapea*, see *Herm.* 2.11.6; Beccadelli's letter in reply (2).

133. *Andria* 189, slightly misquoted: *nunc hic dies aliam vitam defert, alios mores postulat.* Poggio may have known it as a tag from Cic. *Fam.* 12.25.5.

BOOK II

1. Based on Martial 1.107 and other examples of *recusatio*, where the poet claims that he would write epic if only he had the talent or, in this case, the money.

2. I.e., write epic in the dactylic hexameters proper to it. A combination of Hor. *Sat.* 1.2.48: *me pedibus delectat claudere verba*, and Domitius Marsus (Tib. 3.21.4): *forti regia bella pede*; Beccadelli had copied and glossed an important manuscript of Tibullus (see Introduction).

3. *chyrographa < chirographum*, 'written by hand,' used of all sorts of legal documents.

4. *haec . . . haec*: for "the one [law] . . . the other [glory]." For *inebriat aures*, cf. Juv. 9.13, where the metaphor is more appropriate to the context.

5. *excipiam . . . aure*: cf. Mart. 7.12.2.

6. *leges ac iura*: cf. Juv. 2.72; also Plaut. *Epid.* 292, *Most.* 126; Cic. *Caec.* 70, *Flac.* 62; etc.

7. *prostituo . . . foro*: cf. Ov. *Am.* 1.15.6.

8. *ludicra condo*: cf. Hor. *Ep.* 1.1.10 and *Herm.* 1.27.3–4 above.

9. *dum bibo*: Ausonius also claimed to have composed the entirety of his poem 16 (*Griphus ternarii numeri*) between drinks: *dum bibo et paulo ante quam biberem*.

10. For the sentiment, cf. Mart. 1.107, 8.55, 11.3.

11. Cf. *Herm.* 1.4.

12. Thais was the most celebrated of Athenian courtesans, hence a common name and metonymy in Menander, and so into Latin poetry. Cf. Prop. 2.6.3, 4.5.43–44 (on Menander's play); Ov. *Rem.* 385–86, *Ars* 3.604; Mart. 3.8, 3.11, 4.12, 4.50, 4.84, 5.43, 6.93, 11.101.

13. The phallic wand, wrapped in ivy and tipped with a pinecone, which is the attribute of the horned Dionysus (Bacchus).

14. The mixture of gods and goddesses is interesting and sets up the final joke. Cf. [Ov.] *Her.* 15.23–24 (Sappho to Phaon): "sume fidem et

pharetram — fies manifestus Apollo; / accedant capiti cornua — Bacchus eris." ("Take up the lyre string and quiver, you will be the incarnation of Apollo; add horns to your head and you will be Bacchus.")

15. *Ut . . . sic tibi claudatur*: cf. Ov. *Ibis* 570.

16. For another boy-toy past his sell-by date, cf. 1.29 above. The name Philopappa suggests "a lover of old men" (Greek *pappas* 'father', *pappos* 'grandfather') while Sterconus suggests *stercus* 'shit'. Only the form Philopappos is attested.

17. *qui non intelligor ulli*: cf. Ov. *Trist.* 5.10.37.

18. thirty vintages: cf. Ov. *Met.* 14.146.

19. *offa / proluit*: to the extent that this make sense, it seems to be a combination of Verg. *Aen.* 6.420 (*offa*, the sop to Cerberus) and *Aen.* 1.739 (rinse one's mouth with wine).

20. A reminiscence of Aristotle's story in *Nic. Eth.* 1118a (also *Eud. Eth.* 1231a) of a certain gourmet who prayed to have the throat of a crane to prolong his pleasure in food (named in *Eud. Eth.*, and transferred from there to some mss of *Nic. Eth.*, as Philoxenos son of Eryxis, which means 'Burp,' probably a comedy character: see also Aristoph. *Frogs* 934). Though Beccadelli could have read the *Nicomachean Ethics* in Greek (less likely the *Eud. Eth.*), there had long been a flourishing tradition of translations of *Nic. Eth.* into Latin, beginning in the twelfth century.

21. *rubicundula*: from Juv. 6.425.

22. *patula . . . nare*: cf. Vergil *G.* 1.376; Ov. *Met.* 3.686; Lucan 9.813 (in the pl.).

23. *multivolae*: found only at Cat. 68.128; *edo* (*edonis*) found only in Var. *Men.* 529 = Nonius p. 69, 13 Lindsay. For access to Nonius in the years between 1406 and 1425, see Gordan 1974: 34, 233 n. 5; Sabbadini 1971: 27–28 (31, 35, 58–59).

24. I have not been able to identify this story. For *flagro* (OLD 3b, with acc.), cf. Prop. 1.13.23. Beccadelli apparently construes *nescioquis* with a subjunctive.

25. *laudibus . . . ferens*: OLD, s.v. *fero* 11c.

26. Well-endowed Priapus: see *Herm.* 1.18.4 above. From Cat. 47.4, a phrase Beccadelli may not have fully understood, since Priapus is preeminently the fucker, not the fucked. However, the Greek and Roman pederastic esthetic that the boy should have a small penis seems to have pertained in early modern Italy as well.

27. Cf. Tib. 1.9.75–76: "Huic tamen adcubuit noster puer: hunc ego credam / cum trucibus venerem iungere posse feris" ("Yet our boy has slept with that! I would be willing to believe that he could make love with wild animals"). For Libya, cf. Ov. *Fasti* 5.178: *ipse fuit Libycae praeda cruenta ferae.*

28. *immanem . . . stomachum:* cf. *Priap.* 77.1, where *stomachum,* however, means 'anger.'

29. Aurispa's expertise as sexual pharmacist may lie in his role as the translator of Hippocrates.

30. Cf. Verg. *Ecl.* 10.28, "ecquis erit modus?"

31. *femur:* Here inconsistently of the male sexual organs; see above on 1.5.3, 1.23.4, 1.38.24.

32. Not a poem by Aurispa, but Beccadelli's own "reply" in his voice. For the general theme, cf. Mart. 4.4, 6.93.

33. The case of *Ursae* seems to be some sort of loose dative. *Arrigo* in classical Latin takes *in* or *ad; cupio* can also take the dat. but only in the sense "desire good things for."

34. A protestation of sincerity placed immediately after a poem abusing Ursa. For the tone of protest, cf. Prop. 2.20. Cf. Ov. *Am.* 2.7 and 8 for the wittier situation of protest followed by cause.

35. A combination of Ov. *Am.* 3.6.57: *quid fles et madidos lacrimis corrumpis ocellos* ("Why do you weep and ruin your dripping eyes with tears?") and Juv. 6.8 (on Lesbia): *cuius / turbavit nitidos extinctus passer ocellos* (She whose "shining eyes a dead sparrow clouded.")

36. I.e., I've been writing poetry against you.

37. *mea lux:* Cat. 68.120, etc.

38. A mixture of two clauses: "I love you as much as any one ever has" and "No one can love as much as I."

39. A fine line, undercut by the circumstances.

40. *dissidium* is frequent for *discidium* in mss, probably helped by a folk etymology of *dis-sidium*, as if "sitting apart."

41. *per . . . lacrimas*: cf. Verg. *Aen.* 4.314, 12.56; Ov. *Her.* 10.48.

42. For *femur* = sexual organ, see 1.5.3, 1.23.4, 1.38.24 above. Beccadelli has already mentioned the legs (*crura*) and seems to be moving ever higher.

43. *ah, pereat*: A favorite opening of Prop. 1.6.12, 1.17.3, 2.33b.27.

44. *dissabier* = *dissavior*, attested only at Cic. *Fam.* 16.27.2, a letter of Quintus Cicero.

45. Cf. Ov. *Trist.* 1.1.60: *et facto torqueor ipse meo.*

46. *siste . . . lacrimas*: cf. Ov. *Fasti* 1.367: *siste, puer, lacrimas*; Ov. *Fasti* 1.140 (pentameter): *siste, precor, lacrimas*; also *Herm.* 2.21.1 below.

47. *sospite, sospes ero*: cf. Ov. *Her.* 19.206.

48. *merdivomus*: the nonce-word seems to be Beccadelli's creation; not in Du Cange or the standard dictionaries and corpora of medieval Latin.

49. *femur, pedes*: accusatives of respect.

50. For Oddo, see 1.20 above and the letter to Poggio after Book II. For the defense, cf. Cat. 16, Ov. *Trist.* 2.354, Mart. 1. praef., 1.4.8: *Lasciva est nobis pagina, vita proba* ("My page is dirty; my life is pure").

51. Vergil here is not so much the author of the *Eclogues* (especially 2) as the supposed author of the *Priapea*. For *clausere*, see *Herm.* 2.1.4 above.

52. Biberius from *bibo* 'drink', recalling the comic name Biberius Caldius Mero for Tiberius Claudius Nero, given to the Emperor Tiberius because of his drunkenness: Suet. *Tib.* 42. The poem is a distant recollection of *Anth. Pal.* 7.26 (Antipater of Sidon on the grave of Anacreon).

53. Cf. Ov. *Trist.* 1.1.33.

54. The friend is unidentified: a young man, a soldier, a poet, and a native of (or at least resident in) Pistoia. The date is c. 1424 when the

plague hit Siena and forced the closure of the university. See 1.24, 1.25 above. The *sui* in the title refers to the friend, the *se* to the author.

55. Cf. Ov. *Pont.* 2.2.80. Apollo's maiden is Daphne, who was transformed into the laurel, the symbol of poetic victory.

56. *mollis*: suggestive of sensual pleasures and a frequent epithet of the town. Cf. 2.31.2, likewise applied to Siena; *pestifer aer*: cf. Claud. 15 (*In Gildonem*) 514.

57. Beccadelli gets down to business. For *pat(h)icam . . . puellam*, cf. *Priap.* 25.3, 48.5. Roses: cf. Ov. *Fasti* 5.194: *vernas efflat ab ore rosas* ("who breathes spring roses from her mouth"). This seems to be variation for its own sake.

58. A notable line. For *reddere . . . vices*, cf. Ov. *Am.* 1.6.23, *Met.* 14.36.

59. *mersilis*: the nonce-word again seems to be Beccadelli's creation. Not in Du Cange or standard dictionaries and corpora of medieval Latin. For *vivens in amore iocisve*, cf. Hor. *Ep.* 1.6.66.

60. Tagus: a river running through Spain and emptying into the Atlantic at Lisbon, famed for its gold-bearing sands; cf. Ov. *Am.* 1.15.34, etc.

61. Cf. Ov. *Am.* 3.2.60: *pace loquar Veneris, tu dea maior eris*.

62. Castalia, the spring on Mount Parnassus, sacred to the Muses.

63. The subjunctive is copied from Ov. *Am.* 1.8.105: *Haec si praestiteris*, and *Rem.* 635: *Haec ubi praestiteris*.

64. *thyaso*: Beccadelli's preferred spelling for *thiaso*.

65. Sanseverino: An unidentified member of the rich and powerful Neapolitan clan, possibly Amerigo Sanseverino († 1452), baron of Aquara, made count of Capaccio by King Alfonso, with whom Beccadelli served on a diplomatic mission in 1441 (Laurenza 1912: 8). Cossart (1984: 67) identified him as perhaps Roberto Sanseverino, count of Caiazzo, who would have been seven at the time (1418–87).

66. *pectora*: Beccadelli may have intended this word to mean something like 'talent'.

67. Pierian: of the Muses, associated with Mt. Pierus in Thessaly.

68. Beccadelli jokes by unexpectedly repeating the phrase, since *cum . . . tum* leads the reader to expect a contrast.

69. *transitione:* for the sense, cf. Ov. *Rem.* 616.

70. For the loan of Martial, cf. *Herm.* 1.41.19. For the "foot" joke, see *Herm.* 1.10.7–10 above.

71. The joke is not so much that Mattia Lupi is a pederast, but that he can attract only two other pupils. Cf. Mart. 10.60.

72. *arcana . . . aula:* cf. Stat. *Ach.* 1.750, *Theb.* 3.442. The sense is influenced by the Italian *aula*, schoolroom.

73. The situation — Beccadelli acting as poetic Pandarus between a friend, "Marcus Succinus," and a pretty boy of good family, "Lucius Maura" — makes identification of these names with historical characters unlikely. However, there might be a joke or dig at the expense of someone in the Sozzini family, of whom the most famous was Mariano Sozzini the Elder (1397–1467), eminent canon lawyer, friend of Pope Pius II, and founder of a scholarly dynasty (his great-grandson was Socinus, Lelio Sozzini 1525–62). Mariano was cousin by marriage to Francesco Benzi, father of Caterina and Orietta, for whom Beccadelli wrote the epitaphs (1.24, 1,25, 1.32) and of Socino Benzi (b. 1370, who at 55 may have been too old for the role imagined here). Mariano Sozzini would have been in Siena and twenty-eight years old when Beccadelli initially circulated *The Hermaphrodite*, and Nardi (1974: 13) assumes the epigram is directed at him. His sepulchral statue by Vecchietta is now in the Bargello in Florence. See Corso 1953: 145; Nardi 1974; Coppini 1990: 84.

The poem is odd. Beccadelli seems to be offering his Muse in his friend's behalf, but the final lines seem to be a declaration from Beccadelli himself. Or if there meant merely to be ventriloquising Succinus's words, why cannot Succinus write his own poems?

74. Cf. Ov. *Pont.* 2.8.3.

75. Cf. Ov. *Am.* 3.1.9. For the thought, cf. Ter. *Heaut.* 382.

76. Cf. Ov. *Pont.* 2.9.11.

77. *carmine maius:* Ov. *Pont.* 4.8.71.

78. *fama perennis*: Ov. *Am.* 1.15.7–8.

79. Cf. Plaut. *Curc.* 37–38. The framework is Martial 2.28 (ticking off the boxes for possible sex partners), but the poem somewhat misses the point. For Lentulus, see *Herm.* 1.13 above.

80. A curious anecdote. Mathesilanus is probably the jurist Matthaeus Mathesilanus (variously Matthaesilanus, Mattaselanus, etc.), professor of canon law at Bologna, c. 1398–1410. The cook Martino, whom he buries so shabbily, is not to be confused with the later Maestro Martino, author of *Libro de arte coquinaria*, who was still alive in 1457. See Ballerini 2005: 20. Cooks seem to have been very much in the collegiate mind at the time. A decade later, on Shrove Tuesday 1435 at Pavia, Ugolino Pisani presented the *Repetitio Magistri Zanini coqui*, which features the eponymous chef in a parody of a thesis defence. See Pandolfi and Artese 1965: 287–310.

81. Polyphemus, the man-devouring Cyclops from the *Odyssey*.

82. An adaptation of Mart. 1.39. For Aurispa, see 1.42, 2.7–8.

83. Zoilus of Amphipolis, fl. 4th cent. B.C., cynic philosopher and Homeric critic, proverbial for his harshness (Ov. *Rem.* 366, Martial 11.37.1, Vitr. *praef.*).

84. The situation is not that Catullus is unknown — the unnamed girl has read Catullus — but that, for the space of this poem at least, Beccadelli does not possess a copy of his own. Galeazzo, though a favorite name among the Visconti and later the Sforza, cannot be identified.

85. *mollis* here seems to be used in a more positive sense. Cf. *Herm.* 2.13.7 note.

86. *moriger*: *morigerus* is the proper form. There are usually sexual overtones in its use.

87. *teneros . . . poetas*: Ov. *Rem.* 757.

88. A combination of Ov. *Am.* 3.9.62 and 66. *Doctus* is the standard epithet for Catullus: Ov. *Am.* 3.9.62, [Tib.] 3.6.41, Mart. 8.73.

89. *multa prece*: Hor. *Odes* 4.5.33.

90. A new face for the maligned Mattia Lupi: a sexual omnivore, but one who at least does it in private. The adjective *calidus*, 'clever' is surprising. Balbo is unknown. Cossart (1984: 67 n. 15; cf. Thurn 2002: 314) suggests Pietro Balbi (1399–1479), who is not known to have been in Beccadelli's circle.

91. *efflictim*: a Plautine word, *Cas.* 49, *Merc.* 444.

92. *cruscula*: 'little thighs', i.e. boys (implying intercrural intercourse). A rare diminutive, found only in the glossators (Paul. Fest. p. 53 Lindsay, Prisc. 2.103.20) and restored at Plaut. *Cist.* 408, where it means thin, shriveled, or unpleasing thighs (see *Herm.* 1.9.6 note). The text of *Cistellaria* is damaged and the word shows something of Beccadelli's studies in Plautus. *cauda salax*: cf. Hor. *Sat.* 1.2.45.

93. *adeo . . . plena libido*: cf. *Priap.* 33.3.

94. *popisma = poppysma*. A Greek word, onomatopoeic in origin, meaning "smacking the lips." Beccadelli has run across it in Martial 7.18.11 (where it refers to a woman's vagina making noise during sex) and perhaps Juv. 6.584 (where the context is obscure but not sexual). Beccadelli takes it to mean 'a fuck' or the like. Antonio da Rho defined it as "extrema pars coitus" (Rutherford 2005: 317). It was used correctly (as a verb *poppysare*) by Poliziano 1553: 253. For a full treatment, see Coppini 1984.

95. *digito . . . ligato*: the Italian idiom is *legarsela al dito* 'to tie something to one's finger', i.e., 'never forget' (with overtones of 'never forgive').

96. For *paedico* (anal penetrator, implying, though not limited to, boys) vs. *fututor* (vaginal penetrator), cf. Mart. 2.28.3.

97. Cf. Ov. *Am.* 2.13, a prayer for Corinna to recover after an abortion. Though the classical mistresses do not give birth, the heroines of New Comedy do (Plaut. *Aul.*; Ter. *Andr.* 473, *Ad.* 487 for prayers to Lucina). O'Connor (2001: 121) rightly contrasts Pontano's delicate poem *De amore coniugali* I.10. Lucia is perhaps the lover from *Herm.* 1.29 and 30, or else a filler name. Memmo is unknown (a common Italian name and nothing to do with Mercury the god, *pace* Cossart 1984: 68 n. 18).

98. The goddess of childbirth.

99. This is an astonishing sentence. The phrase *paritura deum* could not help but recall the Virgin Mary (e.g. Paulinus of Nola, *Carm.* 6.153: *Sed paritura Deum*; Arator, *Historia apostolica* 1.66: *nunc tumuit paritura Deum*; altered to *non timuit* in some printings!). The only explanation that I can venture is that Beccadelli is alluding to the scene in Plautus *Amphitruo* 1091–1100, where Alcumena, about to give birth to Hercules, calls on the gods and is granted a painless childbirth. Thus Beccadelli hopes to convince Lucina that Lucia's case is similar, and to hurry to the girl's aid. Even so the phrase seems tasteless and perilously blasphemous.

100. *moratam . . . puellam*: that is, she is blocked, her delivery has been checked or held back.

101. Beccadelli does not specify what Lucia's offence had been and her pregnancy would seem to argue that she has already been *mitis facilisque*.

102. Taken from Ov. *Fasti* 3.258: *ut solvat partus molliter illa suos*.

103. An epigram that does not really make any sense. One expects a contrast in the pentameter: "But if I *speak*, I'm three and four times more miserable."

104. See *Herm.* 2.13.29 above.

105. For *puella* of the Muses, cf. Prop. 3.3.33 (though not so bare a use).

106. *contatus < contor*, only at Pl. *Cas.* 571; *percontor* is the regular form.

107. *Pegasis unda*: the fountain Hippocrene on Mt. Helicon, source of poetic inspiration, opened up by a blow from Pegasus's hoof. The phrase is taken from Mart. 9.58.6.

108. Centius: possibly the Cencio de' Rustici (Cincius Romanus), student of Chrysoloras, secretary in the Roman curia, who features as an interlocutor in Poggio Bracciolini's *De avaritia*. He is named in an anonymous invective as one of those who did not praise Beccadelli's work (see Sabbadini 1891: 2). Cencio, however, hardly needed Beccadelli to write verse for him, so perhaps we have another fictive situation. Contes could be anyone, possibly a member of the Conti family of Padua. Thurn (2002: 314) suggests the jurist Giusto de' Conti (b. 1390), who, however, would be too old for the language of this poem. The tone is hard to read

but it seems to be an attempt to lure Conti back to the city by making him jealous of another boy.

109. *dimidiumque animae*: cf. Hor. *Odes* 1.3.8.

110. Cencio, through the poet, now seems to address the boy at hand.

111. *germane*: Cossart (1984: 57) and O'Connor (2001: 76) take this to be Conti's brother (which would explain the resemblance). However, the lack of pronouns makes it equally likely that "brother" is merely a term of affection (Thurn 2002: 59: "mein Bruder"; the Venice ed. glosses as "mi nate"). For the line, cf. Ov. *Her.* 12.13: *At non te fugiens sine me, germane, reliqui.* (Medea about her brother).

112. The surviving manuscripts of Plautus are all heavily damaged (for example, the end of *Aulularia* is missing; *Casina* and *Cistellaria* are mangled). Only eight plays were known (*Amphitruo-Epidicus*) when Beccadelli composed *The Hermaphrodite*. Not until 1429 did Nicolaus Cusanus return to Rome with manuscripts containing twelve other plays. Beccadelli had borrowed a copy of Plautus from Guarino and never returned it, but that seems to have been c. 1432. See Sabbadini 1915–19: I, 200–2 (nos 658–59), 204 (no. 661): Introduction. However damaging to Beccadelli's image as a scholar, such pawning of manuscripts was not uncommon. For example, Petrarch (*Seniles* 16.1) claimed that his teacher, Convenevole da Prato, borrowed the only surviving copy of Cicero's *De gloria* and then pawned it, thus losing it forever: a canard (Nolhac 1907: I.266, Billanovich 1997: 388) but *ben trovato* about what was credible.

113. *Flandria me genuit*: cf. Vergil's supposed epitaph, "Mantua me genuit" (*Vita Vergilii* 36).

114. *candidiora nive*: cf. Ov. *Am.* 3.7.8.

115. Cf. *Priap.* 27.2: *vibratas docta movere nates*.

116. *rapta basia*: cf. *Herm.* 1.35.2 and Ov. *Am.* 3.7.9: *osculaque inseruit cupida luctantia lingua*.

117. *nox erat et*: A favorite phrase of many authors: Verg. *Aen.* 3.147, 4.522, 8.26; Ov. *Am.* 3.5.1, *Fasti* 1.421, 2.792, 6.673, *Pont.* 3.3.5; Hor. *Epod.* 15.1; Prop. 3.15.26; Val. Fl. 3.33; Claud. 24.453. *iuvenum . . . caterva*: cf. Verg. *Aen.* 1.497.

118. *non satiata*: cf. Juv. 6.130 *nondum satiata*. *vices*: for the meaning, cf. Tib. 1.9.63–64: *Illa nulla queat melius consumere noctem / aut operum varias disposuisse vices*.

119. Cf. Ter. *Heaut.* 234: *nil iam praeter pretium dulcest*.

120. On the plague in Siena in 1424, see above on 1.24, 1.25, 1.30, 1.32, 2.13.

121. *quando erit ut*: Ov. *Her.* 7.19, 13.117.

122. Despite the proximity of 2.30, the change of tone is so marked that it is likely that the Nichina here is not the famous whore from Flanders, but rather Nichina, another daughter of Francesco Benzi, whose sisters Caterina and Orietta are honored in 1.24, 1.25, 1.32. She died of the plague on 25 August 1424, seven months after her sisters, which may account for the poem's appearance in Book II. See Corso 1953: 151; Coppini 1990: lxxxiv. The arrangement of poems seems very clumsy.

123. *sitque tuo cineri non onerosa silex*: cf. Ov. *Am.* 3.9.68: *et sit humus cineri non onerosa tuo*.

124. *lyricis . . . sonis*: cf. Ov. *Fasti* 2.94.

125. *Latiis . . . oris*: cf. Stat. *Silv.* 4.4.22.

126. *sanguine clarus avito*: cf. Prop. 2.19.23–24: *sanguine avito / nobilis*.

127. Cf. *Herm.* 2.22.8 above.

128. A curious piece. It may be what it claims to be, or it may be another act of ventriloquising, giving Beccadelli a chance to show off. But line 21 is hard to bear, no matter who wrote it. Lucio Maura is presumably to be thought of as the pretty boy of 2.17–18, who seems to have failed to keep a rendezvous with one of Beccadelli's pupils, who threatens Maura with poetic vengeance from his master. O'Connor's hypothesis (2001: 125) that the title "would indicate that this poem is a later insertion or else belongs to an updated edition of Hermaphroditus, after Panormita had garnered great fame and notoriety," cannot be maintained, since the poem is already found in the manuscripts (M, Ve) of what Coppini calls the "prima fase redazionale" (see Coppini 1990: xcviii–cxiii).

129. Cf. Ov. *Her.* 3.98, Prop. 2.22.44.

130. *āĕrĕā* = *aeria*. For *aërea . . . arce*, cf. Verg. *Aen.* 3.291.

131. *Paganico . . . solo*. Thurn 2002: 315, is probably right to suggest that this is not just a periphrasis for "countryside," but refers to the area of Paganico (Civitella Paganico), roughly midway between Siena and Grosseto. Its principal town is Civitella Marittima, a fortified Sienese hill town which well deserves to be called "aërea arce."

132. Cf. Verg. *Aen.* 1.543: *deos memores fandi atque nefandi.*

133. *O levior foliis, avium ventosior alis*: a combination of Ov. *Her.* 5.109: *tu levior foliis*, with Ov. *Am.* 2.9.49 (to Cupid): *tu levis es multoque tuis ventosior alis* and Verg. *Georg.* 4.473: *quam multa in foliis avium se milia condunt.*

134. *Si te, Maura, iuvat me fallere, falle; sed illum*: cf. Ov. *Ars* 1.310: *Sive virum mavis fallere, falle viro!*

135. *indigus* usually with the gen.; for abl., cf. Lucr. 5. 223: *indigus omni / vitali auxilio.*

136. Cf. Hor. *Ep.* 1.20 (Horace's book as a pretty boy slave about to be put out for sale) and the more direct model, Mart. 3.2.

137. *quo fugis*: cf. Verg. *Aen.* 10.649, Prop. 2.30A.1. *Catones*: Marcus Porcius Cato (234–149 B.C., censor in 184), proverbial as a disapproving spoil-sport. For the generalizing plural and the adj. *rigidus*, cf. Martial 10.20.21: *Tunc me vel rigidi legant Catones.*

138. The sequence of thought is imperfect and implicit. Contrast Mart. 3.2.1–5: "Cuius vis fieri, libelle, munus? / Festina tibi vindicem parare, / ne nigram cito raptus in culinam / cordylas madida tegas papyro / vel turis piperisve sis cucullus." ("Whose present do you want to become, book? Hasten to get yourself a protector, lest you're quickly snatched away into the black kitchen and made to cover sardines with your wet paper or become a hood for incense or pepper"). For similar observations about books being recycled as waste paper, cf. Cat. 95.8, Hor. *Ep.* 2.1.269–70, Pers. 1.43, Mart. 4.86, 13.1.1–2, Sidon. 9.320.

139. Cf. Ov. *Trist.* 4.5.11–12.

140. The curious name *Lelphus* may be meant to recall Francesco Filelfo (1398–1481), while Luscus may point to Antonio Loschi (Antonius Luscus, c. 1368–1441). Neither suggestion is convincing, since Filelfo (who

was in Constantinople from 1420 to 1427) was a fan of Beccadelli's and *The Hermaphrodite*, and did not break with him until Cosimo's exile in 1433 (see Sabbadini 1891: 20–21), and Loschi was the one who introduced Poggio to *The Hermaphrodite*. This poem, too, belongs to the first phase of *The Hermaphrodite* (contra the suggestions by O'Connor 2001: 126–27 and Thurn 2002: 315), though Beccadelli later made some corrections to all the copies he could find, such as changing the end of v. 21 from the unmetrical *fŏdis* to *tundis*. See Beccadelli's letter to Giovanni Toscanella correctly dated to 1426 (Ravenna, Biblioteca Classense MS 349, fol. 169v; Sabbadini 1903: 109; Coppini 1990: cxxviii–cxxix).

141. The line is presumably meant to be scanned *ălĭquāndŏ dŏmĭnūs*, with the false quantity explained in the next verse. The mispronunciation *domĭnus* was a standard example of a "barbarism": see Murethach *In Donati artem maiorem*, ed. Löfstedt 1977: 200; *Ars Laureshamensis*, ed. Löfstedt 1977a: 196; Sedulius Scotus *In Donati artem maiorem*, ed. Löfstedt 1977b: 331; Jacques de Dinant *Breviloquium*, ed. Wilmart 1933: 137; Giovanni del Virgilio *De figuris*, ed. Alessio 1981: 201. For *ălĭquāndŏ*, see Mart. 5.50.8, 10.46.1, 2; Juv. 3.184, etc.

142. The thought, clumsily expressed, is that Lelfo is too cheap even to buy food for himself, so he lives off his own stored excrement, and too cheap to buy drink, so he never needs to urinate. Beccadelli repeats the idea in a poem cited by Coppini 1990: xxx, liv, 133 (in the app. crit.; found in three mss.: Ox, 116v; M₄, 62r; Udine, Bibl. Com. MS 2686, 4v):

> In Iacobum Ianuensem avarum
> Audio quod Iacobus nec mingit nec cacat olim.
> Cur facit hoc Iacobus? Ne bibat aut comedat.
> (Against the miser Giacomo of Genoa
> I hear Giacomo never pisses or shits.
> Why does Giacomo do this? So that he doesn't drink or eat.)

Something similar (and a phrase) is found in Mart. 1.92.11, where Mamurianus is too poor apparently to eat anything but the smell of a kitchen, and so never shits (*non culum, neque enim est culus, qui non cacat olim*): see also Cat. 23.20–24 for someone so dry that he only shits ten times a year.

143. *ex(s)titit*: commonly used by the early humanists for *erat*, etc.; *dira Celaeno*: Verg. *Aen.* 3.211 713; also 3.245, 365: one of the harpies encountered by Aeneas.

144. *ditione* = *dicione*.

145. *ocius affectem*: a periphrasis for *malim*. The mill was a common place of punishment for slaves in Roman comedy.

146. Cf. Ov. *Met.* 1.400: *quis hoc credat, nisi sit pro teste vetustas?* Probably closest to what Beccadelli meant to say.

147. *cornipedi*: Verg. *Aen.* 7.779, Ov. *Ars* 1.280, usually a noble adjective for *equus*. Beccadelli probably meant to have a contrast between the well-fed *equus* and this broken-down *caballus* (as in verse 1 vs. 3), but reuses *caballus* as a synonym for 'horse', under the influence of Italian *cavallo*.

148. *mihi vae misero*: a favorite phrase in Plautus (*vae misero mihi* or *vae mihi misero*): *Capt.* 945, *Epid.* 50, *Merc.* 181, 217, 759, 792, etc.

149. *sim licet informis*: cf. Ov. *Am.* 2.17.3: *sim licet infamis. mage malim*: not used in classical Latin, since *malo < magis volo*, nor is *malo* construed with *quam velim*.

150. *rationis inops et mentis egenus*: a combination of *rationis inops* (Stat. *Theb.* 1.373) with *mentis inops* (a favorite phrase of Ov. *Her.* 15.139; *Ars* 1.465, 3.684; *Rem.* 127; *Met.* 2.200, 6.37; *Fasti* 4.457) and *rationis egentem* (Verg. *Aen.* 8.299; Ov. *Met.* 15.150; Mart. 6.257).

151. *efferitate*: used by Cic. *Tusc.* 2.20, though not in the apparently concrete sense that Beccadelli has here.

152. Cf. Cat. 97.1–2. "Non (ita me di ament) quicquam referre putavi, / utrumne os an culum olfacerem Aemilio" ("God help me, I didn't think it made any difference whether I smelled Aemilius's mouth or his asshole"). *dubius . . . an . . . loquitur*: this should be a subjunctive in an indirect question.

153. *fit mihi de risu nausea saepe suo*: cf. Ov. *Rem.* 356: *Non semel hinc stomacho nausea facta meo est.*

154. *plura equidem . . . sed*: properly *plura quidem . . . sed*; an Ovidian construction: *Her.* 3.1.153, *Met.* 13.497, *Trist.* 1.1.23.

155. *lingua . . . debilitata*: cf. Lucr. 6.1149–50.

156. *procul ite*: Martial 10.72.5; Stat. *Silv.* 1.6.2, 3.3.13.

157. *quo ruitis*: Verg. *Aen.* 12.313; Ov. *Her.* 13.130–31, *Met.* 9.429, *Fasti* 2.225, always of rushing away. Beccadelli probably means to say, "Why are you hurrying?"; *pellis et ossa*: cf. *ossa ac (atque) pellis*: Plaut. *Aul.* 564, *Capt.* 135. Used by Cervantes to describe Rocinante (*Don Quixote*, Ch. 1).

158. Beccadelli's main model was Ov. *Trist.* 3.1. For similar poems of an author's farewell to his book, see the models in Hor. *Ep.* 1.20, Ov. *Trist.* 1.1, *Pont.* 4.5, Martial 1.3, 1.70, 3.4, 3.5, 7.84, 7.97, 9.66, 10.20, 12.2, 12.5. The trope was used by Chaucer ("Go, litel boke, go, litel myn tragedye." *Troilus and Criseyde*, V.1786), and later by, for example, Ramusius Ariminensis (Girolamo Ramusio of Rimini), also for an erotic collection (Mercier 1791: 95–96), and Giovanni Gioviano Pontano (*Parthenopeus* 1.1); see O'Connor 2001: 127.

159. *i, fuge*: Mart. 1.3.12.

160. *parve liber*: Mart. 1.3.2, 3.5.2; Ov. *Trist.* 1.1.1.

161. *Est locus*: a favorite epic line opening, e.g. Verg. *Aen.* 1.530 = 3.163; cf. esp. Ov. *Her.* 16.53: *est locus in mediis nemorosae vallibus Idae*. This passes into Dante (*luogo è, loco è: Inf.* 17.1, 20.67, 24.127; *Purg.* 7.28), Milton (*PL* 9.69), etc.

162. *quove*: Beccadelli has taken the Lucretian form *quo-ve* (for *et quo*) probably from Vergil (*A.* 1.369, 3.88, 5.28, 9.377; also Ov. *Met.* 1.610, 3.455, etc.), where the *quo* is always an interrogative (direct or indirect), and used it for *quo*, the relative.

163. *Reparatae*: The ancient church of Santa Reparata had been completely pulled down by 1375 and incorporated into the Duomo (Basilica di Santa Maria del Fiore) though the name lingered on (e.g. Albertini 1510: a.iii). In 1425, the nave was finished, but Brunelleschi's dome was still under construction and not completed until 1436. For *alta palatia* see Ov. *Trist.* 1.1.69.

164. *agnigeri splendida templa dei*: cf. Ov. *Trist.* 3.1.60: *ducor ad intonsi candida templa dei* (that is Apollo on the Palatine). *Agniger* appears to be Beccadelli's own creation. I.e., the Baptistery of San Giovanni (John the Baptist), where in 1425 Ghiberti had finished the North Doors and had just received the new commission for the East Doors.

165. *hic fueris*, etc.: fairly rocky Latin, but its meaning is clear: "When you have arrived there"; *dextram teneas* for *tene iter in dextram* or the like, modeled on Ov. *Trist.* 3.1.31: *Inde petens dextram*.

166. *vetus . . . forum*. The Foro Vecchio or Mercato Vecchio, site of the original Roman forum and later the Ghetto (1570), which was destroyed in 1890 to make way for the banal Piazza della Repubblica. Beccadelli's directions (borrowed from Ovid's tour of Rome) are unclear: if one is going from the Duomo to the Baptistery (west), one turns *left* (south) down Via Roma to get to the Piazza della Repubblica. The market and its prostitutes were famous. See Mazzi 1991: 249–54; Rocke 1996: 136; Trexler 1981: 1003.

Landino has a verse description of the market, *Xandra* 2.29.7–12 (ed. Perosa 1939: 80: addressing his Muse):

> Exhinc sericeas intervectere tabernas,
> Et Mercatorum compita pulchra Fori.
> Neve Malum post haec Callem transire timebis,
> Namque habet hic falsi nomina vana metus;
> Neve iter inflectes, quamvis sit propter eundum
> Lustra Lupae: fugit hanc nulla matrona viam.

(From here [the Ponte Vecchio], you will be borne in among the silk tents and the lovely cross-roads of the Forum of the Merchants. Nor after this will you fear to cross the Via Calimala ["Bad Alley"; on the east side of the piazza], for it only has an empty name from a false fear, nor will you change your path, even though you have to go through the dens of vice; no married woman avoids this road.")

The most vivid description is Antonio Pucci's "Le proprietà di Mercato Vecchio," which mentions the prostitutes (88–90):

E meretrici vi sono e ruffiani,
battifancelli, zanaiuoli e gaioffi
e i tignosi e scabbiosi cattani.

(And courtesans are there and ruffians, boy-bangers, boy-toys, and louts,
and lousy and scabrous lordlings.) (*battifancelli* = *batti-fanciulli* 'boy-beat-
ers': Sapegno 1952: 406, glosses *maestri, capi-bottega*, i.e. masters in charge
of apprentices; however, the *Tesoro della Lingua Italiana delle Origini* [online
at http://tlio.ovi.cnr.it] has, I think, a better guess as *pederasta*. *zanaiuoli*
is glossed by Sapegno 1952: 406 as 'salarati che portano i cibi a domicilio
nelle ceste'. However, Florio 1611: 613 glosses: "Zanaiuólo, as Záne, as
Zannuolo" (from Zane = Gianni), and glosses: "Zannuólo, a silly Iohn,
a foolish Iacke. Also a wanton darling or dilling.").

For *fesse*, cf. Ov. *Trist.* 3.1.2.

167. *meta viae*: cf. *meta viarum*, Verg. *Aen.* 3.714, 8.594. *geniale lupanar*:
this famous brothel was a municipal utility established in 1403 under the
control of the office of the *Onestà*. See Trexler 1981: 1003; Bracket 1993:
285–287 (citing Beccadelli), 291. Beccadelli's impression of foreign prosti-
tutes is confirmed by the register of 76 women made in 1436, with 26
from the Low Countries, and 16 from Germany.

168. *odore*: cf. Juv. 6.132, *foeda lupanaris tulit ad pulvinar odorem*. "filthy
[Messalina] bore the stench of the brothel to the imperial couch."

169. Cf. *Herm.* 2.30.12 above, note on Nichina. *illa vel illa*: an Ovidian
construction: *Am.* 1.8.84 (of a brothel), *Ars* 1.225, *Fasti* 5.187, *Her.* 15.25;
Martial 7.10.1.

170. Clodia: a suitably classical name. *mammis . . . pictis*: probably refer-
ring to the use of rouge on the nipples (Culiano 1987: 210; Garland 1957:
71), but the topos may be literary; cf. Juv. 6.122–23 (of Messalina): *papillis
. . . auratis*.

171. Galla: perhaps to indicate that she is from France, but a common
filler name in Martial. *iniiciet nullo tacta rubore manus*: cf. Ov. *Am.* 1.4.6,
iniciet collo, cum volet, ille manum?

172. *crissatrix*: *crīsāre* is for a woman to move, wriggle, or buck her hips
during intercourse. See Juv. 6.322, *Priap.* 19.4, Mart. 10.68.10, 14.203.1;

Ps.-Acro *Hor. Sat.* 2.7.50. Adams 1990: 136–37. *Cris(s)atrix* is a new coinage after *fellatrix*. Pīthō (Peithō): the Greek goddess "Persuasion," used by Ovid of a girlfriend at *Am.* 3.7.23.

173. *Ursa*: see 1.4, 1.5, 1.8, 1.21, 1.27, 2.7–10.

174. *vicus / proximus, occiso de bove nomen habens*: the line is modeled on Ov. *Fasti* 1.582: *hic ubi pars Urbis de bove nomen habet* (the Forum Boarium in Rome). Though not, I think, noticed before, Beccadelli is referring to the vanished Chiasso dei Buoi (Oxen Alley), another of the officially designated areas for prostitution; see Brackett 1993: 296; Trexler 1981: 1003; Rocke 1996: 154. Though Chiasso dei Buoi has been identified as the modern Via Teatina (e.g. Mazzi 1991: 250; Cesati 2003: 677), it ran instead slightly south of the modern Via del Giglio and terminated at the north-east corner of San Lorenzo. It was destroyed for the Capella dei Principi (the Medici chapels) but a portion is still preserved in the Piazza di Madonna degli Aldobrandini. For the brilliant detective work involved in locating the street, see Saalman 1985. The other area for prostitution most often mentioned in Florentine accounts was the Malacucina, a street slightly to the north of the Mercato Vecchio, parallel to the eastern end of the modern Via de' Tosinghi.

175. *salutatum*: a supine with *transmitto* (rather than *eo, venio*) is not standard usage (but with *occurro*, see Val. Max. 5.1.ext. 3). For Thais, see 2.2.4.

176. Cf. Cat. 1.

177. For the place of this letter in Beccadelli's defense, see O'Connor 1997: 997–1000.

178. For Loschi, see Letter from Poggio to Beccadelli above. His best known work of poetry was his tragedy *Achilles*.

179. Alluding to Horace, *Ars Poetica* 143 on the good poet and translator: *non fumum ex fulgore, sed ex fumo dare lucem / cogitat*, "He plans not to make smoke from a flash but to bring light out of the smoke."

180. The scurrilous, bow-legged soldier in the *Iliad*.

181. *inter manus adhuc versare*: cf. Cic. *Fam.* 8.3.3.

182. Plato, of course, says nothing of the sort. This seems to be a somewhat garbled version of Augustine's arguments in the *City of God* 8 (esp. ch. 4–5); Beccadelli may also have taken some of this from Apuleius *De deo Socratis* (esp. 14–20) on *daimones*. As for angels, the word in a supernatural sense never occurs in Plato, though Beccadelli may have taken this idea, too, from Augustine (*City of God* 8.24 and 25: *Hi enim diis bonis, quos sanctos angelos nos vocamus . . .* ; and his comments on the overlap of the words among the Platonists in 9.19).

183. For Plato's erotic epigrams to Aster, Alexis, Phaedrus, and Dio of Syracuse, see Diogenes Laertius 3.29–32 (*Greek Anthology* 5.77–79, 7.99–100, 7.110, 7.669–70). This Latin version of an epigram attributed to Plato (*Greek Anthology* 5.78 and Diogenes Laertius 3.32) is taken from Aulus Gellius 19.11 (also found in Macrobius *Sat.* 2.2, but the text of Macrobius had less circulation in the Quattrocento).

184. E.g. frag. 25 (West) from Plutarch *Amatorius* 751c. This whole passage is taken from a passage in Apuleius's *Apologia* 9, where the author gives a list of those eminent personages who are supposed to have written erotic verse to boys, calling Solon *serium virum et philosophum*.

185. *Diogenes the Cynic, Zeno the Stoic*: taken from Apuleius, who does not attribute erotic verse to the philosophers. *Theium*: Beccadelli's misunderstanding (as if a proper name) for Apuleius's *Teius quidam* "a certain man from Teos," a periphrasis for Anacreon. *Lacedaemonium*: likewise a misunderstanding. The "Lacedaemonian (Spartan)" is Alcman. Callimachus may be Beccadelli's guess for what the manuscript of Apuleius gives as *civis* ('the citizen'), an error for *C(e)ius*, the man of Ceos, i.e., Simonides. Beccadelli would know of Callimachus as a love poet mostly from mentions in the Latin poets, e.g., Ov. *Ars* 3.329, *Rem.* 759–60, etc. He is also adduced by Vegio (Appendix, XIII.11). Sappho too is mentioned by Apuleius (*etiam mulier Lesbia*). Beccadelli knew her only through [Ov.] *Heroides* 15, which was taken as a genuine work of Sappho by some (see O'Connor 1997: 999 n. 31; Ludwig 1989: 170 n. 35). His description recasts Apuleius's comments: *lascive illa quidem tantaque gratia, ut nobis insolentiam linguae suae dulcedine carminum commendet.* Nestor and Priam are used as types for very old men, as in *Priapea* 76.

186. *Ars Poetica* 9–10: *pictoribus atque poetis / quidlibet audendi semper fuit aequa potestas.* "To painters and poets there has always been granted the power to dare whatever they wish."

187. *Cat.* 16.5–9, as cited by Guarino in the Prefatory Letter. Shorter citations of these famous lines are also found at Pliny *Ep.* 4.14.5 and Apul. *Apol.* 11.2.

188. 1.35.3–5. Cf. *Herm.* 1.23.

189. For Oddo, see *Herm.* 1.20, 2.11; Appendix, II.9 (Poggio's reply to this letter).

190. Apuleius, cited above. The quotes come from *Apologia* 11.16–19.

191. Apul. *Apol.* 11.3.

192. Seneca's Stoicism in his *Moral Letters* and *Moral Essays* were simply too appealing to be left to a pagan. A set of fourteen letters between him and St. Paul were forged, leading both St. Jerome (*Vir. Ill.* 12, "in catalogo sanctorum") and St. Augustine (*Ep.* 153.14) to claim Seneca as a Christian. Dante knew better and consigned him to the first circle of Limbo with the other virtuous pagans (*Inf.* 4.141). For the tradition, see Sevenster 1961 (Berry 2002 piously believes the story may be true).

193. Seneca is included in the list at Pliny *Ep.* 5.3.5.

194. Forberg (1908: xxxiv) tentatively identified him as San Giovanni da Capestrano (1386–1456), but a more likely candidate is San Bernardino of Siena (1380–1444), who preached for seven weeks solid in Siena in 1425 and devoted close attention to sodomy (see introduction). Beccadelli makes a slight apology for using the classical *praedicatio* ('announcement', 'proclamation') to express 'sermons', *prediche* in Italian.

195. Juv. 1.6. A typical title for a tragedy, which is so long that the author has to continue writing on the back side of the long papyrus roll.

196. The long quote from *Ep.* 5.3.5 becomes one of the proof texts. Beccadelli omits Catulus from Pliny's list. Ennius and Accius were mere names to Beccadelli; the authors are preserved only indirectly in quotation. Beccadelli's manuscript of Pliny apparently read "Maevium" for the correct "Memmium." The quote continues with imperial examples.

197. Taken from Sidonius Apollinaris, *Ep. 8.11.7*: "praeterea quod ad epigrammata spectat, non copia sed acumine placens."

198. Mart. 1.107.5–6.

199. *consilii fuit*: more properly, *consilium fuit*. *Consilii* + *esse* means "is a matter of debate, a judgment call."

200. Malpigli (c. 1375–late 1420s), Italian poet, jurist in Bologna. For unpublished correspondence between him and Beccadelli at this time, see L. Quaquarelli's life of him in the *Dizionario biografico degli italiani*, s.v.

201. *corculum*: a Plautine term of endearment (e.g. *Casina* 837).

202. Source: Cinquini and Valentini 1907: 25 from Brescia, Biblioteca Civica Queriniana 32 (C VII 1), f. 194; Arnaldi et al. 1964: 22–25; O'Connor 1997: 1004–5. See Introduction: a rather sad ending.

203. *Rhŏdī*: The reference is somewhat obscure. Rhŏdos, the island, scans short in all classical and most Renaissance poets (but Antonio Baratella, *Polydoreis* I.771: *Rhōdius heros*). Fubini (1961) assumed that it indicated *Rhōdus*, Beccadelli's usual form for Antonio da Rho in his invective poetry: "intorno al 1435 il Panormita, evidentemente alla ricerca di nuovi favori, sentisse il bisogno di scusarsi presso Cosimo de' Medici e il card. Giordano Orsini delle offese recate a 'Rhodi famam nomenque celebre'." Fubini was followed in this reading by Contini 1995: 19 and Guidi 2007: 240. However, Fubini has chopped off the beginning of the next line and the parallelism of *Rhodi* and *Parnasi* make it clear that Beccadelli was thinking of a trope for poetry (also not *Parnasi* for *Parnasii* with *Rhodi*, since Beccadelli used *Parnaseus*: *Herm.* 2.14.7, and the form is always open). Arnaldi et al. (1964: 24) and O'Connor (1997: 1005, 2001: 13) rightly take it as the island. Rhodes, however, is not especially connected with poetry. Arnaldi et al. (1964: 24) write "Rodi era famosa per il suo Colosso, che rappresentava Febo. Qui dunque la « fama di Rodi » è Apollo, dio della poesia." The Colossus was actually of Helios, but Beccadelli may have thought it made no difference.

APPENDIX: ASSOCIATED LETTERS AND POEMS

1. Source: Sabbadini 1915–19: I, 507–8 (no. 347). Rewritten by Beccadelli for *Epistolae Campanae* 4.6; Beccadelli 1553: 75r–76r = 1746: 176–77. Dated by Sabbadini to February 1426. This is Beccadelli's reply to the letter from Guarino that he used as the preface to Book I of *The Hermaphrodite*.

2. Horace, *Ars Poetica* 371, of flatterers. An allusion to Aesop's fable of the fox who by praising the crow's voice, got it to drop the cheese it held in its beak.

3. *mentem in manibus*: not a classical Latin expression but based on the Italian "avere il cuore in mano."

4. Cf. Plut. *Solon* 21.3: "he placed deceit and compulsion, gratification and affliction, in one and the same category, believing that both alike were able to pervert a man's reason."

5. Source: Poggio 1538: 353–55 = 1832: 180–85 (Book 2.42); Harth 1982: 55–58 (Book 2.4). Poggio wrote to Beccadelli on 2 February 1426 (letter after Book I) and Beccadelli replied around April of the same year (letter after Book II). Beccadelli did not include or circulate this reply from Poggio of perhaps April/May; see Sabbadini 1891: 21. Harth 1982: 55 dates the letter to July 1426.

6. Attributed to Pythagoras by Diogenes Laertius, 8.22.

7. Poggio is on weak ground here, since Beccadelli's list is taken straight from Pliny *Ep.* 5.3.5. In fact, Cicero's poem to his freedman Tiro was notorious (Pliny *Ep.* 7.4), and he wrote a letter on how to use obscenities indirectly (*Fam.* 9.22; analyzed by Richlin 1992: 18–26).

8. For Varro and the others, see Beccadelli's letter to Poggio above. Marcus Terentius Varro (116–27 BC), scholar and poet, was the author of the *Res rusticae*, and *De lingua Latina*, which would have been known to Beccadelli and Poggio, but also of the racy *Menippean Satires*, which they might have heard about from Cic. *Acad.* 1.8–9, but which survived only in scattered quotations.

9. Poggio picks up Beccadelli's appeal to the freedom of painters (from Horace, *A.P.* 9–10).

10. Seneca *De tranquillitate animi* 17.4, 17.9, who also cites the example of Socrates.

11. See above for Beccadelli's quotation of the epigrams ascribed to Plato. Not in fact from a comedy (though we are told by Diogenes Laertius 3.5 that Plato wrote tragedies as a youth but burnt them when met Socrates). Poggio is thinking of the Old Comedy writer, Plato Comicus, who was not always distinguished from the philosopher.

12. Interesting early testimony about attitudes and understanding of ancient pederasty.

13. Cf. Cic. *Orator* 87: "quorum [*sales*, 'wit'] duo genera sunt, unum facetiarum, alterum dicacitatis"; cf. also *De oratore* 2.244 and *Brutus* 143.

14. Terence *Adelph.* 676–77: "Ridiculum: adversumne illum causam dicerem / cui veneram advocatus?"

15. Poggio puns on Oddo and *odium*. See above.

16. Source: *Epistolae Gallicae* 2.23 = 1553: 38r–39r = 1746: 107–8. Part in Sabbadini 1891: 25; see also Sabbadini 1916: 11. On Capra, archbishop of Milan († 1434), see D. Girgensohn's life in *DBI*.

17. *pro virili*: a Renaissance Latin development of classical *pro virili parte* or *portione*, 'as far as I can'.

18. *ad postremos cineres*: a non-classical Beccadellian phrase, cf. *Liber rerum gestarum Ferdinandi Regis* (Resta 1968: 73).

19. Citing again Cat. 16.5–6; see Prefatory Letter from Guarino and Letter from Poggio to Beccadelli after Book I.

20. Again citing the proverb "a pig teaching Minerva"; see Letter from Poggio to Beccadelli.

21. For the phrase *desidiae indormientem*, see Plin. *Ep.* 1.2.3.

22. Source: Sabbadini 1891: 25–26; see also Sabbadini 1916: 10.

23. Scipio Aemilianus (Scipio Africanus the Younger): his friendship with Laelius (Gaius Laelius Sapiens) is the subject of Cicero's *De amicitia*.

24. A reminiscence of Eur. *Andromache* 376–77, "There is nothing private for friends, those who are truly friends, but their possessions are held in common." A commonplace in the form κοινὰ τὰ τῶν φίλων (e.g. Plato *Lysis* 207c, *Rep.* 424a) and variously attributed to Pythagoras or Timaeus; transmitted in Latin by Cicero (*Off.* 1.51, "amicorum esse communia omnia") and in Italian by Dante (*Convivio* 4.1, "in greco proverbio è detto 'De li amici essere deono tutte le cose comuni'.").

25. *Gl(a)ebae adscripti* are, in the phrase of medieval feudal law, men bound to the soil, peasants or serfs.

26. *quoad ocius quivi:* for the regular *quoad potui*, etc.

27. Sabbadini (1916: 11) took the *princeps* as the Duke of Milan, Filippo Maria Visconti, but he is not mentioned in the present exchange of letters and it seems better to take it as referring to the prince of the church, Capra.

28. Aesop (Perry 472): the jackdaw dresses up in a few peacock feathers, but is chased away by the real peacocks. So Robert Greene on Shakespeare: "There is an upstart crow beautified with our feathers" (*Groatsworth of Wit*).

29. *animi* is a loose locative gen., cf. [Caes.] *Bellum Alexandrinum* 56.2; *compereris:* the verb is misused, since *comperio* means 'discover, ascertain' used of facts, knowledge, etc. Beccadelli may have intended some form of *comparo*, 'muster, collect, get'.

30. Presumably from one of Beccadelli's own poems now lost.

31. *Phaedrus* 245a, more or less, but Beccadelli is likely to have taken it from the paraphrase in Seneca *De tranquillitate animi* 19: "Nam sive Graeco poetae credimus 'aliquando et insanire iucundum est', sive Platoni 'frustra poeticas fores compos sui pepulit'." Beccadelli uses this proof text again in his letter to Antonio da Rho (see App. VII below).

32. The monk Ambrogio Traversari (1386–1439), later the prior general of the Camaldolese order.

33. The humanist Giovanni Toscanella (d. 1448/9), a pupil and friend of Guarino's in Florence; see Gualdo 1970, distinguishing the scholar from George of Trebizond's fractious neighbor.

34. Leonardo Bruni of Arezzo (c. 1370–1444), the future chancellor of Florence.

35. We are uncertain about the circumstances that prompted Lamola to leave Bologna for Milan in November 1426 where he encountered Capra (Sabbadini 1910b: 25).

36. Source: Sabbadini 1891: 27. For Giacomo Bracelli (died c. 1466), humanist, geographer, and chancellor of Genoa, see Braggio 1890, Andriani 1924, Grayson 1971.

37. Cic. *Pro Plancio* 95. Beccadelli's text of Cicero had *aram* (listed in apparatuses as a conjecture of Dobree, †1825) for the accepted vulgate *me arcem facere e cloaca*, "make a citadel out of a sewer." Beccadelli has apparently thanked Giacomo profusely for his praises. The phrase was proverbial for the exaggeration of minor services.

38. Neither the ms *quone* or Sabbadini's emendation *quove* is satisfactory. Better is *<et> quo me*; *dives* is construed with abl. and gen. For the thought, cf. Hor. *Odes* 4.8.4–5: "neque tu pessuma munerum / ferres, divite me scilicet artium" ("Nor would you have the worst of gifts — provided, of course, I were rich in works of art . . ."). A reversal of Ov. *Am.* 1.8.25: "Non ego, te facta divite, pauper ero."

39. Anonymous. Source: Rutherford 2005: 265–68 (new edition from the manuscripts; cf. Sommer 1997: 251–54, a defective text). Beccadelli blamed Rho; Rho claimed Beccadelli (or a follower) wrote it himself, a not completely impossible charge.

40. *marisca*: A type of large inferior fig; used of hemorrhoids by Juv. 2.13; used by Mart. 12.96.9 for the less desirable anus of woman compared to the succulent Chian fig of a boy.

41. *Tollite!* Not "Away with such a fellow from the earth," as one might think. Cf. 35.

42. *Ticinum* is the old Latin name of Pavia. By a common poetic periphrasis, Milan is called *anguigeram*, the snake-bearing city, from the snake on the Visconti coat of arms.

43. I have punctuated the sentence thus to try and make some sense of it. If the text is sound, *Nec pigeat* cannot control any part of the rest of the

sentence and appears to be used absolutely (e.g. Ov. *Her.* 9.138; Petrarch *Buc.* 7.15); *pudica* then is ironic, explained by the following *nam*.

44. The meaning is somewhat unclear.

45. Sts. Quirico and Giulitta were a popular mother and son pair in Lombardy. The reference may be very specific. In 1422, the College of the Apothecaries commissioned Michelino da Besozzo to create a set of windows about St. Giulitta and her son Quirico to celebrate the triumphal entrance of Duke Filippo Maria Visconti into the Duomo of Milan.

46. The various prostitutes of *Herm.* 2.37. That the whorehouse is in Florence and this poem addresses Milan is the least of the poem's inconsistencies. The better manuscripts of this poem read *Pytho* for Beccadelli's *P(e)itho* in 2.37 but fluctuations between *ei, i,* and *y* are too common to be any indication.

47. *mores . . . suos* refers to *Beccadelli's* morals, by the indifference to the *suus/eius* distinction common with the early humanists.

48. *spintria:* one of Tiberius's dedicated little band of sexual athletes, Suet. *Tib.* 43.1. See also Tac. *Ann.* 6.1, Petr. 113.11. The name is derived from sphincter.

49. Taken from Juv. 6.121 on the old curtain or blanket (*cento*) that Messallina used in the brothel.

50. Source: Sabbadini 1910b: 7–8; Rutherford 2005: 248–55, who dates the reply to 1431.

51. Unknown. One suspects that this is one of Rho's own verses, referring to a famous line of Naevius: *Laetus sum laudari me abs te, pater, laudato viro* ("I am happy to be praised by you, father, a man who is himself praised"), which learned men would have known from Cic. *Tusc.* 4.67 (Cf. *Fam.* 5.12.7 and 15.6.1).

52. The familiar proof text of Cat. 16 again.

53. "Parthenias," (the Virgin) according to Donatus, *Vita Vergilii* 11.

54. *Phaedrus* 245a (see above, App. IV.5).

55. There is no ancient source for this story, though Donatus's *Life* (46) says he was planning to retire to polish things up in order to satisfy his critics.

56. Modeled on *Rhet. Her.* 4.36: *o virtutis comes invidia.* A commonplace, cf. Velleius Paterculus 1.9.6: "quam sit adsidua eminentis fortunae comes invidia altissimisque adhaereat"; Cornelius Nepos 12.3.3: "est enim hoc commune vitium in magnis liberisque civitatibus, ut invidia gloriae comes sit."

57. Juv. 6.531.

58. Filippo Maria Visconti, Duke of Milan.

59. Ov. *Rem.* 46: *urticae proxima saepe rosa est.* This too becomes a favorite tag for risqué subject matter: e.g. Niccolo Fabrizio Sacca's commentary on *Priapea* (in MS Vat. lat. 4101, cited from O'Connor 1997: 991). There is a pun on *legi* "read/gathered."

60. "Sicilian muses . . . sing things a little more important", Verg. *Ecl.* 4.1–2. For the exchange of insults, see the Introduction and Rutherford's detailed treatment (2005).

61. Cf. Cic. *Off.* 1.20: "iustitiae primum munus est ut ne cui quis noceat, nisi lacessitus iniuria."

62. Source: Gaspary 1886: 475–6; Natale 1902: 22; Arnaldi et al. 1964: 22; O'Connor 1997: 1002–3. The poem was written during the controversy over *The Hermaphrodite*, when Beccadelli was still at Milan, before the fall of his "Maecenas," Francesco Barbavara. For the characters see the introduction. Rho is Antonio da Rho; Lorenzo is Valla. Catone Sacco is Beccadelli's former friend, the legal scholar (the Stoic spokesman in Valla's revised *On the True and the False Good*). The "sons of Crottus" are Luigi and Lancellotto Crotti, secretaries to Filippo Maria Visconti, Duke of Milan, as was Domenico Feruffini. See Arnaldi et al. 1964: 23; O'Connor 1997: 1002–3, and *DBI* ss.vv.

63. Source: Natale 1902: 121; Sommer 1997: 174. On Hylas (and on Ergoteles in the next poem) see Rutherford 2005: 34.

64. Source: Forberg 1824: 166 (from C, lacking the final couplet); Natale 1902: 130; Cinquini and Valentini 1907: 13; Frati 1909: 366; Sommer 1997: 177, 208; Rutherford 2005: 34 n. 155.

65. With *Cum nequeat* understand *mittere*.

66. Source: Cinquini and Valentini 1907: 13; Sommer 1997: 177, 208 (both reporting the reading of N); Coppini 1990: xl reports the first line of V₁. An uncollected poem found in two manuscripts: Vat. lat. 3164 (Coppini's V₁, a copy of *The Hermaphrodite* by Pamphylus Moratus de Martinengo, dated 16 July 1466), f. 51v, where it follows Appendix, X with the heading "eiusdem ad puerum formosum"; and in Naples, Biblioteca Nazionale IV.F.19, 151v (N), where it substitutes for the last couplet of Appendix, X without a break. The poem is clearly a separate work (or fragment). Cinquini and Valentini 1907: 13 call it "welded on" and criticize it for sense and text.

67. A half line from *Herm.* 2.17, where *tua* takes the place of *tibi*, the (perhaps correct) reading of N here.

68. *Bacchus inesse*, etc.: a clumsy borrowing from Ov. *Am.* 1.14.31–32: *comae, quas vellet Apollo, / Quas vellet capiti Bacchus inesse suo* "locks which Apollo, which Bacchus would wish to be on his head."

69. *quod rarum est*: Ov. *Trist.* 4.10.121.

70. The jingle is very medieval; cf. *Carmina Burana* 130.5: *dentes frendentes*, and 39.5: *ut apri frendentes/ exacuere dentes*. The Cecropian woods are the hills of Attica around Athens (cf. Sen. *Phaedra* 1–2). The use of *credo* plus acc. is strained.

71. Son of Atalanta, one of the Seven against Thebes.

72. Source: Coppini 1990: xl. An uncollected poem found in a single manuscript, Vat. lat. 3164, f. 51v–52r (V₁; see above, App. XI headnote). The poem follows Appendix, XI and is headed "eiusdem ad puerum formosissimum."

73. Source: Cinquini and Valentini 1907: 54–55, who date it to 1432. The identity of Andrea of Pisa is unknown. *Iter Italicum* lists the name only for this poem.

74. I.e. the elegiac couplet (cf. *Herm.* 1.10 n.).

75. Vegio has read the *Prostitutes of Pavia* or similar works.

76. Vergil again as the author of the *Priapeia*, before he turned to "crops, pastures, and arms" in the *Georgics, Eclogues,* and *Aeneid.* Not quite as neat as *cecini pascua, rura, duces,* Vergil's supposedly self-composed epitaph, which keeps them in the correct order of composition (*Vita Verg.* 36).

77. Beccadelli himself makes the same point at Appendix, XIV.40–45.

78. Source: Cinquini and Valentini 1907: 23–25; Sommer 1997: 167–68. Rightly assigned by Cinquini and Valentini to Beccadelli. The verses are found with other of his poems (Vat. Urb. lat. 643, fols 83r-84r) and show many of his themes and stylistic features.

79. *Sagitto* is post-classical. The subject should be the shooter; the object, the arrows or target; not normally construed with two acc. Cf. Vulg. Ps. 10.3, 63.6.

80. The etymology connecting *Latium* with *lateo* was commonplace; see Verg. *Aen.* 8.322, with Donatus *ad loc.*; Ov. *Fasti* 8.237–8.

81. The sons of Oedipus, Eteocles and Polynices, killed each other simultaneously in the war over Thebes.

82. The twin sisters are Procne and Philomela. Procne's husband, Tereus, raped Philomela. In vengeance, Procne killed Itys, her son by Tereus. See *Herm.* 1.25.4 above.

83. *sine pectore:* "insensate, brainless"; cf. Hor. *Ep.* 1.4.6, Ov. *Her.* 16.305, *Met.* 13.240.

84. *militia* scanning long at the caesura even in the pentameter, as *obscena* below (50).

85. Source: Cinquini and Valentini 1907: 52–53; Coppini 1985: 334 n. 3; Sommer 1997: 246–47; Rutherford 2005: 268–70. The title is also given as *In Antonium Panormitam apologia,* etc. Cinquini and Valentini 1907: 51 had argued for Pier Candido Decembrio's authorship on the basis that the poem picks up many of his themes in his long prose attack on Panormita "Novis monstris infamis scatet insula." And in fact the work forms part of omnibus editions of Decembrio's output in several manu-

scripts, one of which (Milan, Biblioteca Ambrosiana, MS D 112 inf., fols 156r–157r = A₂; see Zaccaria 1956: 69) has been claimed by Resta (1962: 37–38) as an autograph by Decembrio. Besides the manuscripts collated by Rutherford (2005: 268), Coppini (1985: 334–35 n. 5) records the variants of A₂. This is part of a group including R (Florence, Biblioteca Riccardiana, MS 810, fols 14r–v) and T (Milan, Biblioteca Trivulziana, MS 793, fols 12r–13r; see Rutherford). Coppini argues that some of these changes may be authorial second thoughts, but the alterations usually weaken the verse, and this set of manuscripts omits verses 15–20. I note only departures from Rutherford's text.

86. A reworking of Verg. *Georg.* 325: *magnus alit magno commixtus corpore fetus.*

87. Ital. *bracco*, the English brach or brachet, a hunting dog.

88. The Lemnian women murdered their husbands but later succumbed to the Argonauts. The (singular) Thracian poet is Orpheus, famed for having turned to boys for consolation after the death of Eurydice.

89. The long-delayed *-que* seems to join the phrases. For *dissuadeo* + dat. + acc., cf. Ov. *Met.* 12.307.

90. *gulosus*: Antonio da Rho devotes a section to this word and its cognates' place in invective: Rutherford 2005: 314.

91. *prostibulum* in classical Latin is the person, in medieval Latin the place.

92. Modeled on Lucan 4.377–78: *discite quam parvo liceat producere vitam / et quantum natura petat* ("Learn how little it takes to keep life going and what nature needs"). Note the change from subj. to ind. even in an indirect question.

93. Source: Bottari 1719–26: VII, 500–2; Gaspary 1884: 483–84; Coppini 1985: 358 (lines 17–26); Sommer 1997: 249. Though often assigned to the time of Porcellio's quarrel with Beccadelli in the court of Alfonso of Aragon (e.g. Laurenza 1912: 41), this poem was correctly dated by Sabbadini (1917: 499) to circa 1432, after Beccadelli had left Rome for Pavia. An additional piece of evidence is that Porcellio's poem is a re-

ply to a long abusive elegy by Beccadelli criticizing Porcellio's *Bellum Thebanorum*, which Beccadelli included in his *Poematum et prosarum liber* of the same time (see Introduction; Natale 1902: 130–32). The cause of the quarrel, which Porcellio typically presents as a betrayal of friendship, is unknown, but the charge and tone are similar to Valla's accusation. The poem might be a direct response to Vegio's earlier praise of *The Hermaphrodite*. All in all, a case of pot and kettle, since Porcellio himself wrote pederastic verse and was denounced for it, e.g. by Petrus Siculus in his "In poetas obscoenos precipue Porcellium et Panormitam" (unedited, in Bergamo, Bibl. Civica, MS MM 659). His reputation as a pederast was enshrined in Bandello's *Novelle* of 1554 (see Borris 2004: 35–43 for a translation).

94. *reptile*: post-classical.

95. Cf. *Herm.* 1.18.3–4, where both the violets and the balsam belong to Alda. Corinna with her roses seems a new character.

96. Cf. *Meretrices Papienses* 4 (Appendix, VI).

97. Coppini takes line 24 as a sentence in itself and punctuates: *Hic futuit futuique cupit, nunc ille uel illa.* This must mean "now the boy, now the girl wants to be fucked" (just like Beccadelli). But the point is the sexual voraciousness and polymorphous perversity of Beccadelli, not his minions. The next line then is left as *Materia est inguen, dive Priape, tuum,* "The material (for his poetry) is your member, divine Priapus." This, too, seems inadequate abuse. Rather, the nominatives go with the next line, in which case *inguen* looks like some sort of loose accusative of respect. Replacing *est* with *ad* is the simplest solution (for *ad*, see Liv. 6.22.6, *materia ad omnem laudem*), though *materia* is usually construed with the genitive, less often with a dative (*OLD* s.v. 8).

98. The *sibi* refers to Beccadelli and not the subject.

99. *tenui . . . cothurno*: traditionally the *cothurnus* 'buskin', the high shoe of the tragic actor, is a metonymy for a tragic poet (as opposed to the *soccus*, the flat slipper of the comic actor); here of poetry in general. Callimachus was one of Beccadelli's authorities: see the letter to Poggio.

100. Maeonia in Lydia; a traditional epithet for Homer.

101. *Neque non* is usually an emphatic positive; one cannot avoid the suspicion that Porcellio is misusing it to mean "and you shouldn't be surprised if".

102. Referring to Beccadelli's long legal studies. This dates the poem to around or before 1431, when finally Beccadelli completed his degree (see Introduction).

103. Aonia in Boetia, i.e., the Muses on Mount Helicon. For *Aoniis . . . antris*, cf. Stat. *Silv.* 4.6.31. This may also be a nod to *antris / Aoniis* in Vegio's own *Vellus Aureum* 19–20.

104. *Cirrhaeus*: of Cirrha, the port of, and metonymy for, Delphi. An epithet favored by Statius.

105. The moral tale is not one of the standard fables of Aesop.

106. Porcellio proceeds to list his works: a *Bellum Thebanorum cum Telebois* (based on Plautus *Amphitruo*; selections and summary at Frittelli 1900: 93–103); a lost poem praising Filippo Maria Visconti (see above, Appendix, VI.26 n., on the snake of the Visconti arms). Poems on the Capitoline games and Faunus are also now lost.

107. While still at Rome, before leaving for Naples, Porcellio had written verses for his patron, Cardinal Prospero Colonna and for Martin V of the same house, including an allegory "Bos Prodigiosus," (see Frittelli 1900: 18–19), and a celebration of Martin V becoming pope (Bottari 1719–26: 7, 503).

108. Porcellio declares that he is not hostile to proper love poetry. For his poem "Qui legitis Floram," see Bottari 1719–26: 7, 504–5, and for mildly pederastic verse, 506.

109. Lines 67–70 are not in the mss as reported by Sommer, but are printed by Bottari and Gaspary. They are too specific to be an unauthorized addition.

110. The Venetian Giacomo Languschi, professor at Padua 1423–31, and from 1428 secretary to Pope Martin V; he continued under Eugenius IV and Nicholas V. He was famed as a wit and a poet in both Italian and Latin, but of his poetry only two Italian sonnets have survived. See

Davies 1988. Beccadelli had insulted his poetry in his elegy against Porcellio.

111. Bornio da Sala (c. 1400–1469), law professor at Bologna (1438–66). See Ballistreri 1970; Bianchi 1976.

112. In these last two verses Porcellio suddenly shears off and addresses Vegio.

113. Source: Cinquini and Valentini 1907: 57; Marletta 1941: 149 n. 3; Coppini 1985: 359; (cf. Sommer 1997: 248). For the polemics, see Sabbadini 1917. In two manuscripts (Vat. lat. 2858, fol. 4v; Brescia, Queriniana, A VII 7, fol. 159r) this poem carries the heading *Persuasio Antonii Panormite (An. Panor.) ad lecturam,* and this has led most to read the piece as an ironic recommendation. However, Coppini (1985: 359–63) has cogently argued that this interpretation really does not work (especially in the face of the direct denial of Beccadelli's authorship in line 2). Marletta 1941: 5 correctly noted that the lines were written "per dissuadere dalla lettura dell'*Ermafrodito,* in modo che sembrino un invito a leggere il proprio libretto." Porcellio is setting himself up as the anti-Panormita, a more worthy recipient for Cosimo's favors and the poet's laurels. The likeliest scenario is that a scribe added Panormita's name to the title in confusion. The poem is still "ironic," however, in that it condemns Beccadelli's language by using the same primary obscenities.

114. *properate puellae:* cf. Ov. *Fasti* 2.745.

115. See *Herm.* 1.5.

116. Cf. Appendix, XVI.18–20 and *Herm.* 2.3.

117. See *Herm.* 1.18.4.

118. Coppini (1985: 360) thought that the final couplet did not sit well at the end of the poem, and argued that since it exists as apparently a separate fragment entitled "In <in>vidos" in a collection of Porcellio's works (Florence, Biblioteca Nazionale Centrale, Conventi Soppressi, J IX 10 (240), fol. 112v) it may have been added accidentally. However, the sequence of thought, though rough, can still be followed: if you have picked up this poem hoping for smut, these final lines will be the last you need to read in your disappointment.

119. Source: Marletta 1941: 5 n. 3; Coppini 1985: 360 n. 19, 361–62 (Florence, Biblioteca Nazionale Centrale, Conventi Soppressi, J IX 10 (240), fol. 138r-v). From Porcellio's *Laureae*, Book VI, a collection of his poems.

120. Porcellio was not above reusing his material: here we have vv. 1–3 of the previous poem plus a rewrite of 5. He also adapts line 5 for a picture of the good old days in "Francisco Patavino Cubiculario Apostolico": *Non hic furta Jovis metuere aut Pana puellae* (Bottari 1719–26: 7, 513).

121. *pharetratus:* an epithet of Cupid in Ov. *Am.* 2.5.1.

122. The manuscript *facilesque* is clearly the wrong word. It seems to be based on Mart. 3.69.5: *Haec igitur nequam iuvenes facilesque puellae*, but the sense is the exact opposite: "easy" girls are not to read these decent verses. Coppini suggested *castaeque* or *doctaeque*, with no confidence, as fitting the sense but without an explanation of how *facilesque* crept into the text. I suggest *pueri atque puellae* (from Hor. *Sat.* 1.1.85) as in keeping with the title but with the same lack of confidence.

123. Alluding not only to the title of the collection but to Porcellio's jealousy of Panormita's laureation and his own (frustrated) hopes to become poet laureate: Coppini 1985: 360 n. 19, 364–65.

124. Though this seems to contradict what he has said in line 6, Porcellio recommends his milder erotic poetry (see above Appendix, XVI.61–62). For *vaga fama*, cf. *Homerus Latinus* 238; Ov. *Met.* 8.267, and Vergil *Aen.* 2.17: *ea fama vagatur*. This refers to his martial epic (Appendix, XVI.55).

125. In lines 11–15 Porcellio turns around and takes Beccadelli's apologia for himself. Despite the title, these verses seem to appeal directly to Cosimo: Porcellio can provide all the relaxation that Beccadelli claimed to, but in cleaner vein.

126. Source: Valla 1540: 364; Sabbadini 1891: 102–3; Valla 1984: 240–41. Appendix, XIX and XX are two epigrams that Valla included in a letter to Pier Candido Decembrio (*Ep.* 18 in Besomi and Regoliosi's edition), and which also circulated separately (nos. 4 and 5 in the enumeration of Lo Monaco 1986: 146). For additional MS sources see Besomi and Regoliosi 1986: 83 and Lo Monaco 1986: 164. Sabbadini (1891: 101–03) dated the letter to 1444, since Beccadelli is married; however, Sabbadini was thinking of the second wife and dating that marriage to 1444; Mancini 1891: 205–

06 dated it to around the same year. Besomi and Regoliosi (Valla 1984: 226–27, 238), realizing that the *uxor* must be Beccadelli's first wife, correctly date it to 1442–43.

127. *tonso*: i.e. sufficiently over the proper age for a boy-love that he now needs to shave; the phrase seems to be adapted from Mart. 10.98.9.

128. Note the incorrect scansion here (and in line 10) of *muliĕris*.

129. Cf. Appendix, VI.4: Beccadelli is sometimes the penetrator, sometimes the penetrated.

130. For *puellus* in the sexual sense, see the Latin translation of lines said to be by Plato, which Beccadelli quotes in his letter to Guarino (Appendix, I).

131. she: *illa*, Beccadelli's wife, apparently, punning *Hyla* and *illa*. For Hylas as the beloved youth, see *Herm.* 1.7.13 n. and Appendix, IX n. above.

132. Oedīpus is occasionally scanned as if Oedippus in humanist verse. This is Oedipus as the proverbial answerer of riddles (Plaut. *Poen.* 443: "nam isti quidem hercle orationi Oedipo / opust coniectore, qui Sphingi interpres fuit"; Ter. *Andria* 194). For *bechus*, see Du Cange (1883–87: I, 645, s.v.), standing for Italian *becco*, 'goat', i.e., with horns, a cuckold, punning on Beccadelli.

133. *dare verba* is an idiom for 'to deceive'; Valla takes the pun on *verba*, *verbera* from Ter. *Heauton Timorumenos* 356. A double share of punishment for a double sin.

134. Source: Soldati 1902: 401–02; Oeschger 1948: 447–48. Praise for Beccadelli's talent, his marriage, and a lover's complaint. A poem not placed by Pontano in any of his collections of poetry. The reference to the end of the embassy to Venice allows us to date this poem to 1452 (see Introduction), showing that Beccadelli's friends were not afraid of resurrecting *The Hermaphrodite* (at least in a limited circle) at that late a date.

135. Delights: *delicias*, a Catullan word: Cat. 2.1, 3.4, 6.1, etc. Balbus is probably Pietro Balbi (1399–1479) of Pisa, a leading Platonist at Rome.

136. See *Herm.* 1.38.2: Aonia is the part of Boeotia where Mt. Helicon is located, hence Aonian, a conventional epithet for the Muses.

137. Calliope is by late tradition the Muse of epic poetry, but is often used for any Muse.

138. A spring in Pieria, and so a metonymy for the Muses. Cf. Mart. 12.11.3.

139. Alluding to Catullus's description of his book: Cat. 1.1–2.

140. Mount Cirrha: see Appendix, XVI.42 above.

141. Laura Arcella, his second wife, whom he married in 1447; see Introduction.

142. We hear nothing else about Laura's talents.

143. Though a variation on a trope of Catullus (68b.119–20), one cannot help wondering if this is not a small dig at the fifty-three-year-old man who married a sixteen-year-old girl; for *deserta cubili* (line 33 below), cf. Cat. 66.21.

144. *Ah pereant*: cf. Prop. 1.11.30, 2.23.12; Ov. *Ars* 2.272, 3.494; *Fasti* 4.240–1.

145. Alfonso of Aragon, King of Naples, and Beccadelli's employer.

146. *Cinnama*: "Cinnamon," a favorite addressee in Pontano's *Parthenopaeus* (*Amores*) 1.19–21, 23–24, 29, 31.

147. I include here four early summaries of Beccadelli's life and work that relate more directly to the reception of his *Hermaphrodite*.

148. Source: Mehus 1745: 4. The text was completed in 1456. Pius II thanks the author for being included amongst the famous in a letter of 25 March 1457 (Mehus 1745: 107–08). For Facio's friendship with Beccadelli and their quarrel with Valla, see the Introduction.

149. Source: Graziosi 1973: 42. Paolo Cortesi (1465–1510) was apostolic secretary in the papal curia and one of the leading Ciceronians of his age.

150. Source: Giovio 1577a: 23–24; 1577b: 16–17; Natale 1902: 103 n. 1. Paolo Giovio (1483–1552), professor of moral philosophy at the university of Rome, physician to Cardinal Giulio di Giuliano de' Medici (Pope Clement VII); an important historian (*Historiarum sui temporis libri XLV*, among many works). See Zimmermann 1995.

151. Pontano, *Parthenopaeus* 1.27.1–2, addresses Beccadelli as: "Antoni, decus elegantiarum / atque idem pater omnium leporum" ("Antonio, the glory of elegance and the father of all wit").

152. Cat. 11.12; Hor. *Odes* 1.35.29.

153. Not the current arms of Beccadelli di Bologna, which feature three winged claws. Beccadelli was granted the right to quarter his arms with those of Aragon.

154. The epitaph appears in Beccadelli 1475: 166 (unpaginated) under the heading: "Sequens epitaphium clarissimus poeta Antonius Panhormita suis dulcissimis carminibus composuit et in sepulcrum suum affigi mandavit." ("The most famous poet, Antonio Panormita composed this epitaph for his sweet songs and ordered it to be placed on his tomb.") The detail that he did so on his deathbed seems to derive from Giovio. The epitaph was frequently repeated in various collections and in Beccadelli 1746: 133 with the heading "Epitaphium Antonij Panhormitae, quod ipse moriens sibi scripsit." The inscription there bears a final line, not by Beccadelli, "Antonine decus nostrum letare: resurgam." ("Antonio, our glory, rejoice." "I shall arise.") The epitaph is followed by additional poetic praises of Beccadelli (by Pontano, Eliseo Calenzio, Giano Vitali, and Latomus) in the editions of Giovio.

155. Source Giraldi 1894: 18–19. Pandolfi 1999: 70. Lilio Gregorio Giraldi (1479–1552) of Ferrara. See Giraldi 1894. The fictive date is the celebrations in Ferrara following the marriage by proxy of Anna d'Este to François de Lorraine, Duc de Guise, on 15 September 1548. The text was written c. 1549 and published in 1551. Giraldi here is largely dependent on Giovio.

Bibliography

᠍᠍᠍᠍

Adams, J. N. 1990. *The Latin Sexual Vocabulary*. Baltimore: Johns Hopkins University Press.

Albertini, Francesco. 1510. *Memoriale di molte statue et picture di Florentia*. Rome. Repr. in *Five Early Guides to Rome and Florence*, ed. Peter Murray. Farnborough: Gregg International Publishers, 1972.

Alessio, Gian Carlo. 1981. "I trattati grammaticali di Giovanni del Virgilio," *Italia medioevale e umanistica* 24: 159–212.

Andriani, Giuseppe. 1924. "Giacomo Bracelli e la storia della geografia," *Atti della Società ligure di storia patria* 52: 129–248.

Aretino, Pietro. 1969. *Pietro Aretino. Sei giornate: Ragionamento della Nanna e della Antonia (1534); dialogo nel quale la Nanna insegna a la Pippa (1536)*. Ed. Giovanni Aquilecchia. Bari: Laterza.

——. 1971. *Aretino's Dialogues*. Trans. Raymond Rosenthal. New York: Stein and Day.

Arnaldi, Francesco, Lucia Gualdo Rosa, and Liliana Monti Sabia, eds. 1964. *Poeti latini del Quattrocento*. Milan: Ricciardi.

Ballerini, Luigi, ed. 2005. *The Art of Cooking: The First Modern Cookery Book Composed by Maestro Martino*, translated and annotated by Jeremy Parzen. Berkeley: University of California Press.

Ballistreri, G. 1970. "Bornio da Sala," *Dizionario biografico degli italiani* 12: 801–03.

Baron, Hans. 1955. *The Crisis of the Early Italian Renaissance: Civic Humanism and Republican Liberty in an Age of Classicism and Tyranny*. 2 vols. Princeton: Princeton University Press.

Beccadelli, Antonio. 1475. *Antonii Panormite epistolae familiares*. Naples: Sixtus Riessinger.

——. 1538. *Antonii Panormitae De dictis et factis Alphonsi regis Aragonum libri quatuor*. Basel: Ex officina Hervagiana. Published with Pius II's commentary on the work. http://daten.digitale-sammlungen.de/~db/bsb00006233/images/index.html

——. 1553. *Antonii Bononiae Beccatelli cognomento Panhormitae Epistolarum libri V. Eiusdem orationes.* Venice: apud Bartholomaeum Caesanum.

——. 1746. *Antonii Beccatelli . . . Epistolarum Gallicarum libri quatuor. Accedit etiam eiusdem Epistolarum Campanarum liber.* Naples: Ex typographia Johannis de Simone.

Belloni, A. 1986. *Professori giuristi a Padova nel secolo XV. Profili bio-bibliografici e cattedre.* Frankfurt am Main: Vittorio Klostermann.

Bentley, Jerry H. 1987. *Politics and Culture in Renaissance Naples.* Princeton: Princeton University Press.

Berry, Paul. 2002. *The Encounter between Seneca and Christianity.* Lewiston, N.Y. : Edwin Mellen Press.

Bertini, Ferruccio, ed. 1976–2000. *Commedie latine del XII e XIII secolo.* 8 vols. Genoa: Università di Genova, Facoltà di Lettere, Istituto di filologia classica e medievale.

——. 1998a. "Guglielmo di Blois, *Alda,*" in Bertini, Ferruccio, ed. 1976–2000, 6: 11–109.

——. 1998b. "Iacopo da Benevento, *De uxore cerdonis,*" in Bertini, Ferruccio, ed. 1976–2000, 6: 429–503.

Besomi, Ottavio. 1966. "Dai 'Gesta Ferdinandi regis Aragonum' del Valla al 'De Orthographia' del Tortelli," *Italia medioevale e umanistica* 9: 75–121.

——, ed. 1973. *Laurentii Valle gesta Ferdinandi regis Aragonum.* Padua: Antenore.

——, and Regoliosi, Mariangela. 1986. "'Laurentii Valle Epistole'. Addendum," *Lorenzo Valla e l'Umanesimo italiano.* Padua: Antenore. 77–109.

Bettella, Patrizia. 2005. *The Ugly Woman: Transgressive Aesthetic Models in Italian Poetry from the Middle Ages to the Baroque.* Toronto: University of Toronto Press.

Bianchi, Bianca. 1976. *Ein Bologneser Jurist und Humanist: Bornio da Sala.* Wiesbaden: Steiner.

Billanovich, Giuseppe. 1951. "Petrarch and the Textual Tradition of Livy," *Journal of the Warburg and Courtauld Institutes* 14: 137–208.

———. 1997. "Ser Convenevole Maestro Notaio e Chierico," in *Petrarca, Verona, e l'Europa: Atti del Convegno internazionale di studi (Verona: 19–23 settembre 1991).* Padua: Antenore. 367–90.

Borris, Kenneth. 2004. *Same-Sex Desire in the English Renaissance: A Sourcebook of Texts, 1470–1650.* New York: Routledge.

Bottari, Giovanni Gaetano, ed. 1719–26. *Carmina illustrium poetarum italorum.* II vols. Florence: Apud J. C. Tartinium et S. Franchium.

Botterill, Steven. 1996. "Minor Writers of the Trecento," in *The Cambridge History of Italian Literature,* ed. Peter Brand and Lino Pertile. Rev. ed. Cambridge: Cambridge University Press. 108–27.

Bowen, Barbara. 1986. "Renaissance Collections of Facetiae, 1344–1490: A New Listing," *Renaissance Quarterly* 39: 1–15.

Bracciolini, Poggio. 1538. *Poggii Florentini oratoris et philosophi opera.* Basileae: Apud Henricum Petrum. Repr. as Vol. 1 of *Poggii Opera Omnia,* ed. R. Fubini. Turin: Bottega d'Erasmo, 1964.

———. 1832. *Poggii Epistolae,* ed. Thomas Tonelli. Florence: L. Marchini. 3 vols. Repr. as Vol. 3 of *Poggii Opera Omnia.* Turin: Bottega d'Erasmo, 1964.

Brackett, John K. 1993. "The Florentine Onestà and the Control of Prostitution, 1403–1680," *Sixteenth Century Journal* 24: 273–300.

Braggio, Carlo. 1890. "Giacomo Bracelli e l'Umanesimo dei Liguri al suo tempo," *Atti della Società ligure di storia patria* 23: 5–295.

Braun, Lugwig. 1980. *Scenae Suppositiciae oder Der falsche Plautus.* Göttingen: Vandenhoeck & Ruprecht.

Butrica, J. L. 1984. *The Manuscript Tradition of Propertius.* Toronto: University of Toronto Press.

Campbell, Stephen J. 1997. *Cosmè Tura of Ferrara: Style, Politics, and the Renaissance City, 1450–1495.* New Haven: Yale University Press.

Cappelletto, Rita. 1988. *La "lectura Plauti" del Pontano: con edizione delle postille del cod. Vindob. lat. 3168 e osservazioni sull'"Itala recensio."* Urbino: QuattroVenti.

Cesarini Martinelli, Lucia, ed. 1977. "Leon Battista Alberti, *Philodoxeos fabula,*" *Rinascimento* n.s. 17: 111–234.

Cesati, Franco. 2003. *La grande guida delle strade di Firenze.* Rome: Newton & Compton.

Chambers, D. S. 1976. "Studium Urbis and *Gabella Studii*: the University of Rome in the Fifteenth Century," in *Cultural Aspects of the Italian Renaissance; Essays in Honour of Paul Oskar Kristeller*. Manchester: Manchester University Press. 68–110.

Charlet, Jean-Louis. 1997. "Éros et érotisme dans la *Cinthia* d'Enea Silvio Piccolomini," in *Eros et Priapus. Érotisme et obscénité dans la littérature néolatine*, ed. Ingrid De Smet and Philip Ford. Geneva: Droz. 1–19.

Chatfield, Mary P., ed. and trans. 2008. *Cristoforo Landino: Poems*. I Tatti Renaissance Library. Cambridge, MA: Harvard University Press.

Cinquini, Adolfo, and Roberto Valentini. 1907. *Poesie latine inedite di A. Beccadelli detto il Panormita*. Aosta: Giuseppe Allasia.

Classen, Albrecht. 1991. *Die autobiographische Lyrik des europäischen Spätmittelalters: Studien zu Hugo von Montfort, Oswald von Wolkenstein, Antonio Pucci, Charles d'Orléans, Thomas Hoccleve, Michel Beheim, Hans Rosenplüt und Alfonso Alvarez de Villasandino*. Amsterdam and Atlanta, GA: Rodopi.

Colangelo, Francesco. 1820. *Vita di Antonio Beccadelli, soprannominato il Panormita*. Naples: Angelo Trani.

———. 1826. *Vita di Gioviano Pontano*. Naples: Angelo Trani.

Contini, Gianfranco, ed. 1995. *Letteratura italiana del Quattrocento*. Florence: Sansoni.

Coppini, Donatella. 1984. "Storia di una parolaccia: 'poppysma' nel Quattrocento," *Rinascimento* 24: 231–49.

———. 1985. "Un'eclisse, una duchessa, due poeti," in *Tradizione classica e letteratura umanistica. Per Alessandro Perosa*, ed. Roberto Cardini et al. 2 vols. Rome: Bulzoni. 333–73.

———, ed. 1990. *Hermaphroditus Antonii Panhormitae*. Humanistica 10. Rome: Bulzoni.

———. 1998. "I modelli del Panormita," in *Intertestualità e smontaggi*, ed. Roberto Cardini and Mariangela Regoliosi. Rome: Bulzoni. 1–29.

———. 2006-7. "Cosimo togatus. Cosimo dei Medici nella poesia latina del Quattrocento," *Incontri triestini di filologia classica* 6: 101–19.

Corbellini, Alberto. 1930. "Note di vita cittadina e universitaria pavese nel Quattrocento," *Bollettino della Società pavese di storia patria* 30: 1–282.

Corso C. 1953. "Il Panormita in Siena e l'Ermafrodito," *Bullettino senese di storia patria*, serie 3, 12: 138–88.

Cossart, Michael de, ed. 1984. *Antonio Beccadelli and The Hermaphrodite*. Liverpool: Janus.

Culiano, Ioan Petru. 1987. *Eros and Magic in the Renaissance*. Chicago: University of Chicago Press.

D'Amico, John F. 1983. *Renaissance Humanism in Papal Rome: Humanists and Churchmen on the Eve of the Reformation*. Baltimore: Johns Hopkins University Press.

Daude, Juliette Desjardins, ed. 2008. *Pacifico Massimi: Hecatelegium. Les Cent nouvelles élégies*. Paris: Les Belles Lettres.

Davies, Martin C. 1984. "The Senator and the Schoolmaster: Friends of Leonardo Bruni in a New Letter," *Humanistica Lovaniensia* 33: 1–21.

———. 1988. "An Enigma and a Phantom: Giovanni Aretino and Giacomo Languschi," *Humanistica Lovaniensia* 37: 1–30.

De Robertis, Domenico, ed. 1986. *Guido Cavalcanti: Rime, con le rime di Iacopo Cavalcanti*. Torino: Einaudi.

Dennis, Rodney G., ed. and trans. 2006. *Giovanni Gioviano Pontano: Baiae*. I Tatti Renaissance Library. Cambridge, MA: Harvard University Press.

Doglio, Federico. 1990. "Rapporti fra le diverse esperienze drammatiche europee nel Medio Evo: La commedia elegiaca, ambito italiano," in *Il teatro scomparso: Testi e spettacoli fra il X e il XVIII secolo*. Rome: Ente dello Spettacolo. 161–81.

Donati, Gemma. 2000. *Pietro Odo da Montopoli e la Biblioteca di Niccolò V*. Rome: Roma nel Rinascimento.

Du Cange, Charles. 1883–87. *Glossarium ad scriptores mediae & infimae Latinitatis. Ed. nova*. 10 vols. Niort: Léopold Favre.

Duprè Theseider, Eugenio. 1956. *La politica italiana di Alfonso d'Aragona*. Bologna: R. Pàtron.

Elliott, Alison Goddard, trans. 1984. *Seven Medieval Latin Comedies*. New York: Garland.

Fantazzi, Charles. 1996. "The Style of Quattrocento Latin Love Poetry," *International Journal of the Classical Tradition* 3: 127–46.

Ferri, Ferruccio. 1909. *La poesia popolare in Antonio Pucci*. Bologna: Beltrami.

Filelfo, Francesco. 1502. *Francisci Philelfi viri Grece & Latine eruditissimi Epistolarum familiarium libri xxxvij*. Venice: Ex aedibus Ioannis & Gregorii de Gregoriis.

Fioravanti, Gianfranco. 1999. "Librerie e lettori a San Gimignano nel '400: Onofrio Coppi e Mattia Lupi," *Interpres* 18: 58–73.

Florio, John. 1611. *Queen Anna's New World of Words*, London: Printed by Melch. Bradwood [and William Stansby], for Edw. Blount and William Barret. Reprint Menston, Yorkshire, UK: Scolar Press, 1968.

Forberg, Friedrich Karl (Carl). 1824. *Antonii Panormitae Hermaphroditus. Primus in Germania edidit et Apophoreta adjecit Frider. Carol. Forbergius*. Coburg: sumptibus Meuseliorum.

———. 1884. *Manual of Classical Erotology (De figuris Veneris) by Fred. Chas. Forberg*. Manchester: Privately printed. Reprint New York: Grove Press, 1966.

———. 1908. *Antonii Panormitae Hermaphroditus: Lateinisch nach der Ausgabe von C. Fr. Forberg (Coburg 1824), nebst einer deutschen metrischen Übersetzung und der deutschen Übersetzung der Apophoreta von C. Fr. Forberg / besorgt und herausgegeben von Fr. Wolff-Untereichen; mit einem sexualwissenschaftlichen Kommentar von Alfred Kind*. Leipzig: A. Weigel. Reprint Leipzig: Edition Leipzig, 1986.

Frati, Ludovico, ed. 1892–93. *Vite di uomini illustri del secolo XV scritte da Vespasiano da Bisticci*. Bologna: Romagnoli-dall'Acqua.

———. 1909. "Due umanisti bolognesi alla Corte ducale di Milano," *Archivio storico italiano*, ser. 5, 43: 359–74.

Frittelli, Ugo. 1900. *Giannantonio de' Pandoni detto il Porcellio: studio critico*. Florence: Paravia.

Fubini, Riccardo. 1961. "Antonio da Rho," *Dizionario biografico degli italiani* 3: 574–577.

———. 2003. *Humanism and Secularization: From Petrarch to Valla*, trans. Martha King. Durham, NC: Duke University Press.

Furstenberg Levi, Shulamit. 2006. "The Fifteenth Century Accademia Pontaniana: An Analysis of its Institutional Elements," *History of Universities* 21.1: 33–70.

Gabotto, Ferdinando. 1893. "L'attività politica di Pier Candido Decembrio," *Giornale ligustico di archeologia, storia e letteratura* 20: 161–98, 205–14, 241–70.

Gagliardi, Roberto, trans. 1980. *L'Ermafrodito: Antonio Beccadelli*. Milan: Savelli.

Gaisser, Julia Haig. 1993. *Catullus and his Renaissance Readers*. Oxford: Clarendon Press.

Garin, Eugenio. 1955. "La cultura milanese nella prima metà del XV secolo," in *Storia di Milano*. Vol. 6. *Il ducato visconteo e la repubblica ambrosiana (1392–1450)*. Milan: Fondazione Treccani degli Alfieri. 545–608.

Garland, Madge. 1957. *The Changing Face of Beauty: Four Thousand Years of Beautiful Women*. New York: Barrows.

Gaspary, Adolf. 1886. "Einige ungedruckte Briefe und Verse von Antonio Panormita," *Vierteljahrschrift für Kultur und Litteratur der Renaissance* 1: 474–84.

——. 1887–1901. *Storia della letteratura italiana*. 2 vols. Turin: Loescher.

Giovio, Paolo. 1577a. *Elogia virorum literis illustrium*. Basel: Petrus Perna. http://bibliothek.uv.es/search*val/aGiovio

——. 1577b. *Elogia virorum literis illustrium*. Basel: Petrus Perna. http://www.uni-mannheim.de/mateo/camenaref/giovio1.html [Though the title pages are identical the pagination is different.]

Giraldi, Lilio Gregorio. 1894. *De poetis nostrorum temporum*, ed. K. Wotke. In M. Herrmann and S. Szamatólski, eds, *Lateinische Litteraturdenkmäler des XV. und XVI. Jahrhunderts*, 10. Berlin: Weidmann.

Godman, Peter. 1988. "Johannes Secundus and Renaissance Latin Poetry," *Review of English Studies* 39: 258–72.

——. 1990. "Literary Classicism and Latin Erotic Poetry of the Twelfth Century and the Renaissance," in *Latin Poetry and the Classical Tradition: Essays in Medieval and Renaissance Literature*, ed. Peter Godman and Oswyn Murray. Oxford: Clarendon Press. 149–82.

Gordan, Phyllis Walter Goodhart. 1974. *Two Renaissance Book Hunters. The Letters of Poggius Bracciolini to Nicolaus de Niccolis*. New York: Columbia University Press.

Grayson, Cecil, ed. 1954. *Leon Battista Alberti, Opuscoli inediti: Musca-Vita S. Potiti.* Florence: Olschki.

———. 1971. "Bracelli, Giacomo," *Dizionario biografico degli italiani* 13: 652–53.

Graziosi, Maria Teresa. 1973. *Paolo Cortesi, De hominibus doctis dialogus.* Rome: Bonacci.

Greco, Aulo, ed. 1970–76. *Vespasiano da Bisticci. Le vite.* 2 vols. Florence: Istituto Nazionale di Studi sul Rinascimento. (The text available at http://imagohistoriae.signum.sns.it/works.php.)

Gregorovius, Ferdinand. 1870. *Geschichte der Stadt Rom im Mittelalter. Vom fünften bis zum sechzehnten Jahrhundert.* 2., durchgearb. Aufl. Stuttgart: Cotta.

Grund, Gary R., ed. and trans. 2005. *Humanist Comedies.* I Tatti Renaissance Library. Cambridge, MA: Harvard University Press.

Gualandri, Isabella, and Giovanni Orlandi, eds. 1998. "Arnolfo di Orleans, Lidia," in Bertini, Ferruccio, ed. 1976–2000, 6: 111–318.

Gualdo, Germano. 1970. "Giovanni Toscanella. Nota biografica," *Italia medioevale e umanistica* 13: 29–58.

Guidi, Remo L. 2007. *L'inquietudine del Quattrocento.* Rome: Tielle Media.

Halperin, David M., John J. Winkler, and Froma I. Zeitlin, eds. 1990. *Before Sexuality: The Construction of Erotic Experience in the Ancient Greek World.* Princeton: Princeton University Press.

Hankins, James. 1990. *Plato in the Italian Renaissance.* 2 vols. Leiden and New York: Brill.

Harth, Helene, ed. 1984. *Poggio Bracciolini: Lettere II. Epistolarum familiarium libri.* Florence: Olschki.

Haskins, Charles Homer. 1928. "Latin Literature under Frederick II," *Speculum* 3: 129–51.

Hausmann, Frank-Rutger. 1976. "Martial in Italien," *Studi Medievali* 17, 173–218.

———. 1986. "Datierte Quattrocento-Handschriften lateinischer Dichter (Tibull, Catull, Properz, Ovid-Epistula Sapphus ad Phaonem, Martial, 'Carmina Priapea') und ihre Bedeutung für die Erforschung des italienischen Humanismus," in Ulrich Justus Stache, Wolfgang Maaz, and Fritz Wagner, eds., *Kontinuität und Wandel. Lateinische Poesie von*

Naevius bis Baudelaire. Franco Munari zum 65. Geburtstag. Hildesheim: Weidmann. 598–632.

Helas, Philine. 1999. *Lebende Bilder in der italienischen Festkultur des 15. Jahrhunderts.* Berlin: Akademie Verlag.

Heyworth, S. J. 1986. *The Elegies of Sextus Propertius: Towards a Critical Edition* (diss. Cambridge).

——, ed. 2007. *Sexti Properti Elegi* (OCT). Oxford: Oxford University Press.

Holtz, Louis, ed. 1977. *Murethach, In Donati artem maiorem.* Corpus Christianorum, Continuatio Mediaevalis 40. Turnhout: Brepols.

Jacodetius, Ennius, ed. 1790. *Fescennina seu Antonii Panormitae Hermaphroditus, Pacifici Maximi Elegiae iocosae, Ioannis Secundi Basia.* [n. p.]: typis Joa. Giraltii. [Not seen. I cite this volume from Coppini 1990, lxviii, ccxii, 1. Copies are recorded in Berlin and Vicenza].

Kendall, Paul M., and Vincent Ilardi, eds. and trans. 1970. *Dispatches with Related Documents of Milanese Ambassadors in France and Burgundy (1450–1483).* 3 vols. Athens, OH: Ohio University Press.

Kidwell, Carol. 1991. *Pontano: Poet and Prime Minister.* London: Duckworth.

Kleinhenz, Christopher. 1986. *The Early Italian Sonnet: The First Century (1220–1321).* Collezione di Studi e Testi 2. Lecce: Milella.

——. 2000. "Erotismo e carnalità nella poesia italiana del Due e Trecento," in *"Por le soie amisté": Essays in Honor of Norris J. Lacy,* ed. Keith Busby and Catherine M. Jones. Amsterdam and Atlanta, GA: Rodopi.

Landino, Cristoforo. 1939. *Carmina omnia,* ed. Alessandro Perosa. Florence: Olschki.

Lanza, Antonio. 1985. "Aspetti e figure della poesia comico-realistica toscana del secolo XV," *Rassegna della letteratura italiana* 89: 403–43.

Laurenza, Vincenzo. 1912. "Il Panormita a Napoli," *Atti dell'Accademia Pontaniana* 42, memoria no. 8: 1–60.

Lefèvre, Eckard. 2002. "Beccadellis 'homerische' Bitte um einen Martial," in *Epea pteroenta: Beiträge zur Homerforschung; Festschrift für Wolfgang Kullmann zum 75. Geburtstag,* ed. Michael Reichel. Stuttgart: Steiner. 93–98. Available at http://www.freidok.uni-freiburg.de/volltexte/

5149/pdf/Lefevre_Beccadellis_homerische_Bitte_um_einen_Martial
.pdf

Limbeck, Sven. 1999. *Theorie und Praxis des Übersetzens im deutschen Humanismus: Albrecht von Eybs Übersetzung der 'Philogenia' des Ugolino Pisani.* Diss. Freiburg. http://www.freidok.uni-freiburg.de/volltexte/2147/pdf/limbeck.pdf.

Lo Monaco, Francesco. 1986. "Per un'edizione dei 'Carmina' di Lorenzo Valla," *Italia medioevale e umanistica* 29: 139–64.

Löfstedt, Bengt. 1977a. *Ars Laureshamensis: Expositio in Donatum maiorem.* Corpus Christianorum, Continuatio Mediaevalis 40A. Turnhout: Brepols.

———. 1977b. *Sedulius Scotus. In Donati artem maiorem.* Corpus Christianorum, Continuatio Mediaevalis 40B. Turnhout: Brepols.

Lopez, Pasquale. 1972. *Sul libro a stampa e le origini della censura ecclesiastica.* Naples: Regina.

Lorch, Maristella de Panizza. 1968. "The Attribution of the 'Janus Sacerdos' to Panormita: An Hypothesis," *Quaderni urbinati di cultura classica* 5: 115–35.

———, ed. 1970. *Lorenzo Valla, De vero falsoque bono.* Bari: Adriatica.

Ludwig, Walther. 1989. *Litterae Neolatinae: Schriften zur neulateinischen Literatur.* Munich: W. Fink.

———. 1990. "The Origin and Development of the Catullan Style in Neo-Latin Poetry," in *Latin Poetry and the Classical Tradition: Essays in Medieval and Renaissance Literature,* ed. Peter Godman and Oswyn Murray. Oxford: Clarendon Press. 183–97.

Mancini, Girolamo. 1891. *Vita di Lorenzo Valla.* Florence: Sansoni.

Marletta, Fedele. 1941. "Distici latini attribuiti al Panormita," *Rassegna di lingue e letterature* 19: 3–8.

———. 1942. "L'umanista Francesco Pontano," *Nuova rivista storica* 26: 32–41.

Martelli, Mario. 1989. "Il capitolo 'Di vecchiezza' di Francesco d'Altobianco degli Alberti," *Interpres* 9: 35–63.

Martène, Edmond, and Ursin Durand, eds. 1724–33. *Veterum scriptorum et monumentorum historicorum, dogmaticorum, moralium amplissima collectio.* 9 vols. Paris: Apud Montalant. Reprint New York: Burt Franklin, 1968.

Marti, Mario. 1953. *Cultura e stile nei poeti giocosi del tempo di Dante.* Pisa: Nistri-Lischi.

———, ed. 1956. *Poeti giocosi del tempo di Dante.* Milan: Rizzoli.

Martin, Adrienne Laskier. 1991. *Cervantes and the Burlesque Sonnet.* Berkeley: University of California Press.

Mazzi, Maria Serena. 1991. *Prostitute e lenoni nella Firenze del Quattrocento.* Milan: Saggiatore.

Mehus, Lorenzo. 1745. *Bartholomaei Facii De viris illustribus liber nunc primum ex ms. cod. in lucem erutus.* Florence: ex typographio Joannis Pauli Giovannelli (text at http://www.bibliotecaitaliana.it/).

Ménage, Gilles. 1729. *Menagiana ou Les bons mots et remarques critiques, historiques, morales & d'érudition,* ed. Bernard de La Monnoye. Paris: Chez Florentin Delaulne.

Mercier, abbé de Saint-Léger, attrib. ed. 1791. *Quinque illustrium poetarum: Ant. Panormitae; Ramusii, Ariminensis; Pacifici Maximi, Asculani; Joan. Joviani Pontani; Joan. Secundi, Hagiensis: Lusus in Venerem.* Paris: Prostat ad pistrinum in vico suavi.

Mesdjian, Béatrice (Charlet-Mesdjian). 1997. "Éros dans l'*Eroticon* de T. V. Strozzi," in *Eros et Priapus. Érotisme et obscénité dans la littérature néo-latine,* ed. Ingrid De Smet and Philip Ford. Geneva: Droz. 25–42.

Migliore, Ferdinando Leopoldo del. 1684. *Firenze città nobilissima illustrata.* Florence: Stella. Repr. Bologna: Forni, 1968.

Mormando, Franco. 1999. *The Preacher's Demons: Bernardino of Siena and the Social Underworld of Early Renaissance Italy.* Chicago: University of Chicago Press.

Murgatroyd, Paul, ed. and trans. 2000. *The Amatory Elegies of Johannes Secundus.* Leiden and Boston: Brill.

Murphy, Stephen. 1997. *The Gift of Immortality: Myths of Power and Humanist Poetics.* Madison: Fairleigh Dickinson University Press.

Nardi, Paolo. 1974. *Mariano Sozzini, giureconsulto senese del Quattrocento.* Milano: A. Giuffrè.

Natale, Michele. 1902. *Antonio Beccadelli, detto il Panormita: studio.* Caltanissetta: Tip. dell'Omnibus.

Nolhac, Pierre de. 1907. *Pétrarque et l'humanisme.* 2nd ed. 2 vols. Paris: Champion.

O'Connor, Eugene. 1996. "Hell's Pit and Heaven's Rose: The Typology of Female Sights and Smells in Panormita's *Hermaphroditus*," *Medievalia et humanistica*, n.s. 23: 25–51.

———. 1997. "Panormita's Reply to His Critics: The 'Hermaphroditus' and the Literary Defense," *Renaissance Quarterly* 50: 985–1010.

———. 2001. *Antonio Panormita: Hermaphroditus*. Lanham, MD.: Lexington Books.

Oeschger, Giovanni, ed. 1948. *Ioanis Ioviani Pontani Carmina: ecloghe, elegie, liriche*. Bari: Laterza.

Orlandi, Giovanni. 1990. "Classical Satire and the Medieval Elegiac Comedy," in *Latin Poetry and the Classical Tradition: Essays in Medieval and Renaissance Literature*, ed. Peter Godman and Oswyn Murray. Oxford: Clarendon Press. 97–114.

Orvieto, Paolo, and Lucia Brestolini. 2000. *La poesia comico-realistica: dalle origini al Cinquecento*. Rome: Carocci.

Ottolini, Angelo, ed. and trans. 1922. *Antonio Beccadelli: L'Ermafrodito. Pacifico Massimo: L'Ecatelegio*. Milan: Corbaccio.

Pandolfi, Claudia. 1999. *Lilio Gregorio Giraldi da Ferrara, Due dialoghi sui poeti dei nostri tempi*. Ferrara: Corbo.

Pandolfi, Vito, and Erminia Artese, eds. 1965. *Teatro goliardico dell'Umanesimo*. Milan: Lerici.

Perosa, Alessandro. 1965. *Teatro umanistico*. Milan: Nuova Accademia.

Petrocchi, Giorgio. 1965. "I poeti realisti," in *Storia della letteratura italiana*. Vol. 1, *Le origini e il Duecento*, ed. Emilio Cecchi and Natalino Sapegno. Milan: Garzanti. 575–607.

Pittaluga, Stefano. 1986. "Riccardo da Venosa: De Paulino et Polla," in *Commedie latine del XII e XIII secolo*. Genoa: Università di Genova, Facoltà di lettere, Istituto di filologia classica e medievale. Vol. 5: 81–227, 233–35.

Pius II. 1571. *Aeneae Sylvii Piccolominei Senensis, qui post adeptum pontificatum Pius eius nominis secundus appellatus est, opera quae extant omnia*. Basel: ex officina Henricpetrina.

Poliziano, Angelo. 1553. *Opera omnia*. Basel: Apud Nicolaum Episcopium. Repr. Turin: Bottega d'Erasmo, 1970.

Pontano, Giovanni Gioviano. 1943. *I dialoghi*, ed. Carmelo Previtera. Florence: Sansoni.

Questa, C. 1962. "Plauto diviso in atti prima di G. B. Pio (Codd. Vatt. latt. 3304 e 2711)," *Rivista di cultura classica e medioevale* 4: 209–30.

Ramorino, Felice. 1883. "Antonionio [*sic*] Beccadelli a Pavia," *Archivio storico siciliano* n.s. 7: 249–73.

Rao, Ennio I., ed. 1978. *Bartolomeo Facio, Invective in Laurentium Vallam*. Studi e testi di letteratura italiana 15. Naples: Società Editrice Napoletana.

Raponi, Nicola. 1964. "Barbavara, Francesco," *Dizionario biografico degli italiani* 6: 141–42.

Reeve, M. D. 1990. [Review] "Plautus, Pontano and Panormita," *Classical Review* n.s. 40: 24–27.

Regoliosi, Mariangela. 1980. "Per la tradizione delle 'Invective in Laurentium Vallam' di Bartolomeo Facio," *Italia medioevale e umanistica*, 24: 389–97.

——— . ed. 1981a. *Laurentii Valle: Antidotum in Facium*. Padua: Antenore. (The text, but not the introduction, is available at http://imagohistoriae.signum.sns.it/works.php.)

——— . 1981b. "Lorenzo Valla, Antonio Panormita, Giacomo Curlo e le emendazioni a Livio," *Italia medioevale e umanistica* 24: 287–316.

Resta, Gianvito. 1954. *L'Epistolario del Panormita. Studi per una edizione critica*. Messina: Università degli studi.

——— . 1962. *Le epitome di Plutarco nel Quattrocento*. Padua: Antenore.

——— . 1965. "Beccadelli, Antonio," *Dizionario biografico degli italiani* 7: 400–06.

———, ed. 1968. *Antonii Panhormitae Liber rerum gestarum Ferdinandi Regis*. Palermo: Luxograph.

———, ed. 1976. *Johannis Marrasii Angelinetum et carmina varia*. Palermo: Centro di studi filologici e linguistici siciliani.

Ribuoli, Riccardo. 1981. "Polemiche umanistiche: a proposito di due recenti edizioni," *Res publica litterarum* 4: 339–54.

Richlin, Amy. 1992. *The Garden of Priapus: Sexuality and Aggression in Roman Humor*, rev. ed. New York: Oxford University Press.

Ritschl, Friedrich Wilhelm. 1845. *Parerga zu Plautus und Terenz. Parergon Plautinorum Terentianorumque*. Leipzig: Weidmann.

Rocke, Michael. 1996. *Forbidden Friendships: Homosexuality and Male Culture in Renaissance Florence.* New York: Oxford University Press.

Rozzo, Ugo. 2001. "Italian Literature on the Index," in *Church, Censorship, and Culture in Early Modern Italy,* ed. Gigliola Fragnito, trans. Adrian Belton. Cambridge: Cambridge University Press. 194–222.

Rutherford, David. 2005. *Early Renaissance Invective and the Controversies of Antonio da Rho.* Renaissance Text Series 19. MRTS 301. Tempe, AZ: Arizona Center for Medieval and Renaissance Texts and Studies.

Ryder, Alan Frederick Charles. 1976a. *The Kingdom of Naples under Alfonso the Magnanimous: The Making of a Modern State.* Oxford: Oxford University Press.

——. 1976b. "Antonio Beccadelli: A Humanist in Government," in *Cultural Aspects of the Italian Renaissance. Essays in Honour of Paul Oskar Kristeller,* ed. Cecil H. Clough. Manchester and New York: Manchester University Press. 123–40.

——. 1990. *Alfonso the Magnanimous: King of Aragon, Naples, and Sicily, 1396–1458.* Oxford: Oxford University Press.

Saalman, Howard. 1985. "The New Sacristy of San Lorenzo before Michelangelo," *Art Bulletin* 67: 199–228.

Sabbadini, Remigio. 1891. "Cronologia documentata della vita del Panormita e del Valla," in Barozzi, Luciano, and Remigio Sabbadini, *Studi sul Panormita e sul Valla.* Florence: Le Monnier.

——. 1903. "Un biennio umanistico (1425–1426) illustrato con nuovi documenti," *Giornale storico della letteratura italiana,* Supplemento 6: 74–119.

——. 1910a. "La più antica lettera del Panormita," *Il libro e la stampa: Bullettino ufficiale della Società bibliografica italiana* n.s. 4: 113–17. (http://emeroteca.braidense.it/)

——. 1910b. *Ottanta lettere inedite del Panormita tratte dai codici milanesi.* Catania: Giannotta.

——. 1915–19. *Epistolario di Guarino Veronese.* 3 vols. Venice: A spese della Società.

——. 1916. "Come il Panormita diventò poeta aulico," *Archivio storico lombardo* 43: 5–28. (http://emeroteca.braidense.it/)

———. 1917. "La polemica fra Porcelio e il Panormita," *Rendiconti del reale istituto lombardo di scienze e lettere* 50: 495–501.

———. 1922. *Il metodo degli umanisti.* Florence: Felice Le Monnier.

———. 1931. *Carteggio di Giovanni Aurispa.* Rome: Tipografia del Senato.

———. 1971. *Storia e critica di testi latini.* Seconda edizione. Padua: Antenore.

Santoro, Mario. 1975. "La cultura umanistica," in *Storia di Napoli,* ed. Ernesto Pontieri et al. 11 vols in 15. Vol. 7: 115–291. Naples: Edizioni scientifiche italiane.

———. 1984. "Il Panormita 'aragonese'," *Esperienze letterarie* 9: 3–24.

Sapegno, Natalino. 1952. *Poeti minori del Trecento.* Milan: Ricciardi.

Schalk, F. 1980. "Beccadelli, Antonio," *Lexikon des Mittelalters* 1: 1769.

Sevenster, Jan Nicolaas. 1961. *Paul and Seneca.* Leiden: Brill.

Soldati, Benedetto. 1902. *Ioannis Ioviani Pontani Carmina.* Florence: Barbèra.

Sommer, Anton F. W., ed. 1997. *Literarische Schätze der Renaissance und des Humanismus: Das gesamte lyrische Oeuvre von Franciscus Pontanus und Antonius Becadelli genannt Panormita: aus den Handschriften zum ersten Mal veröffentlicht.* Editiones neolatinae, vol. 9. Vienna: Eigenverlag Sommer.

Stacey, Peter. 2007. *Roman Monarchy and the Renaissance Prince.* Cambridge: Cambridge University Press.

Starrabba, R. 1902. "Notizie concernenti Antonio Panormita," *Archivio storico siciliano* n.s. 27: 119–33.

Stäuble, Antonio. 1968. *La commedia umanistica del Quattrocento.* Florence: Istituto Nazionale di Studi sul Rinascimento.

Symonds, John Addington. 1877. *Renaissance in Italy: The Revival of Learning.* London: Smith, Elder & Co.

Tenenti, Alberto. 1957. *Il senso della morte e l'amore della vita nel Rinascimento (Francia e Italia).* Turin: Einaudi.

Thurn, Nikolaus. 2002. *Drei neapolitanische Humanisten über die Liebe: Antonius Panormita—Hermaphroditus, Ioannes Pontanus—De amore coniugali, Michael Marullus—Hymni naturales.* St. Katharinen: Scripta Mercaturae.

Tognelli, Jole, ed. and trans. 1968. *L'ermafrodito di Antonio Beccadelli detto il Panormita*. I Classici per tutti 86. Rome: Avanzini e Torraca.

Traversari, G. 1903. "Di Mattia Lupi (1380–1468) e de' suoi 'Annales Geminianenses'," *Miscellanea storica della Valdelsa* 11: 10–27, 108–28.

Trexler, Richard. 1981. "La prostitution florentine au XVe siècle: patronages et clientèles," *Annales: Economies, Sociétés, Civilisations* 36: 983–1015.

Tuohy, Thomas. 1996. *Herculean Ferrara: Ercole d'Este, 1471–1505, and the Invention of a Ducal Capital*. Cambridge: Cambridge University Press.

Turner, James. 2003. *Schooling Sex: Libertine Literature and Erotic Education in Italy, France, and England, 1534–1685*. Oxford: Oxford University Press.

Ullman, B. L. 1933. "Poggio's Manuscripts of Livy — Alleged and Actual," *Classical Philology* 28: 282–88.

Valentini, R. 1907. "Sul Panormita. Notizie biografiche e filologiche," *Rendiconti della reale Accademia dei Lincei, Classe di scienze morali, storiche e filologiche*, serie 5a, 16: 456–90.

Valerius Probus, Marcus. 1499. *De interpretandis Romanorum litteris*. Venice: Per Ioannem Tacuinum.

Valla, Lorenzo. 1540. *Opera Omnia*. Basel: Apud Henricum Petrum. 2 vols. Repr. Turin: Bottega d'Erasmo, 1962.

——. 1977. *On Pleasure = De Voluptate*, trans. A. Kent Hieatt and Maristella de Panizza Lorch. New York: Abaris Books.

——. 1984. *Laurentii Valle Epistole*, ed. Ottavio Besomi and Mariangela Regoliosi. Padua: Antenore.

Viti, Paolo. 1982. *Due commedie umanistiche pavesi: "Janus sacerdos", "Repetitio magistri Zanini coqui"*. Padua: Antenore.

——. 1999. *Immagini e immaginazioni della realtà. Ricerche sulla commedia umanistica*. Florence: Le Lettere.

Voigt, Georg. 1880–81. *Die Wiederbelebung des classischen Alterthums oder das erste Jahrhundert des Humanismus*. 2. umgearb. Aufl. Berlin: G. Reimer.

——. 1893. *Die Wiederbelebung des classischen Alterthums oder das erste Jahrhundert des Humanismus*. 3. Aufl. Berlin: G. Reimer.

Waters, William George, and Emily Waters, trans. 1926. *The Vespasiano Memoirs. Lives of Illustrious Men of the XVth Century, by Vespasiano da Bisticci, Bookseller*. New York: Dial Press.

Wilmart, A. 1933. "L'Ars arengandi' de Jacques de Dinant avec un Appendice sur ses ouvrages 'De dictamine'," in *Analecta Reginensia*. Studi e Testi 59. Città del Vaticano: Biblioteca Apostolica Vaticana. 135–39.

Wilson, Allan M., ed. and trans. 1995. *The Erotopaegnion: A Trifling Book of Love of Girolamo Angeriano*. Nieuwkoop: De Graaf.

Zaccaria, Francesco Antonio. 1777. *Storia polemica delle proibizioni de' libri*. Rome: Generoso Salomoni.

Zaccaria, Vittorio. 1956. "Sulle opere di Pier Candido Decembrio," *Rinascimento* 7: 13–74.

Zimmermann, T. C. Price. 1995. *Paolo Giovio: The Historian and the Crisis of Sixteenth-Century Italy*. Princeton: Princeton University Press.

Index

☙§℘֍

Note: Lowercase roman numerals refer to pages in the introduction. References to *The Hermaphrodite* are by book, poem, and line numbers, preceded by "H." References to the letters and poems in the Appendix are by number and line (or paragraph) number, preceded by "App." "Pref" refers to the Prefatory Letter of Guarino at the head of Book I; "Pogg" refers to the the letter of Poggio to Beccadelli after Book I; "Becc" refers to the letter of Beccadelli to Poggio after Book II; "Recant" refers to Beccadelli's Recantation at the end of *The Hermaphrodite*. Notes to the introduction are listed by page and note number; notes to the translation are listed by the location of the note number in the text. Thus "xlii n114" refers to note 114 on page xlii, while "H.1.7.12n18" refers to *The Hermaphrodite*, Book I, poem 7, line 12, note number 18. Italicized numbers in subentries refer to sections of a work.

Publication of this volume has been made possible by

The Myron and Sheila Gilmore Publication Fund at I Tatti
The Robert Lehman Endowment Fund
The Jean-François Malle Scholarly Programs and Publications Fund
The Andrew W. Mellon Scholarly Publications Fund
The Craig and Barbara Smyth Fund
for Scholarly Programs and Publications
The Lila Wallace–Reader's Digest Endowment Fund
The Malcolm Wiener Fund for Scholarly Programs and Publications